Introducing Pragmatics in Use

Introducing Pragmatics in Use is a lively and accessible introduction to pragmatics, which both covers theory and applies it to real spoken and written data.

Pragmatics is the study of language in context, yet most textbooks rely on invented language examples. This innovative textbook systematically draws on language corpora to illustrate features such as creativity in small talk or how we apologise in English. The authors investigate the pragmatic implications of the globalisation of the English language and focus on the applications of pragmatics for teaching languages. In addition, a practical chapter on researching pragmatics aimed at developing students' research skills is included.

With a range of tasks aimed at putting theory into practice and chapter by chapter further reading recommendations, this is the ideal textbook for advanced undergraduate or postgraduate students of pragmatics and corpus linguistics within applied language/ linguistics or TEFL/TESOL degrees.

Anne O'Keeffe is Senior Lecturer in Applied Linguistics, Department of English Language and Literature, Mary Immaculate College, University of Limerick, Ireland.

Brian Clancy lectures on undergraduate courses including academic writing and research methods at Mary Immaculate College, University of Limerick, Ireland. His research expertise and publications centre on pragmatic and sociolinguistic aspects of family discourse.

Svenja Adolphs is Professor of English Language and Linguistics, School of English Studies, University of Nottingham, UK.

Introducing
Pragmatics in Use

ANNE O'KEEFFE

BRIAN CLANCY

SVENJA ADOLPHS

Routledge
Taylor & Francis Group

LONDON AND NEW YORK

First published 2011 by Routledge
2 Park Square, Milton Park, Abingdon, OX14 4RN

Simultaneously published in the USA and Canada by Routledge
711 Third Avenue, New York, NY 10017

Routledge is an imprint of the Taylor & Francis Group, an informa business

Typeset in Akzidenz Grotesk by
Swales & Willis Ltd, Exeter, Devon

British Library Cataloguing in Publication Data
A catalogue record for this book is available from the British Library

Library of Congress Cataloging in Publication Data
O'Keeffe, Anne.
Introducing pragmatics in use / Anne O'Keeffe, Brian Clancy, Svenja Adolphs.
— 1st ed.
        p. cm.
    Includes bibliographical references.
    1. Pragmatics.   2. Linguistics.   I. Clancy, Brian, 1975–   II. Adolphs, Svenja.
III. Title.
P99.4.P72O44 2011
401'.45–dc22   2010034568

ISBN: 978-0-415-45092-8 (hbk)
ISBN: 978-0-415-45091-1 (pbk)
ISBN: 978-0-203-83094-9 (ebk)

Contents

List of illustrations   vii
Acknowledgements   ix

Chapter 1   Introduction   1
    1.1   What is pragmatics?   1
    1.2   Pragmatics in use   2
    1.3   The structure of this book   4
    1.4   What is corpus linguistics?   6
    1.5   Using a corpus to study pragmatics   8
    1.6   Further reading   16

Chapter 2   Researching pragmatics   18
    2.1   Introduction   18
    2.2   Diversity of studies in pragmatics: five diverse case studies   19
    2.3   Ways of researching pragmatics   20
    2.4   Conclusion   34
    2.5   Further reading   34

Chapter 3   Deixis   36
    3.1   What is deixis?   36
    3.2   Deictic versus non-deictic expression   37
    3.3   Gestural versus symbolic deixis   39
    3.4   The deictic centre   42
    3.5   Basic categories of deixis   44
    3.6   Conclusion   57
    3.7   Further reading   58

Chapter 4   Politeness in context   59
    4.1   The linguistic study of politeness   59
    4.2   Penelope Brown and Stephen Levinson   60
    4.3   Impoliteness   71
    4.4   Richard Watts   74

4.5 Conclusion   80
4.6 Further reading   81

Chapter 5   Speech acts in context   83
                 5.1 Introduction   83
                 5.2 Speech Act Theory   84
                 5.3 Identifying and analysing speech acts   91
                 5.4 What is a speech act context?   93
                 5.5 Speech act classification in discourse analysis 96
                 5.6 Conclusion   98
                 5.7 Further reading   98

Chapter 6   Pragmatics across languages and cultures   100
                 6.1 Introduction   100
                 6.2 Defining the area: a tricky task   102
                 6.3 The issue of *universality* of pragmatic norms 104
                 6.4 Studies of pragmatics across languages and cultures   107
                 6.5 Pragmatic variation within the same language   109
                 6.6 Conclusion   112
                 6.7 Further reading   113

Chapter 7   Pragmatics in specific discourse domains   115
                 7.1 Introduction   115
                 7.2 Comparability at the level of turns   116
                 7.3 Comparability using a corpus   120
                 7.4 Other ways of investigating pragmatics in specific
                      discourse domains using a corpus   127
                 7.5 Conclusion   135
                 7.6 Further reading   135

Chapter 8   Pragmatics and language teaching   137
                 8.1 Introduction   137
                 8.2 Pragmatics in the language classroom   138
                 8.3 What can be taught?   142
                 8.4 Teaching politeness   143
                 8.5 Conclusion   162
                 8.6 Further reading   163

                 References   165
                 Index   183

Illustrations

TABLES

1.1 Description of frequently referred to corpora in this volume   4

1.2 Top 25 most frequent words in the BNC and LCIE   10

1.3 Ten most frequent 2-word, 3-word and 4-word units in LCIE results per million words   11

1.4 Top ten positive and negative keywords when comparing C-MELT and LCIE   12

1.5 Top ten most frequent collocates for *Democrat* and *Republican* in the COCA corpus   15

2.1 Typical codes used in a broad transcription of spoken corpora   30

3.1 Top 20 most frequent words in LCIE (personal pronouns in bold)   45

3.2 Comparison of frequency of occurrence of *yesterday*, *today* and *tomorrow* with the lexicalised names for days of the week   52

3.3 Word frequency counts for the 20 most frequent words in LCIE   57

4.1 Culpeper's (1996) impoliteness strategies   72

4.2 Frequency of *please* in family sub-corpus (LCIE), (not normalised)   80

6.1 Schneider and Barron's (2008) levels of pragmatic analysis   111

7.1 Identifying characteristics of situational variation based on Biber *et al.* (1999: 15–17)   116

7.2 Comparison of NHS and BNC 1–40 wordlists   121

7.3 Keywords of NHS Direct corpus   123

7.4 Keywords of C-MELT   125

7.5 Keywords, minus content items, of C-MELT corpus of teacher meetings using LCIE as a reference corpus   125

7.6 30 most frequent three-word units in ELT classes from LIBEL   130

7.7 30 most frequent three-word units in corpus of soap opera scripts   132

8.1 Formulaic address in different spoken and written contexts   145

8.2 Ways in which we make what we say less direct (marked in bold)   148

8.3 A summary of hedging forms   152

8.4 Examples of discourse markers (in bold) and their core functions in speaking   157

8.5 Examples of interactional markers (in bold) and their functions   159

FIGURES

1.1 A Key Word in Context (KWIC) of the word *now* using WordSmith Tools Version 5.0 (Scott, 2009), using LCIE ... 13

2.1 An example of a Discourse Completion Task ... 21

2.2 An example of a freer DCT (adapted from Tanck, 2002) ... 22

2.3 An example of a freer DCT (adapted from Beebe and Zhang Waring, 2004: 245) ... 22

2.4 Samples of scenarios from a DCT presented to American and Mandarin students in Liang and Han (2005) ... 24

2.5 Example of broad transcription (an extract from a political science lecture from the LIBEL corpus) ... 29

2.6 Example of narrow transcription from the Hong Kong Corpus of Spoken English (HKCSE) (Cheng and Warren, 2006) ... 30

2.7 Concordance lines for *us* in a corpus of radio phone-ins ... 32

3.1 Possible uses of a deictic expression ... 42

4.1 Brown and Levinson's (1987) strategies for performing FTAs ... 65

4.2 The semantic categorisation of in-group terms of address (adapted from Leech, 1999) ... 67

6.1 Summary of Grice's Co-operative Principle, Leech's politeness maxims and Brown and Levinson's politeness theory ... 105

7.1 Concordance extracts of *sort* in the NHS Direct corpus ... 124

7.2 Concordance line extracts for search item *it's* ... 124

7.3 Extract of concordance lines for *maybe* + we + modal/semi-modal verb in C-MELT ... 126

7.4 Extract from concordance lines for *now* in shop recordings from LCIE ... 127

7.5 Examples of concordance lines of <$E> inhales <\$E> ... 128

7.6 Concordance lines for *no* reduplication from *Fair City* soap opera scripts ... 133

8.1 Short- and long-term goals in teaching pragmatic competence ... 143

8.2 Concordance lines from LCIE using the search word *hours* ... 154

8.3 Concordance lines from BNC using the search word *year* ... 155

Acknowledgements

In putting this book together, we have had inspiration, support and feedback from many quarters. First and foremost, we wish to thank both our editorial assistant and publisher at Routledge, Sophie Jaques and Louisa Semlyen, for their help and great patience. Further involved along the way at Routledge were Eloise Cook, Ursula Mallows and particularly Samantha Vale Noya. Additionally, we acknowledge and value the feedback that we received on the manuscript from Randi Reppen and Nancy Drescher, and the reviews on early drafts of chapters that were provided by Joan Cutting, Christoph Rühlemann and Camilla Vásquez. Friends and colleagues, Ron Carter, Mike McCarthy and Elaine Vaughan were also kind enough to provide feedback on individual chapters, for which we are very grateful. Needless to say, the weaknesses of this book are ours rather than theirs! And to our partners Ger, Elaine and Nick, respectively, we say thank you for your love and support throughout.

This book contains a lot of real data drawn from corpora and we wish to acknowledge these sources: the British National Corpus, the Corpus of Contemporary American English, the Michigan Corpus of Academic Spoken English, the Limerick Corpus of Irish English, the Limerick and Belfast Corpus of Academic Spoken English, the Corpus of Meetings of English Language Teachers (very kindly lent to us by Elaine Vaughan) and the Nottingham Health Communication Corpus (NHS Direct component). We also acknowledge the use of the Nottingham Multi-Modal Corpus which has been funded by the UK Economic and Social Research Council (ESRC), grant numbers RES-149-25-1016 and RES-149-25-0035. Reproduced in Chapter 1 is a screenshot from WordSmith Tools (Lexical Analysis Software Ltd) with the kind permission of Mike Scott. In Chapter 2, we are grateful for the permission granted to use an extract from the Hong Kong Corpus of Spoken English. In Chapter 4, we use material from wikiHow: http://www.wikihow.com/Be-Polite-at-a-Dinner.

Every effort has been made to contact copyright holders. If any have been inadvertently overlooked, the publishers will be pleased to make the necessary arrangement at the first opportunity.

CHAPTER 1

Introduction

1.1 WHAT IS PRAGMATICS?

The term *pragmatics* is often used in linguistic research to refer to the study of the interpretation of meaning. Although it has proven difficult to determine an exact definition for the term pragmatics (Levinson discusses the issue over more than 50 pages in his influential 1983 work *Pragmatics*), a user-friendly definition is suggested by Fasold (1990: 119): 'the study of the use of context to make inferences about meaning'. In this definition, inferences refer to deductions made by participants based on available evidence (Christie, 2000). This available evidence is, according to pragmaticists, provided by the context within which the utterance takes place. Cutting (2008: 3–11) distinguishes between three different types of spoken context: *situational*, what speakers know about what they can see around them; *background knowledge*, what they know about each other (interpersonal knowledge) and the world (cultural knowledge); and *co-textual*, what they know about what they have been saying (see also Chapter 3). Therefore, the pragmatic choices made by conversational participants can simultaneously encode indications of position and time and interpersonal and cultural indicators such as power, status, gender and age. Thus, as Christie (2000: 29) maintains, pragmatics provides 'a theoretical framework that can account for the relationship between the cultural setting, the language user, the linguistic choices the user makes, and the factors that underlie those choices'.

The modern usage of the term *pragmatics* in the study of language is attributable to the philosopher Charles Morris (1938), who envisaged a three-part distinction: *syntax, semantics* and *pragmatics*.

For example, the utterance *I've got a headache* carries a variety of meanings according to when it is used, who uses it, who the person is talking to, where the conversation takes place, and so forth:

- If a patient said it to a doctor during a medical examination, it could mean: *I need a prescription*.

- If a mother said it to her teenage son, it could mean: *Turn down the music.*
- If two friends were talking, it could mean: *I was partying last night.*
- If it were used as a response to an invitation from one friend to another, such as *Do you fancy going for a walk?*, it could simply mean: *No.*

Therefore, depending on the context it occurs in, the utterance *I've got a headache* can function as an appeal, an imperative, a complaint or a refusal, and so on. In any language, what is *said* is often quite distinct to what is *meant*, or to put it another way, *form* is often very different to *content.* As such pragmatics does not assume a one-to-one relationship between language form and utterance function, but is concerned instead with accounting for the processes that give rise to a particular interpretation of an utterance that is used in a particular context. As Romero-Trillo (2008) lyrically puts it, pragmatics sails the sea between sentence meaning and intended meaning.

on Fri: Think at diff. interpretations/contexts

There are many other single utterances that can have a variety of meanings according to the contexts in which they occur. Consider the number of meanings that can be attributed to:

The door is open.
It's raining.

Utterances such as these provide evidence that speakers frequently mean *more* than they say. Rühlemann (2010) claims that pragmatics is particularly interested in this 'more', while Mey (1991: 245) refers to pragmatics as 'the art of the analysis of the unsaid.'

Hymes (1974) refers to two different types of competence: the first, *grammatical competence*, relates to the ability to create and understand grammatically correct sentences; and the second, *communicative competence*, is associated with the ability to produce and understand sentences that are appropriate and acceptable in a particular situation. Christie (2000) notes that it is axiomatic to pragmatics that our grammatical competence does not provide conversational participants with sufficient knowledge to be able to understand examples of language use. Therefore, it is within Hymes' notion of communicative competence that the study of pragmatics is located.

1.2 PRAGMATICS IN USE

The title of this book places a strong focus on the notion of *in use* both from the point of view of the linguistic data used and the study of pragmatics. In terms of language in use, traditionally, research within the area of pragmatics has not used attested, or 'real-life', examples of language in use and has not been concerned with the link between language form and function. Recently, however, there has been a marked shift towards the use of real-life, naturally-occurring data, as evidenced in journals such as the *Journal of Pragmatics* or *Historical Pragmatics* (see Chapter 2). Indeed, one of the major developments in pragmatics in recent years has been the advent of language corpora (i.e. large databases of naturally-occurring spoken and written language available on computer for empirical study) which provide the researcher with access to naturally-occurring data. Romero-Trillo (2008: 1) maintains that 'pragmatics and corpus linguistics have not only helped each other in a relationship of mutualism, but, they have also made common cause against the voices that have derided and underestimated the utility of working with real data to elucidate the patterns of language use.'

Despite this, many areas of pragmatics which address how language is used do not actually use real language, for example in interlanguage pragmatics (see Chapters 2 and 6), Discourse Completion Tasks (DCTs) or role-plays (see Chapter 2) are the norm. DCT data are elicited by the researcher, which results in parameters which are focused, specific and confined. There can be valid reasons for this, for example when one is examining a widely used but difficult to record speech act, such as (face-to-face) complaining. The naturally-occurring language evident in many modern corpora is precisely that, authentic, spontaneous, unrehearsed and uncensored. The extent to which DCT data is different to corpus data has not been explored sufficiently to assess the value of these different approaches. However, as Schauer and Adolphs (2006) illustrate in a study of expressions of gratitude in DCT data versus corpus data, the fact that data generated through DCTs is based around single utterances distorts the overall picture of a speech act which is often negotiated and developed over a number of turns in a dynamic discourse event. It is therefore unclear whether DCT or role-play data displays the same patterns and attributes as naturally-occurring data stored in a spoken corpus. We will return to this discussion in greater detail in Chapter 2.

When we look at language in use, we find that it is highly context-dependent and many of its forms and uses have to be explained beyond the sentence, in other words within the realms of pragmatics. As previously stated, pragmatics can be defined as the study of the relationship between context and meaning. This book approaches context and meaning as features of authentic language in use and employs corpus data as an evidential base for their exploration. Through this corpus data, some of the major areas of investigation associated with pragmatics such as deixis, Speech Act Theory and politeness are covered. Our aim is to operationalise pragmatics for those interested in the study of empirical data, by drawing on real contexts of use from language corpora. Therefore, by providing the critical theoretical knowledge required to access the area and by applying this to real data, we investigate how to research pragmatics using corpus linguistic techniques. In Chapter 2, we survey a number of approaches to eliciting data in the study of pragmatics, including DCTs, interviews and role-plays as well as using language corpora. We also give practical advice on how to build your own corpus and transcribe it.

The main corpora that we draw on are described in Table 1.1 (more details of many of these corpora are provided throughout the book).

Table 1.1 Description of frequently referred to corpora in this volume

Corpus name	Size (words)	Description
The Corpus of Contemporary American English (COCA)	400+ million	The COCA corpus is the largest freely available corpus of English. It contains 20 million words of spoken and written American English collected each year from 1990 to 2009 (see www.americancorpus.org).
The British National Corpus (BNC)	100 million	The BNC is a corpus of samples of spoken and written language from a wide range of sources, designed to represent a cross-section of current British English (see www.natcorp.ox.ac.uk).
Michigan Corpus of Academic Spoken English (MICASE)	1.8 million	The MICASE corpus consists of almost 200 hours of spoken discourse recorded in a wide range of academic settings (see Simpson et al., 2002).
The Limerick Corpus of Irish English (LCIE)	1 million	LCIE is a corpus of naturally-occurring, contemporary spoken Irish English (for more details see Farr et al., 2004).
The Limerick and Belfast Corpus of Academic Spoken English (LIBEL CASE)	1 million	The LIBEL corpus consists of spoken data collected in two universities on the island of Ireland; one in the Republic of Ireland and one in Northern Ireland (see Walsh et al., 2008).
Corpus of Meetings of English Language Teachers (C-MELT)	40,000	C-MELT is a corpus of English language teachers recorded in different settings (see Vaughan, 2007, 2010).
The Nottingham Multi-Modal Corpus (NMMC)	250,000	The Nottingham Multi-Modal Corpus consists of video-recorded academic supervision meetings and lectures. The transcribed interactions are fully aligned with the video recordings in a multi-modal interface (see Knight et al., 2009).
The Nottingham Health Communication Corpus (NHS Direct component)	61,981	The National Health Service (NHS) Direct corpus is a sub-corpus of the Nottingham Health Communication Corpus and comprises recordings of phone calls made to the UK National Health Service phone line (see Adolphs et al., 2004).

1.3 THE STRUCTURE OF THIS BOOK

This book is organised into eight chapters. This introductory chapter has already presented the term pragmatics and outlined our rationale for writing the book. It also mentioned, in brief, some of the corpora we will refer to throughout. This chapter proceeds to set out in detail some of the essential information needed to apply corpus linguistics to the study of pragmatics. We will explain what a corpus is and explore the development of corpora in the digital age. In addition, we will demonstrate how corpus tools such as frequency lists can contribute to the study of pragmatics.

Each chapter also features a series of 'information boxes' such as this one (all marked with the notebook symbol). These are designed to complement the material presented in the main body of the text. In addition, at the end of each chapter is an annotated bibliography that points towards further key readings.

The rest of the book is structured in the following way:

Chapter 2 Researching pragmatics

This chapter builds on the introduction. We review the major research methods commonly used in pragmatics and the different ways in which these intersect with other sub-disciplines of linguistics. We go into detail on the many ways in which data can be collected and discuss the pros and cons of different approaches to eliciting data. We look at DCTs, role-plays, interviews and corpus data. Key to this chapter is the section *Corpus data* which outlines the fundamental considerations involved in the building and transcribing of a corpus.

Chapter 3 Deixis

This chapter furthers our exploration of key concepts within the study of pragmatics. We deal with an area that is integral to the study of pragmatics – that of *deixis*. Deixis represents the intersection of grammar and pragmatics and the chapter explores many of these grammatical items such as the personal pronouns *you* and *I* and the demonstratives *this* and *that*. This chapter demonstrates how corpus linguistics can be used to examine the relationship between the context of the utterance and the referential practices therein. This relationship is shown to characterise the very nature of our pragmatic systems.

Chapter 4 Politeness in context

This chapter introduces two of the seminal theories in politeness research. Brown and Levinson's model of politeness is compared and contrasted with Watts' by demonstrating key features of these models using corpus linguistic techniques. It also presents Grice's notion of *conversational implicature*, one of the foundation stones of pragmatic research. In addition, we address the growing literature on impoliteness.

Chapter 5 Speech acts in context

Chapter 5 examines the link between linguistic forms in the shape of speech acts and their function in context. We provide an overview of Speech Act Theory and discuss the main arguments and underlying assumptions on which this theory is based. This includes a discussion of direct and indirect speech acts, and the broad taxonomy of different speech act categories such as *directives* or *commissives*. The chapter also looks at the way in which context and co-text impact on the analysis of speech acts in a discourse framework.

Chapter 6 Pragmatics across languages and cultures

This chapter addresses the distinction between *cross-cultural* and *interlanguage* pragmatics and it surveys some of the many studies in this area. We consider the notion of the universality of pragmatic norm across all languages. By looking at Asian norms of politeness in contrast to Western norms, we see that the notion of 'universal' norms is quite limited. We also employ corpus-based techniques to examine pragmatic variation both across and within languages.

Chapter 7 Pragmatics in specific discourse domains

Chapters 7 and 8 bring together many of the issues discussed in Chapters 1–6 by considering pragmatics in specific discourse domains. Using corpus techniques, Chapter 7 examines the concept of *comparability* by focusing on five specific domains: casual conversation, healthcare communication, the classroom, service encounters and soap operas. The chapter examines features such as turn-taking, discourse markers, personal pronouns and hedges which are emblematic of many pragmatic systems.

Chapter 8 Pragmatics and language teaching

In this chapter we address pragmatics in the specific domain of English language teaching, learning and teacher training. The chapter takes a two-pronged approach. The first half of the chapter explores the issue of teaching pragmatics in the language classroom using a variety of illustrative corpus-based studies. The second half of the chapter employs corpora to generate a series of task-based activities designed for the language classroom in order to promote the learning of specific pragmatic features of English.

1.4 WHAT IS CORPUS LINGUISTICS?

Corpus linguistics most commonly refers to the study of machine-readable spoken and written language samples that have been assembled in a principled way for the purpose of linguistic research. At the heart of empirically-based linguistics and data-driven description of language, it is concerned with language use in real contexts. Access to ever larger spoken and written corpora has already revolutionised the description of language in use, but the impact of corpus linguistics has reached far beyond the disciplines that are purely concerned with descriptions of language. As an approach, corpus linguistics continues to gain recognition and popularity, with an increasing number of researchers across different disciplines exploring innovative ways of using corpus-based research as part of their methods toolkit.

Corpora as language data

Common distinctions are made between *specialised* and *general* corpora, where the former includes texts that belong to a particular type, e.g. academic prose, while the latter includes many different types of texts, often assembled with the aim of serving as reference resources for linguistic research or to produce reference materials such as dictionaries. Specialised corpora are usually quite small (less than one million words) while general corpora are usually large (at the time of writing, the largest corpora are held by publishing houses and some comprise over 2.5 billion words). Other types of corpora include *historical* and *monitor* corpora, *parallel* corpora and *learner* corpora. Historical corpora include texts from different periods of time and allow for the study of language change when compared with corpora from other periods. Monitor corpora can be used for a similar purpose, but tend to focus on current changes in the language. New texts from the same variety are added to the existing corpus at regular intervals, thus contributing to a constantly growing text database. Parallel corpora include texts in at least two languages that have either been directly translated, or produced in different languages for the same purpose. Such corpora are often used for translation studies (see Kübler and Aston, 2010; Kenning, 2010). Learner corpora contain collections of texts produced by learners of a language. They allow the researcher to identify patterns in a particular variety of learner language and to compare the language of the learner to that of other users of a language.

In terms of the history of corpus design, a distinction is often made between the early corpora developed in the 1950s, 1960s and 1970s and the larger corpora developed from the late 1980s onwards. Early corpora include the London-Lund Corpus of Spoken English (LLC), the Brown Corpus, based on American written English, and the Lancaster-Oslo/Bergen Corpus, based on written British English. The parallel design of the latter two corpora allowed for a corpus-based comparison between British and American English. Early corpora were often limited in size to a one-million word threshold which is partly a reflection of the technological possibilities at the time.

Two of the most substantial corpus projects developed in the 1980s and 1990s are the Collins and Birmingham University International Language Database (COBUILD) and the British National Corpus. Both offer a valuable resource for the study of everyday spoken and written English. The COBUILD corpus, which is also referred to as The Bank of English, was developed in the 1990s as a monitor corpus. This means that new texts are constantly added to this database. At the time of writing, the size of the corpus stands at 650 million words. One of the main aims of this project has been to provide a textual database for the compilation of dictionaries and lexicography research. The corpus contains samples of mainly British written language, as well as transcribed speech from interviews, broadcast, and conversation. The British National Corpus (BNC) was compiled in the late 1980s and early 1990s, and is a 100 million word corpus of modern British English, consisting of 90 per cent written and 10 per cent spoken texts (including speeches, meetings, lectures and some casual conversation). Apart from these two major corpora, many publishing houses have developed their own corpora which serve as a resource for authors, mainly in the area of lexicography. Examples are the Cambridge International Corpus (CIC), the

Longman Corpus Network, the Oxford English Corpus and the Collins Corpus. Another large corpus project is the International Corpus of English (ICE), which was initiated in 1990 as a resource for comparing different varieties of world English. At the time of writing, there are 23 ICE teams working on one-million word corpora, each representing a regional variety of English, for example Canadian, Irish, Kenyan or Singapore English. Two substantial American English corpora have also been developed, the American National Corpus (ANC) and the Corpus of Contemporary American English (COCA). At the time of writing, the ANC contains 22 million words of written and spoken texts in American English produced since 1990. The COCA consists of more than 400 million words of American English, with 21 per cent spoken and 79 per cent written material. With 20 million words added each year, the COCA can also be used as a monitor corpus to capture language change. For a more wide-ranging overview of available corpora, see Lee (2010).

The main aim of the large general corpora above is to capture the use of general English rather than English used in a particular domain. Domain-specific corpora are compiled into usually smaller specialised corpora which range from those that represent the language of a particular group of people, such as the Bergen Corpus of London Teenage Language (COLT), to those that represent a particular mode of discourse. Some of the major developments of specialised corpora have taken place in the domain of academic discourse and include, for example, the Michigan Corpus of Academic Spoken English (MICASE), and its British counterpart, the British Academic Spoken English corpus (BASE).

Another category of corpora are those that capture the language use of learners. The analysis of learner corpora makes it possible to track developmental aspects of learner language, as well as to highlight particular areas of difficulty for the learner. At the same time, learner corpora can be used as a basis for better descriptions of different varieties that emerge from communication between speakers whose first language is not the language in which they communicate at that time. The design criteria for learner corpora have a slightly different focus to native speaker corpora in that particular emphasis has to be placed on the level of consistency of the resource in terms of the language background of the speakers, including their level of proficiency and first language. Examples of learner corpora include the Cambridge Learner Corpus of written English, which consists of Cambridge exam data, the Longman Learners' Corpus of written English, and the International Corpus of Learners' English (ICLE). Examples of corpora which are used as the basis for exploring the use of English as a lingua franca include the Vienna-Oxford International Corpus of English (VOICE) and the English as a Lingua Franca in Academic Settings (ELFA) Corpus.

Many of the corpora outlined above come with their own concordancing interface, often accessible via the internet. Only some of those mentioned are freely available, others are available for a licence fee while others, usually held by publishers, are not publically available (see O'Keeffe *et al.*, 2007 for a summary of which corpora are available). The next section will consider in more detail the various tools and methods which may be used to explore the language captured in spoken and written corpora for pragmatics research.

1.5 USING A CORPUS TO STUDY PRAGMATICS

Corpus linguistics offers a research tool which benefits the study of pragmatics in a number of ways. One of the primary benefits that corpus linguistics offers the researcher is large amounts of naturally-occurring data, i.e. large amounts of language in use. However, as

Orpin (2005: 39) cautions, 'an attendant danger in using a large corpus is that the researcher may feel swamped by the huge amount of data s/he is faced with'. She maintains that a good entry point for the researcher is the corpus frequency list and this corpus tool, in addition to keyword lists and concordance lines, will be explored in this section. In Chapter 2, we discuss the limitations of using a corpus for pragmatics research.

Corpus word frequency lists

The frequency of a word or a phrase in different contexts is an important part of its description. Tognini-Bonelli (2001: 4) claims that 'frequency of occurrence is indicative of frequency of use and this gives a good basis for evaluating the profile of a specific word, structure or expression in relation to a norm'. Therefore, frequency lists are often a good starting point for the analysis of a corpus. According to Baker (2006: 47), 'used sensitively, [frequency lists] can illuminate a variety of interesting phenomena'. Wordlists also provide a good starting point for subsequent searches of individual items at concordance level and can be useful in the comparison of different corpora. Wordlists can be generated to account for individual items or for recurrent sequences of two or more items. Lemmatised frequency lists group together words from the same lemma, i.e. all grammatical inflections of a word. For example, the words 'say', 'said', 'saying', 'says' are all part of the lemma SAY. Lemmatised lists also have a place in more applied contexts, including English Language Teaching where it can be beneficial to teach all forms of one lemma together and to give priority to the most frequently used form.

When applied to the study of pragmatics, a word frequency list may allow the identification of both the presence (and absence) of items that may be characteristic of the pragmatic system of a particular language variety. For example, Table 1.2 shows a direct comparison of the frequency lists for the top 25 words of the spoken component of the British National Corpus (BNC) and the Limerick Corpus of Irish English (LCIE). Both frequency lists are unlemmatised and the spoken BNC frequency list is taken from Leech *et al.*, 2001.

Table 1.2, in addition to highlighting some *potential* pragmatic similarities between British and Irish English, also may point toward likely differences. For example, the personal pronouns *I* and *you* (positions 2 and 3 in the BNC and 2 and 4 in LCIE), characteristic of the deictic system in many languages, feature prominently and appear to be comparable. In contrast, the pronoun *we* is in 13th position in the BNC but does not appear in the top 25 words in LCIE (see Chapter 3 for a further discussion of these pronouns). Furthermore, the response token *yeah*, a word used to show that a listener is engaged with what a speaker says, occurs in 19th place in the BNC but it appears in 10th position in LCIE. This could indicate a predominance of *yeah* as a response token in Irish English as opposed to British English. O'Keeffe and Adolphs (2008) explored response tokens in British and Irish English and their findings are consistent in relation to the use of *yeah*; however, they found that in British English there is an (almost) equal tendency to use *yes* as a response token. In Irish English, *yes* was not found as a high frequency response item. Finally, two tokens with the potential to hedge in Irish English, *like* and *know*, both appear in LCIE (positions 14 and 15 respectively) but do not feature within the top 25 items on the BNC list. This may indicate that speakers of Irish English hedge more than their British counterparts or that these hedges take different forms (see Chapter 4 for a further discussion of hedges).

Table 1.2 Top 25 most frequent words in the BNC and LCIE

	BNC	LCIE
1	the	the
2	I	I
3	you	and
4	and	you
5	it	to
6	that	it
7	a	a
8	's	that
9	to	of
10	of	yeah
11	n't	in
12	in	was
13	we	is
14	is	like
15	do	know
16	they	he
17	er	on
18	was	they
19	yeah	have
20	have	there
21	what	no
22	he	but
23	to	for
24	but	be
25	for	what

Frequency lists can be generated for recurrent strings or sequences, as well as for individual words. Table 1.3 below shows the most frequent 2-, 3- and 4-word units in LCIE.

Although the kinds of sequences generated in this way do not necessarily fully reflect the underlying structure of a language, the output is strongly suggestive of common expressions of which the sequences evident in Table 1.3 form a part. These include expressions such as *you know, I think, I don't know, I don't think, know what I mean*, and so on. In terms of the pragmatics of Irish English, it could be argued that these items are characteristic of the importance of relational language, the language we use to negotiate or build our relationships with others, in everyday casual conversation. Irish English is characterised by a high degree of markers that function as hedges, many of which are centred around the verbs *know* and *think* (see also Chapter 4). These multi-word units can also be referred to as 'lexical bundles', 'chunks' or 'clusters' (see Greaves and Warren, 2010).

A useful distinction when looking at units is between those which seem complete (*I don't know*) or integrated compared with those that seem incomplete or fragmented (*know what I mean*). There is a temptation to dismiss the latter fragmented units but these are in fact operating as frames for different structures, for example:

You know what I mean?
If you know what I mean?
Do you know what I mean?

Table 1.3 Ten most frequent 2-word, 3-word and 4-word units in LCIE results per million words

Frequency rank	2-word units		3-word units		4-word units	
1	you know	4406	I don't know	1212	you know what I	230
2	in the	3435	do you know	769	know what I mean	215
3	of the	2354	a lot of	522	do you know what	208
4	do you	2332	you know what	379	I don't know what	134
5	I don't	2200	do you want	373	do you want to	121
6	I think	2003	I don't think	338	are you going to	103
7	It was	1939	you know the	323	you know the way	103
8	I was	1891	you have to	308	I don't know I	91
9	going to	1849	going to be	307	thank you very much	91
10	on the	1801	yeah yeah yeah	297	the end of the	85

Does he know what I mean?
Does she know what I mean?
Do you know what I mean **by X**?
Does he know what I mean **by X**?
Does she know what I mean **by X**? . . . etc.

However, a mere frequency-based list of continuous sequences is limited in its explanatory power when it comes to the study of pragmatics. Current research in the area of computational linguistics has introduced new techniques for extracting meaningful units from corpora, both on the basis of frequency information (see, for example, Danielsson, 2003) and on the basis of part-of-speech (POS) tagged corpora. POS tagging involves assigning a grammatical tag to each word in a corpus. One of the most famous POS tagging systems is called Constituent-Likelihood Automatic Word Tagging System or CLAWS. CLAWS automatically assigns a POS tag and is reported to have a 97 per cent success rate on general written English (see Garside and Smith, 1997).

Keyword list

A keyword can be described as a word (or cluster of words) which occurs with unusual frequency in a given text or set of texts when compared to a reference corpus (Scott, 2010). A word or cluster of words may be found to occur much more frequently than would otherwise be expected (a positive keyword) or much less frequently (a negative keyword). Keywords are identified on the basis of statistical comparisons of word frequency lists derived from the target corpus and the reference corpus. Each item in the target corpus is compared with its equivalent in the reference corpus and the statistical significance of difference is calculated using chi-square or log-likelihood statistics (see Dunning, 1993). Both of these statistics compare actual observed frequencies between two items with their expected frequencies, assuming random distribution. If the difference between observed and expected frequency is large, then it is likely that the relationship between the two items is not random, but that other factors influence their relationship. In this way, the procedure generates words that are characteristic, as well as those that are uncharacteristic in a given target corpus. The choice of the reference corpus used as the basis for such a comparison is crucial in this context, as it will affect the output of keywords. For example, in a comparison of a transcript of medical consultation with a reference corpus that consists solely of written texts, the characteristics of spoken versus written language may interfere with the analysis of keywords in the medical consultation genre. The reference corpus can include the corpus for which one is generating keywords. For example, in generating the keywords of one article from a particular newspaper, one might use a reference corpus of all of the articles from that newspaper in the same year (which would include the target article).

Table 1.4 illustrates the positive and negative keyword lists when comparing C-MELT, a corpus of the meetings of English language teachers, with LCIE as the reference corpus. The positive keywords are those which are unusually frequent whereas the negative keywords are those which are not unusually frequent.

Table 1.4 Top ten positive and negative keywords when comparing C-MELT and LCIE

Positive keywords	Negative keywords
KET	ah
PET	he
students	was
semester	now
class	am
exam	like
we	you
English	on
classes	she
think	there

As can be seen, the positive keyword list is dominated by words that characterise the nature of language teaching such as *KET*, *PET* (both names of Cambridge ESOL exams) and *English*, and those that characterise teaching in general such as *students*, *class* and *exam*. In terms of pragmatics, the words *we* and *think* are notable in the positive keyword list. As Chapter 3 further explores, *we* can be used by speakers to create inclusivity and solidarity or to create an out-group consisting of the speaker and others that are not present in the conversation. In common with Tables 1.2 and 1.3, *think*, which is often used to hedge, again appears. In contrast, other items characteristic of the deictic system in everyday conversation such as *you*, *he*, *she* and *now* appear in the negative keyword list (see also Chapter 7). Keyword (or cluster) lists therefore are another good starting point in tandem with word and cluster frequency counts.

Concordance lines

Corpus word frequency lists are, admittedly, a raw measure of comparability, based on, as Table 1.2 demonstrates, the potential of a word form rather than its actual function. Therefore, many corpus studies recommend that frequency analysis be complemented by a detailed consideration of the environment of key words through the use of concordances

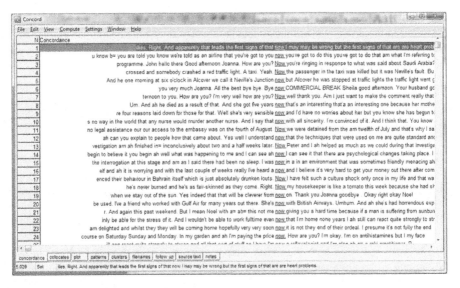

Figure 1.1 A Key Word in Context (KWIC) of the word *now* using WordSmith Tools Version 5.0 (Scott, 2009), using LCIE.

and collocational tools (see, for example, Farr and O'Keeffe, 2002; O'Keeffe and Adolphs, 2008). According to Sinclair (2003: 173), 'a concordance is an index to the places in a text where particular words and phrases occur'. Visually, as Figure 1.1 shows, the software programmes used to generate concordances generally present results in a Key Word in Context (KWIC) format, which features a *node* word (underlined in Figure 1.1), the subject of the query by the researcher, surrounded by the *co-text*, words that occur before and after it.

Corpus users can normally specify the number of words to the left and to the right of the search word that are displayed as part of the output. If a corpus is tagged for POS, then users may also carry out a concordance search based on word class or grammatical structure (see Tribble, 2010 for an overview of the use and history of concordances).

A single item can, at times, produce a very large number of concordances (for example, the number in the bottom left-hand corner of Figure 1.1 tells us there are 5,029 concordance lines for *now* in this instance). Much of the concordancing software available allows the researcher to re-sort the concordance lines in a number of ways, for example, re-sorting to the left enables us to see what occurs before the node word, whereas to the right enables us to see what occurs after it. This can prove useful in discovering different patterns associated with the node word.

On first viewing, concordance lines can prove difficult to interpret because they are generated in the order in which they occur in the corpus. Sinclair (2003: xvi-xvii) recommends a seven-step procedure for 'uncovering the mysteries of most concordances' (p. xvi). These steps are:

(1) *Initiate*: Look at the words that occur directly to the left and right of the node (Sinclair recommends working with no more than a single screen of concordances at any one time). Note any that are repeated. Employ the strongest pattern you find as a starting point.
(2) *Interpret*: Look at the repeated word and formulate a hypothesis that may link them or most of them (for example, they may all have similar meanings).
(3) *Consolidate*: Look for other evidence, for example from adjoining words, to support your hypothesis. Be prepared to 'loosen' your hypothesis based on this.
(4) *Report*: When you have exhausted the patterns you can observe, formulate an explicit, testable hypothesis.
(5) *Recycle*: Following from the *initiate* step, employ the next strongest pattern in the vicinity of the node and repeat steps 2–4. Continue until all repeated patterns have been exhausted.
(6) *Result*: Make a final list of hypotheses based on the node.
(7) *Repeat*: Gather a new selection of concordances of your node word from the corpus. Repeat the steps and confirm, extend or revise your hypotheses as you progress.

There are, however, some caveats concerning concordance lines. The first is that although they provide information on a node (the search word), they do not interpret it. As is evident in Sinclair's (2003) seven-step process to concordance analysis, it is the responsibility of the researcher to determine the patterns that are salient and construct hypotheses as to why these patterns occur. Therefore, as Baker (2006: 89) states, 'a concordance analysis is . . . only as good as its analyst'.

There are many ways of examining and interpreting concordance data. A concordance output can often be useful in providing a representation of language data which allows the user to notice patterns relating to the way in which a lexical item or a sequence is used in context. In order to describe the nature of individual units of meaning, Sinclair (1996) suggests four parameters: *collocation, colligation, semantic preference* and *semantic prosody. Collocation* refers to the habitual co-occurrence of words, for example *blonde* and *hair*. As McCarthy *et al.* (2009) define it, collocation means the way words combine to form pairs which occur frequently together: *make an effort, do one's duty, torrential rain, strictly forbidden. Colligation* is the co-occurrence of grammatical choices which 'gives the phrase its essential flexibility, so that it can fit into the surrounding co-text' (Sinclair, 1996: 83). For example, we say *I was discharged from the hospital* rather than *I was discharged out of the hospital.* Even though *from* and *out of* both work on a semantic level in the sense of exiting from the building, only *from* colligates with *discharge. Semantic preference* of a lexical item or expression is a semantic abstraction of its prominent collocates. In his discussion of the expression *the naked eye*, Sinclair (1996) finds that most of the verbs and adjectives preceding this expression are related to the concept of 'vision'. The verbs 'see' and 'seen' together occur 25 times within 4 words to the left of the expression in a sample of 151 examples of *the naked eye*.

Table 1.5 shows the top ten most frequent collocates for the nouns *Democrat* and *Republican* taken from the COCA corpus.

Table 1.5 Top ten most frequent collocates for
Democrat and *Republican* in the COCA corpus

Democrat	Republican
ruling	extremist
Russian	mean-spirited
yellow	anti-tax
hard-core	hard-line
Christian	country-club
communist	Californian
constructive	greedy
beleaguered	later
electable	slick
fun	ambitious

Semantic prosodies allow the researcher to assess the pragmatic impact of these collocates. First discussed by Sinclair (1987) and Louw (1993), semantic prosodies are associations that arise from the collocates of a lexical item and are not easily detected using introspection. Semantic prosodies have mainly been described in terms of their positive or negative polarity (Sinclair, 1991; Stubbs, 1995; Partington, 1998) but also in terms of their association with 'tentativeness/indirectness/face saving' (McCarthy, 1998: 22). As we can see, there are 'unpleasant' adjectives such as *hard-core*, *mean-spirited* or *greedy* used to describe the groups of politicians. However, the majority of these collocate with Republican rather than Democrat; with Democrats also being attributed the adjectives *constructive*, *electable* and, indeed, *fun*. Therefore, it seems that in the COCA corpus, the item *Republican* displays a negative prosody.

Corpus-based pragmatic analysis can be further complemented by demographic speaker information such as gender, age, educational background or region that accompanies conversations contained in many modern spoken corpora (this demographic information is often referred to as *metadata*). This metadata allows the researcher a more detailed interpretation of the corpus results. As referred to above, O'Keeffe and Adolphs (2008) analyse the form and function of response tokens such as *yeah*, *lovely*, *great* or *absolutely* across British and Irish English. To examine form, they analysed two one-million-word corpus samples from the Cambridge and Nottingham Corpus of Discourse in English (CANCODE) and LCIE. From these samples, they generated word and cluster lists and these were manually cross-checked with transcripts using concordancing. They demonstrate that, in terms of overall frequency, listener response tokens are far more frequent in British English than in Irish English. In order to compare the data functionally, they analysed two smaller 20,000 word corpora of casual conversation taken from LCIE and CANCODE. The demographic information provided by CANCODE and LCIE allowed them to closely match their data in terms of gender, age, social relationship, socio-economic class and genre of discourse. Accordingly, in both smaller corpora the participants were female university students in shared accommodation, who were close friends and of similar age (around 20 years old). By controlling for categories such as gender, age and socio-economic class, O'Keeffe and Adolphs were able to make more accurate generalisations across two varieties of the same language. While they found that listener response tokens were more frequent among the British participants, their analysis revealed no variation in the pragmatic function of the response tokens across the two smaller corpora.

Further evidence of the usefulness of semantic prosody is provided by Carter and McCarthy (1999) who noticed a consistently negative prosody associated with the *get*-passive in the corpus data they examined, for example, *get arrested, get sued, get nicked*.

Rühlemann (2010) notes the negative prosody of *set in*, for example, *boredom can easily set in*. Furthermore, he suggests that collocational rules can, at times, be deliberately broken, such as in the case of the phrasal verb *break out* (usually associated with *war*) following the noun *peace*.

Using corpora for pragmatic research is, however, limiting on some levels. There are obviously some aspects of pragmatic analysis that are more suited to corpus analysis than others (we will discuss this in greater detail in Chapter 2). For example, many corpora are not yet tagged for pragmatic features such as a speech act and, therefore, it is necessary to manually search for instances of individual speech acts. This process can be quite time-consuming. This particular aspect can, however, be overcome by the use of small corpora such as those advocated for here. Another issue particular to most spoken corpora is that transcripts are a written representation of a spoken text and are characterised by a tension between accuracy, readability and issues of representation (see, for example, Roberts, 1997; Bird, 2005). However, the continued development of multi-modal corpora will ensure that, in the future, the researcher will be able to align transcription with its audio-visual context (see Knight *et al.*, 2009 for an overview of emerging research in this area). The comparability of corpora across language varieties can also be an issue because of the differing design criteria used in the construction of different corpora. There have been attempts within corpus linguistics to address this. For example, the International Corpus of English is designed for comparability across different varieties and the design framework for LCIE is based on the CANCODE matrix (see McCarthy, 1998). Despite these issues, corpus linguistics affords the researcher access to (often large amounts of) naturally occurring text, the ability to explore both form and function, and the background information necessary to control for various macro- and micro-social factors, thereby providing pragmatics with a very compatible methodological tool.

1.6 FURTHER READING

Adolphs, S. (2006) *Introducing Electronic Text Analysis: A Practical Guide for Language and Literary Studies*. London: Routledge.
This book is a practical introduction to corpora. Written specifically for students studying this topic for the first time, the book begins with a discussion of the underlying principles of electronic text analysis. It then examines how these corpora enhance our understanding of literary and non-literary works. The book contains abundant illustrative examples and a glossary with definitions of main concepts.

Anderson, W. and **Corbett, J.** (2009) *Exploring English with Online Corpora: An Introduction.* Basingstoke, Hampshire: Palgrave Macmillan.
This book provides a valuable entry point for those involved in the initial stages of corpus design and analysis. The book centres on available online corpora, namely the BNC, COCA, the TIME corpus, MICASE and the SCOTS corpus. These corpora generate the potential for the novice researcher to explore the use of English around the world making the book particularly relevant to both learners and teachers of English.

McEnery, T., Xiao R. and **Tono, Y.** (2006) *Corpus-based Language Studies: An Advanced Resource Book.* London: Routledge.
This book provides an extremely comprehensive overview of the field of corpus linguistics. Divided into three sections, *Introduction, Extension* and *Exploration,* the book's stated goal is to engage the reader with an increasing depth and intensity as s/he progresses. It is a valuable resource for the corpus researcher, regardless of the level of expertise.

O'Keeffe A. and **McCarthy, M.** (eds) (2010) *The Routledge Handbook of Corpus Linguistics.* London: Routledge.
This corpus handbook provides the researcher with a comprehensive guide to the area of corpus linguistics. Organised around six thematic sections, the handbook features 45 chapters dealing with all facets of corpus linguistics from building your own corpus to analysing a corpus to applied corpus studies. Each chapter also contains a further reading section in order to facilitate further investigation of a particular topic.

Verschueren, J. (1999) *Understanding Pragmatics.* London: Arnold.

Grundy, P. (2008) *Doing Pragmatics.* London: Hodder Education.
Both of these books provide a comprehensive introduction to the major theoretical and methodological aspects of the field of pragmatics. They are both engaging and accessible texts and assume no prior knowledge of the field. Each is noteworthy for both suggestions for further reading and research topics for further study.

CHAPTER 2

Researching pragmatics

2.1 INTRODUCTION

Looking at how pragmatics has been studied is a challenging endeavour. Even though the span of its existence is relatively short, it has diversified considerably in its application. The differing and varied development of pragmatics as an area of research is bound up with its link to meaning in context. Let us revisit the definition of pragmatics, which we addressed in Chapter 1, so as to get a view on how this diversity has come about. Crystal provides us with a broad definition:

> Pragmatics is the study of language from the point of view of users, especially of the choices they make, the constraints they encounter in using language in social inter-action and the effects their use of language has on other participants in the act of communication.

> (Crystal, 1985: 240)

This definition accommodates not only speech acts but also the social context of discourse in its many different manifestations (e.g. power and politeness, use of metaphor and irony, and so on). It also focuses on the user and the intended meaning but all within a social context. To use Leech's terms, it focuses on how writers and speakers, as social actors, both get things done with language and simultaneously attend to their interpersonal relationships with other participants (Leech, 1983).

'Research' in the area of pragmatics suggests purely empirical enquiry; however, pragmatics has its origin in the philosophy of language and there remains an important ongoing dialectic process whereby core concepts of pragmatics are debated, critiqued, revisited and refined. Such intellectual debate is as important to pragmatics (and linguistics in general) as it is to philosophy. This is attested by looking at the signature journals in pragmatics where you will find such philosophical debate sitting comfortably alongside empirical studies. Lindblom (2001), for example, looked at Grice's Co-operative Principle. The debate was also taken up by Davies (2007), who highlights the confusion which arises from the use of the word 'co-operative'. Confusion between Grice's technical notion of 'co-operative' and its general meaning has led to what Davies terms 'co-operation drift'. She attributes the misinterpretation, in part, to 'the relocation of the Co-operative Principle from philosophy to linguistics' (ibid.: 2308). (For a more detailed overview of Grice's Co-operative Principles, see Chapter 4.)

2.2 DIVERSITY OF STUDIES IN PRAGMATICS: FIVE DIVERSE CASE STUDIES

As we have discussed, the breadth of application of pragmatics is immense, thus leading to comments such as '[f]ears of uncontrolled expansion far beyond the limits of what could be called "linguistic" are, [therefore], not entirely without grounds' (Verschueren, 1999: 10). However, it is a testimony to the pervasive power of pragmatics as a framework that it has had such a wide-ranging application empirically and theoretically. Pragmatics, as a framework for the study of intended meaning in social context, has proved inclusive rather than delimiting.

It is very worthwhile to take a close look at any issue of the main journals in the field, for example, the *Journal of Pragmatics*, *Pragmatics* (the journal published by the International Pragmatics Association (IPrA)) and the *Journal of Historical Pragmatics*.

Taking just five papers (out of ten) from one issue of the *Journal of Pragmatics* (2007, vol. 39, issue 12), we find the following eclectic range of studies all using 'pragmatics' as a framework for research:

- The pragmatics of conversation and communication in noisy settings (McKellin *et al.*, 2007);
- Performing texts/performing readings: a pragmatic understanding of the revisionist interpretation of American literature (Bollobás, 2007);
- Manner-of-motion verbs in wine description (Caballero, 2007);
- Voicing folk for the academy: interdiscursivity and collective identity in a north Dalmatian ethnography (Plas, 2007);
- Grice's Co-operative Principle: meaning and rationality (Davies, 2007).

Let us compare these briefly to see how they all lay claim to the field of pragmatics. McKellin *et al.* (2007) take as their focus real conversations in two noisy settings, the restaurant and the classroom, and they collect real spoken and audio visual recordings in these settings. They focus on three questions:

(1) How does noise affect grammatical and discourse structures?
(2) How does noise affect the ability of the conversational participants to engage in co-construction of conversational themes through collaborative talk and reciprocal turn-taking?
(3) What insight does the analysis of conversation in noisy environments provide about the relationships among speech perception, cognitive language processing, and language pragmatics? (ibid.: 2160).

On the basis of their in-depth multimodal empirical work, they reach a far-reaching conclusion: that their data indicate that the strategies employed in these settings are similar to those employed by people who are hard-of-hearing. They claim that usage-based and cognitivist theories of language processing, interaction and pragmatics that ignore language perception are inadequate.

Bollobás (2007) looks at written data, namely American literature (two texts by Henry James), and sets out to show that the pragmatic understanding of reading can help explain recent revisionary interpretations of the canon of American literature. Meanwhile, Caballero

(2007) looks at the use of manner-of-motion verbs in wine description ('earthy flavors *run through* this firm-textured red' or 'hints of milk chocolate and vanilla *sneak in* on the palate' are two of her examples). Plas (2007) examines realisations of 'folk identities' in a north Dalmatian ethnographic account from the end of the nineteenth century. This study illustrates how pragmatics can help us understand ethno-cultural identity formation in a dialogue which took place among a group of participants in a particular socio-cultural context in the past.

Davies (2007), in the same volume, looks at one of the core concepts of pragmatics, Grice's Co-operative Principle. She suggests that there is a tendency to confuse Grice's term 'co-operative' with a 'folk-linguistic notion of co-operation' (p. 2308) which is often used in linguistic literature to refer to 'human behaviour in conversation'. By looking at Grice's philosophical writings as a whole, Davies tells us that it is only sometimes used in this manner and it is sometimes used independent of this meaning. She makes a strong argument for the case that knowledge of the philosophical background to the Co-operative Principle not only demonstrates the relative unimportance of 'co-operation' to the Co-operative Principle, it also enables an interpretation which is closer to Grice's original intentions.

The scope and diversity of what constitutes pragmatics research is clear from our brief focus on five diverse papers from one issue of the *Journal of Pragmatics*. What connects all of these is their quest for the understanding of meaning in context, both in theory and in practice. As Verschueren (1999: 10) puts it, it is particularly important to remember that '*meaning* [his emphasis], as a defining feature of what pragmatics is concerned with, is not seen as a stable counterpart of linguistic form. Rather it is dynamically generated in the process of using language.' In tandem with our investigation of meaning as something dynamic, it is important that we continue to grapple with meaning in context as a philosophical concept. As illustrated by Davies' (2007) study, the transfer from philosophical concepts about language to the study of linguistics is not without complication.

2.3 WAYS OF RESEARCHING PRAGMATICS

Pragmatics is a framework for understanding language use. In itself it is not methodology which can be applied. As we have seen with the diverse sample from one past issue of the *Journal of Pragmatics*, there are many means of arriving at a pragmatic understanding of language, ranging from the analysis of texts to philosophical debate. In other words, a number of methodologies are used in pragmatics-based research. Here we will look at some of the main approaches to gathering data in pragmatics research. Studies which employ a methodology are those which are empirical in nature, that is, those which look at language in use. As we discussed briefly at the outset, much of the research in the area of pragmatics is philosophical rather than empirical. This strand of research is no less important. It provides us with a deeper understanding of what we do. The refinement of the models and frameworks that we apply and the delineation of what is and what is not pragmatics is crucial.

Attested data

If you are interested in conducting a pragmatics-based study of language in context, the first issue which faces you is how to get data. There are a number of means to this end. Here we survey the two main types of attested data, *elicited* and *corpus-based*. Attested data is language which we have said, heard, written or read and which we have recorded usually by noting it down or recording it. Attested data is the opposite of intuitive data. Intuitive data is language that we have introspected about. For example, one might reflect on which is more common: *She helped me to wrap the presents* or *She helped me wrap the presents*. Both of these examples and the conclusion that one might reach as a result of one's introspection are intuitive; they are created and reflected upon within one's mind. They are not based on what you have attested, or witnessed. Basing your research on real data can bring rich rewards but it will involve many challenges, a lot of time and effort and, at times, expense. In research in the area of pragmatics, there are different ways of gathering real language.

Elicited data

Elicited data are those which are gained in a very focused way as opposed to data which are selected from an existing collection of recordings or texts or data, and so forth. For example, if you want to look at how people make offers, apologies, refusals and so on, the most common method is to set up a type of task whereby you survey many speakers as to what they would say in a certain situation. Figure 2.1 is typical.

You are a student. You are one day late with your end-of-term assignment. You knock on your tutor's door. What do you say?

Figure 2.1 An example of a Discourse Completion Task.

These tasks are usually referred to as Discourse Completion Tasks or Discourse Completion Tests (DCTs). DCTs have been widely and successfully used in the study of speech acts (see Chapter 5) and speech events (e.g. asking the time). They are particularly favoured as a methodology in the study of second language pragmatic competence (Blum-Kulka *et al.*, 1989; Sasaki, 1998; Billmyer and Varghese, 2000). They are essentially a type of language questionnaire whereby you elicit what a speaker thinks they would say in a situation. In addition to their use in the study of speech acts and events, they are used in dialect studies where they can focus on very specific structures (see Barron, 2005; Schneider and Barron, 2008).

DCTs can be written tasks or they can be presented orally. The degree to which they are controlled can vary. In Figure 2.1 a scenario is presented and the informant has a choice, albeit rather limited, as to the speech act which they opt for. DCTs can be more controlled when they are presented in a turn-based format. The example in Figure 2.2 illustrates how a scenario is set up and then a turn is provided. This is followed by 'write on lines' (a blank turn) which the informant must complete, and so on.

You are applying for a position with a multinational company. The interview committee has requested that you have your professors send letters of recommendation directly to the company. When you call the interview committee to check the status of your application, you are told that one of the recommendation letters has not arrived. You are concerned because you asked your professor for the letter over a month ago.

You stop by your professor's office to find out what has happened.

Professor: Hi, [your name].

You: _____

_____

_____

Figure 2.2 An example of a freer DCT (adapted from Tanck, 2002).

A further example, Figure 2.3, is taken from Beebe and Zhang Waring (2004). Here the authors set out to investigate pragmatic tone.

The attraction of DCTs is their 'discreteness'. The researcher has a lot of control over the language which they want to elicit. The focus can be limited to a very specific context of use, as the examples in Figures 2.1, 2.2 and 2.3 illustrate. As Schauer and Adolphs (2006: 120) put it, 'the aim of discourse completion task research is to investigate a linguistic act within highly predefined parameters'.

The level of control in DCTs has come in for criticism over the years (see Beebe and Cummings, 1996; Schauer and Adolphs, 2006). It is argued that DCTs cannot be used to appraise pragmatic competence in the study of foreign language users because, apart from providing too little context, they cannot constrain discourse options without contaminating the response (Yoon and Kellogg, 2002). In an effort to redress this, Yoon and Kellogg (2002) used a cartoon DCT so as to provide a pictorial context to constrain the response while allowing freedom to elaborate language. Their study which gathered data from 505 Korean learners of English showed that picture DCTs yielded more elaborated language from respondents, whereas written DCT results were more lexicalised. Cultural

You go to a tourist bookstore where the books are kept behind a counter. You ask to see a book on display. The lady behind the counter says, 'If you want to browse, go to a library.'

You would say: _____

_____

_____

You would feel like saying: _____

_____

_____

Figure 2.3 An example of a freer DCT (adapted from Beebe and Zhang Waring, 2004: 245).

considerations are also at play. Rose (1994) conducted a study of requests in Japanese and American English using both DCTs and questionnaires (see more on questionnaires below) and concluded that DCTs may not be culturally appropriate for Japan. As mentioned in Chapter 1, Schauer and Adolphs (2006) illustrate, in a study of expressions of gratitude in DCT data compared with corpus data, that because DCT data is normally based around single utterances, this distorts the overall reality of a speech act which is typically negotiated and developed over a number of turns in a dynamic discourse event.

Boxer and Cohen (2004) note that DCTs are used particularly when:

- Gathering examples of rarely occurring speech acts, speech events or listener responses (see Kasper and Dahl, 1991; Kasper and Rose, 1999; Schauer and Adolphs, 2006)
- Researching speech acts that readily occur but which are difficult to capture on recorded data (for example, requests or complaints)
- Looking at speech acts comparatively and it may be difficult to find corresponding acts that readily occur in data from two languages.

Despite their limitations, a rich body of research into speech acts has amassed as a result of the use of DCTs. Without this methodology, it would have been difficult if not impossible to conduct such research because some speech acts are very difficult to 'obtain' in any other way. Speech acts of conflict and disagreement are particularly elusive (essentially because informants are reluctant to be recorded in such situations) and DCTs have been used as a means of gathering these and many contrastive speech act studies have resulted. For instance, Liang and Han (2005) looked at disagreement strategies between American English and Mandarin Chinese. They based their study on five scenarios for disagreement within a college context. The scenarios vary in the power relationships, ranging from higher to lower status, including peer–peer interactions. Three of the scenarios are shown in Figure 2.4.

Among other findings, Liang and Hạn (2005) tell us that Chinese students employ more politeness strategies when disagreeing with higher status interactants. Both the Chinese and the American students showed fewer politeness strategies when disagreeing with peers. In other studies, Beebe *et al.* (1990) looked at refusals produced by American English speakers and Japanese EFL learners. Chen (1996) used semantic formulae to analyse speech act sets of refusals produced by American and Chinese speakers of English (refusing, requests, invitations, offers and suggestions). The direct refusal, *no*, she found was not a common strategy, regardless of first language background. Chen also shows that an expression of regret is common in American speakers' refusals but is generally not produced by the Chinese speakers.

Varghese and Billmyer (1996) conducted a multi-layered DCT-based study of requests, which elicited data from 55 American English university students. In addition to looking at the request itself, they also focused on social distance and social dominance. They provided an elaborated version of the DCT with additional information on interlocutor's gender, role

---

The English Version of the Discourse Completion Test

Thank you very much for your time and help. Three scenarios are described below in which you are expected to disagree with the speaker on different occasions. How would you respond? Please write out what you are to SAY in real life scenarios.

Your Age: _____   Gender: _____   Hometown: _____

1. Your supervisor questions the originality of the term paper you submit. S/he says to you, 'I'm sorry, but I don't think these ideas are yours.' However, they are yours. In response, you will say:

'..'

2. Your friend makes the following comment on your thesis, 'I think you should supply more data to support your arguments. You know, your conclusion is a little bit weak.' However, you think that there has been enough evidence and the problem is how to give a better explanation of the data. In response, you will say:

'..'

3. In a seminar class on the effect of modern technology, one of your classmates says, 'The so-called modern technology is endangering the environment. It causes too much pollution.' However, you believe such problems are only temporary and can be solved gradually. In response, you will say:

'..'

Figure 2.4 Samples of scenarios from a DCT presented to American and Mandarin students in Liang and Han (2005).

relationship, length of acquaintance, interaction frequency, whether the relationship was optional, and a description of setting. Students were asked to reflect for 30 seconds before responding. They found no significant response differences in the act of requesting across the various versions of the task, but one of their most significant findings was the variation in the length of the request act.

Tanck (2002) looked at both refusals and complaints in native and non-native English speakers. Unlike other studies, Tanck looked at a range of first language backgrounds including non-native speakers whose first language was Chinese, Haitian Creole, Korean, Polish, Russian, Serbian, Spanish or Thai. She found that over time, with focused instruction, the pragmatic competence of the non-native speakers improved. However, Tanck (2002) notes that while DCTs are a time-efficient instrument, they may not be the best way to obtain authentic data because subjects are writing, not speaking, and have the opportunity to contemplate and change their responses, something that is less possible in a naturalistic spoken setting (in her study, 20 per cent completed the survey outside the researcher's presence, and many took a number of days before returning the completed survey).

Role-plays

Role-plays offer another means of collecting data. Boxer and Cohen (2004: 17) point out that in certain contexts role-play data are similar to spontaneous spoken data, 'with the caveat that the researcher is able to set up a context for studying speaking'. Demeter (2007) sees role-play as a method which brings the researcher closest to authentic data in the study of the production of speech acts. He claims that role-play 'tries to provide as natural a setting as possible while allowing for the control of certain variables in the study' (p. 85). This is supported by Rosendale (1989), who used role-plays to elicit data for a study on the speech act of invitation. Konishi and Tarone (2004) used role-plays in their study of English constructions employed in compensation strategies. Thirty native-speaking university students took part in the study. One of the researchers, a Japanese male, took on the role of a Japanese man who had a low level of proficiency in English. Each participant was asked to role-play a series of 15 situations in which they were interacting with the Japanese man. As Konishi and Tarone describe, in each situation the participant needed to refer to an item from a list that they had drawn up (e.g. caretaker, rhinoceros, ostrich, pliers, punch, carburettor, and so on). Participants were told that they would have to use alternative expressions for the items as the Japanese man did not know the word. They were not allowed to use mime, body language or gesture. One example they give is the following:

> You hear on the news that a rhinoceros has run away from the Minnesota Zoo. You try to tell Koji [the Japanese man] the news. However, he doesn't know the word 'rhinoceros' in English. Please explain it to him.
>
> (Konishi and Tarone, 2004: 179)

Konishi and Tarone reflect that they would ideally have liked to use 'a referential communication task' (p. 179) with actual exchange of information rather than a role-play. However, they wanted at least 30 speakers and it was unlikely that they would have been able to find a corresponding number of Japanese participants who collectively did not know the same set of English words.

Based at a Romanian university, Demeter (2007) used role-play as a means of data-gathering for a study of apologies. One of the explicit aims of his study was to demonstrate that the use of role-plays is a valid and effective method of collecting data for the analysis of apologies. To support this, he compared data collected through role-plays with data collected via a DCT. His study involved 19 university students majoring in English. They were asked to role-play an apology in six situations adapted from the US television show *Friends*. Among the situations were these:

- You did not have time to change before going to the wedding of your best friend, and therefore you are wearing sports clothes.
- You had promised your spouse that you would stop smoking. However, you started again, and your wife can tell that you were smoking again.
- You arrive late to your friend's birthday dinner.
- You took your friend's blue jeans without telling him or her. Now your friend has found out and you admit to taking them.

The negative side of role-plays is covered by Rintell and Mitchell (1989), Kasper and Dahl (1991), Sasaki (1998), Jung (2004) and Demeter (2007) among others. They point out that role-plays:

- Can sometimes result in unnatural behavior.
- Are difficult and time-consuming to transcribe and code.
- Offer less control over the situational variables and produce a wider range of speech act production strategies than Discourse Completion Tests as well as considerably longer responses.

DCTs were also used to collect apology data (in Romanian) based on these and some additional situations (also from *Friends*). Comparing role-plays with DCTs, Demeter notes that in some instances, role-plays can offer a better choice, as they solve some of the concerns raised by DCTs, most notably that the DCT may not be an accurate representation of what the speaker would actually say in naturally-occurring situations in real time. Because role-plays require the participant to actually speak instead of write, a more naturalistic response is more attainable as it is easier for the participants to imagine themselves in the respective situations and they do not have a protracted amount of time in which to think about what they might or should say. Role-plays potentially offset Schauer and Adolphs' (2006) criticism that speech acts elicited through DCTs do not capture their dynamic nature over extended turns. In addition, the role-play is conducted in spoken mode whereas a DCT is conducted in writing.

Interviews

Oral interviews are another means of collecting data for the purposes of pragmatic research. These involve the elicitation of conversation using various prompts; they can also be unstructured. The recordings are then transcribed and used for analysis. The main difference between an oral interview and a role-play is that the participants do not take on new identities or roles. There are a number of examples of pragmatic studies which have used this method. Bardovi-Harlig and Salsbury (2004) conducted a longitudinal study of non-native and native English speaker pairings. They look at disagreement between native and non-native speakers. Their focus was on the development of turn organisation over the study period (two semesters) of 12 non-native speakers who were paired with native speaker graduate students. The participants met for an hour every week and their encounters were part semi-structured and part open-ended. Picture cards and emotion cards were used as prompts for conversational topics and in later sessions emotion cards were replaced with open-ended questions. Half of every session was totally unstructured and involved spontaneous conversations. Bardovi-Harlig and Salsbury comment that the richness of the data for analysis which resulted far outweighed the transcription workload. Because they conducted their interviews longitudinally, they were able to track the changes in how non-native speakers organised their turns in disagreements. They found that they moved from making bald statements of disagreement, through to the inclusion of agreement components with disagreement components and, eventually, they were able to postpone disagreement turns within a sequence of turns.

Yuan (2001) conducted an in-depth study which compared written and oral DCTs, natural observational field note data and audio-taped interview data. The study was conducted in China and focused on the compliment speech act. Twelve situations to elicit compliments were devised, plus twelve dialogues to elicit compliment responses. Participants were given the opportunity not to give any answer if they felt that they would not say anything in a particular situation. In the case of the written DCTs, participants filled out the questionnaire in their own time and no time limit was set. The oral DCTs were presented in individual face-to-face encounters where the recorded situations were played to the participants by the researcher. The participants responded to each situation orally and a tape recorder was used to record this. Yuan explains that a second recorder was kept running in order to record the oral sessions in their entirety. In addition, Yuan used a field work notebook to record any compliments and compliment responses encountered during a four-month period. In these notes, Yuan recorded what was said as well as the gender, age and social relationships of the interactants.

Questionnaire data

In addition to Discourse Completion Tasks (which can be categorised as an open-ended written questionnaire: Kasper and Roever, 2005), multiple choice questionnaires can be used to give participants a number of plausible pragmatic options or interpretations of utterances in given situations. Another type of questionnaire involves scaled response tasks where participants assess situational contexts and speech act or discourse samples according to certain variables. Kasper and Roever (2005: 327) note that all questionnaire types, including DCTs, probe into 'offline self-reporting states of knowledge or beliefs'. Respondents are not required to produce language. They are not put in the position of having to comprehend utterances in real time. However, Kasper and Roever (2005) point out that written questionnaires do impose a certain cognitive load on respondents. DCTs require the respondent to recall. Multiple choice demands recognition while scaled response rating means respondents have to perform judgement tasks.

The positive side to using questionnaires is that they are quick to administer and analyse compared to role-play and other elicitation methods. Kasper and Roever (2005) warn, however, that they have to be carefully designed to suit the individual research context. The design of multiple choice questionnaires is particularly demanding. All of the response options must be plausible (unlike multiple choice options in an assessment context where only one response is plausible and all others are implausible distractors). Kasper (2000) and Kasper and Roever (2005) note that multiple choice questionnaires in pragmatics research have varying success depending on their purpose. Multiple choice studies which probe situational routines and implicatures were found to have a satisfactory degree of consistency (see Kasper, 2000) while multiple choice studies which look at speech act realisation strategies 'tend to achieve notoriously poor reliability scores' (Kasper and Roever, 2005: 328).

Corpus data

As discussed in Chapter 1, a corpus is a collection of spoken or written language which is stored on a computer and available for analysis (Biber *et al.*, 1998). Many large corpora are commercially available and some are free (see Lee, 2008 and 2010, and O'Keeffe *et al.*, 2007, for extensive listings). Corpora can be very large; for example, the British National Corpus (BNC) stands at 100 million words, 10 million of which are spoken English. However, to conduct research into pragmatics, one does not necessarily need to use a 'mega-corpus'. In fact a small 'home-made' corpus is often more valuable for pragmatics research because the researcher has access to all of the contextual details and, because of its size, it can be used qualitatively and quantitatively.

Some guidelines for a 'home-made' spoken corpus:

- One hour of talk yields between 10–15,000 words approximately (it varies according to rate and the nature of the speech).
- It takes about ten hours to transcribe one hour of talk. It may take more than this depending on how much detail you wish to add to your transcription (e.g. do you want to add codes for when people overlap when they talk? Do you want to add codes for intonation? Etc.).

In order to build a small spoken corpus, you need to do the following:

(1) Before you start recording, design a speaker information form to log details on each recording such as date, location and setting of recording, speaker age, gender, geographical origin, socio-economic background, the number and relationship of the speakers, and so forth. This will be very useful when you are conducting your analysis.
(2) Electronically record your data (either using an audio or audio-visual recording device; see below on multi-modal corpora).
(3) Transcribe your data using a coding system that suits your research question(s) (see below).
(4) Create a database for each recording, giving each sound file a number which will correspond with its transcription and the details from your speaker information form. This will allow you to readily access detailed information about each transcript when you are conducting your research.

Note that when you record someone speaking, you need to tell them in advance and you need to have their written consent to use the recording for your research. Each speaker recorded in your corpus should sign a consent form. This essentially signs their consent to record the data, transcribe it and use it for research and publications. It is a good idea to make the consent form part of the speaker information form so that both are completed simultaneously.

When you transcribe your data, you have a number of choices and decisions to make. How you will go about it depends on your research aims. For example, if you are researching disagreement, you may wish to use a special code or 'tag' for every instance of disagreement in your data. That way you can automatically find all instances of disagreement. A broad transcription is the quickest but it is very general (see Figure 2.5). A narrow transcription goes into great detail marking prosodic features for example (see Figure 2.6).

<$1>	Okay? So if ye just take three minutes or four minutes and talk to the people around you there and come up with a few things that make us different. <$E> three minutes of group work <\$E>. Okay. Did you come up with things? Finished talking? Yeah? Okay so. What you come up with?
<$2>	Religion.
<$1>	Do you have to have an ethnic do you have to does religion?
<$2>	No it's not necessary but+
<$1>	Okay so. So we'll just put religion over here one second. We can keep it on the final list. Okay. Another one? <$G?>.
<$5>	I think that for <$G?> ethnic difference have a a set of customs and symbols and a well defined location and has to be considerably different from another ethnic group as well. So that's it.
<$1>	Right. What what did you say? You said? Culture and you said a set of customs.
<$5>	Yeah that's sort of the same difference.
<$1>	Okay? So and you said? Language. Okay well we'll start with these. So a set of customs and traditions. Now I'll leave it up to you to argue the point. Is religion a separate point from customs and traditions? What do you think?
<$2>	Yes and no.
<$4>	No. Religion is a is <$G?> of amm like customs and rituals and kind of practice that has to do with being kind of a higher power. Amm and so that would really be amm traditional and <$G?>.

Figure 2.5 Example of broad transcription (an extract from a political science lecture from the LIBEL corpus).

In this book, we use broad transcriptions in a lot of our featured extracts. Table 2.1 shows the basic codes often included in broad transcription and these will serve as a guide for this book.

Narrow transcription goes into great depth to capture as many aspects of the spoken language as possible. The Hong Kong Corpus of Spoken English uses a narrow transcription (see Cheng and Warren, 2007), using the following codes:

- Tone group boundaries are marked with '{ }' brackets.
- The referring and proclaiming tones are shown using combinations of forward and back slashes: rise '/', fall-rise '\/', fall '\', and rise-fall '/\'.

- Level tones are marked '=' and unclassifiable tones '?'.
- Prominence is shown by means of UPPER CASE letters.
- Key is marked with '[ ]' brackets, high key and low key are indicated with '^' and '_' respectively, while mid key is not marked (i.e. it is the default).
- Termination is marked with '< >' brackets with high, mid, and low termination using the same forms of notation used for key choices.
- Points in the discourse where simultaneous talk occurs are marked with a single * in the utterance of the current speaker, and ** in the utterance of the 'interrupter'.

A key concern in building a corpus, no matter what size, is whether it is representative (see Atkins *et al.*, 1992; Biber, 1993; O'Keeffe *et al.*, 2007; Reppen, 2010), that is, whether it represents what it claims to represent. Any chance collection of data will not make a valid corpus. For example, if you wanted to study pragmatic markers in English language

---

A: { = do you [STILL] have the BOARding < PASS > }
B: { ? < ER > } { ? < ER > } { ? < LET > me } { \ [LET] me < SEE > }
   { \ the [^ BOARding] < PASS > } { \ no i am < NOT > } (.) { ? i am
   not < TAking > }
A: { \ oh you < MEAN > } { \/ the [CHECK] in STAFF collect the
   boarding CARD < alREAdy > }
B: { \ < YEAH > } * { \ < _ YEAH > }

Figure 2.6 Example of narrow transcription from the Hong Kong Corpus of Spoken English (HKCSE) (Cheng and Warren, 2006).

Table 2.1 Typical codes used in a broad transcription of spoken corpora

Example of code	What it means
<$1>	*Speakers*: Every time there is a new speaker, a number is given to it in order of 'appearance'. The first person to speak in a recording is <$1>, the second <$2> and so on.
<$E> ... <\$E>	*Background noises and extralinguistic information*: it is useful to note background noises and extralinguistic information such as 'dog barks', 'door opens' or 'sound of cash register' in the transcript as these may have relevance to the interaction.
+	*Speaker interruptions*: when a speaker is interrupted, + marks where their utterance ends. If they resume what they were saying, this can also be marked with +
=	*Incomplete word*: incomplete words can be marked with =
<$G?>	*Unintelligible word(s)*: when you cannot make out what has been said, <$G?> can be used. If you can figure out the number of syllables, then this can be noted, for example a two syllable unintelligible word could be transcribed as <$G2>.

teachers' talk, a corpus of around 20,000 words, just about two hours of classroom talk from one classroom, will not yield results that can be generalisable because the corpus only represents two classes given by the same teacher. Any conclusions can only be seen within a case study and other case studies would be needed as a follow up. A corpus of around 40,000 words, approximately four hours of classroom talk, drawn equally from eight classes (30 minutes each), all at the same language level (e.g. beginners) and of similar composition in terms of gender, nationality and age, with four male and four female teachers, all recorded in different institutions, though still a small study, would offer more generalisable results. Therefore, before one begins recording data, one must carefully consider the corpus 'design matrix' – in other words, what will go into it? Begin by looking at your research questions. Consider how much and what type of data you need to have in order to be able to address these questions.

The key instruments of analysis when looking at a corpus are covered in Chapter 1, namely concordancing, word and cluster frequency counts, and key word analyses. There are a number of software applications which can be used, some commercially available and some free to download. Evison (2010), Scott (2010) and Tribble (2010) provide excellent introductions to what a corpus, corpus software and concordances can do (respectively).

Among the aspects of pragmatics that have become part of the growing body of work in corpus-based studies are pragmatic markers. Pragmatic markers, in their broadest sense, include a gambit of markers such as hedges, discourse markers, boosters, markers of shared knowledge and hesitation devices (see Carter and McCarthy, 2006). Aijmer and Simon-Vandenbergen (2006) compiled an interesting volume on pragmatic markers across a number of languages and using a variety of approaches. Stenström (2006) looks at the Spanish pragmatic markers *o sea* and *pues* and their English equivalents using a corpus-based approach. Lewis (2006) studies adversative relational markers in French and English. *Surely* and its Spanish counterpart are the focus of Downing's study (2006), while Johansson conducts a corpus-based study of *well* and its equivalent in Norwegian and German. Another growing strand of pragmatic research in the area of discourse markers seems to be the comparison of native and non-native speaker usages. Müller (2005) built a parallel corpus of American students and German non-native speakers of English retelling and discussing a silent movie. The study focuses on the discourse markers *so, well, you know* and *like*. Fung and Carter (2007) compare native and non-native use of discourse markers in a pedagogic setting. Amador Moreno *et al.* (2006) look at the use of discourse markers in classroom recordings of Spanish and French language classes and make the case for the use of such data in language teacher education so that teachers who are non-native speakers of the target language can be exposed to the typical classroom use of certain discourse markers.

Hedging has also received wide attention, particularly in relation to its use in academic genres (see, for example, Hyland and Milton, 1997; Hinkel, 1997 and 2002). Hedging in spoken Irish English is compared by Farr and O'Keeffe (2002) in two specific institutional contexts, radio interviews and post-observation teacher education meetings. Lewis (2005) creates a corpus of online political discussion fora in French and English. She looks at this new communicative situation where there is 'many-to-many interaction, physical distance and particularly low contextual information' among other things. She notes the use of two concession markers which appear to resemble more closely that of conversation than that of monologic political discourse.

Vague language has also been well-covered in corpus-based studies. Cutting (2007) brings together a number of studies on vague language. Most of the studies in Cutting's volume are based on small 'self-assembled' corpora. Cook (2007) looks at vague language structure in a Bob Dylan song and in public relations web-pages from global food and tobacco companies. Koester (2007) analyses the use of vague language in North American office talk while Adolphs *et al.* (2007) look at vague language in the context of health communication (specifically in NHS Direct phone calls and hospital chaplain–patient interactions). Other corpus-based contexts for the study of vague language include courtrooms (Cotterill, 2003 and 2007), radio phone-ins and academic seminars (Evison *et al.*, 2007) and the cross-cultural context of the Hong Kong Spoken Corpus (which includes native and non-native speakers of English) (Cheng *et al.*, 2008)).

Corpora have also been used to conduct research into irony (Clift, 1999), humour (Vaughan, 2007) and metaphor (Charteris-Black, 2004a, 2004b and 2006; Charteris-Black *et al.*, 2006). Modality is also well-researched using corpus-based methods (Biber, 1988; Hyland, 1996a and 1998; Farr, 2005). Aspects of deixis are also well-researched using corpus linguistics. Notably Rühlemann (2007) looks at *I* and *you* in the BNC spoken corpus and notes that these two highly frequent items in conversation have far fewer occurrences in writing and that this clearly suggests that personal deixis is much less important in writing than in conversation. O'Keeffe (2002 and 2006) looks at deictic centring and othering in corpora of media discourse, particularly through the pronouns *we* and *they*. Chang (2002) uses a small corpus of an American radio talkshow to look at pronoun use by radio hosts. Generic pronouns were investigated by Holmes (1998) in the Wellington Corpus of Spoken New Zealand English. Mason and Şerban (2003) used a corpus of Oscar Wilde's novel, *The Picture of Dorian Gray,* comparing its English text with its Romanian translation for their study of deixis in monologue and dialogue.

Clearly, the strength corpus linguistics brings to the study of pragmatics is its power to automatically search for and retrieve items. This allows for patterns of use to be brought into relief, particularly those features which have become pragmatically-specialised in small concentrated corpora. For example, in a corpus of 55,000 words of radio phone-in calls to an Irish radio programme, *Liveline*, patterns of deixis can be mapped through patterns of pronoun use (see O'Keeffe, 2002 and 2006). For example, the use of *us* by the presenter deictically aligns the listener and the presenter vis-á-vis the caller: *Thank you very much indeed for talking to **us**.* The pattern [vocative] + *thank you very much indeed for talking to us* is brought to light as a pragmatically-specialised closing device in the dataset illustrated in Figure 2.7.

very much indeed for talking to **us** and thank you Una. Thank you.
ry much indeed for talking to **us**. Thank you. Thank you all the
ank you very much indeed for talking to **us**. Not at all. Thank you nd Felix thank you
d for talking to **us**. Thank Marian.
deed for talking to **us**. Thank you Marian
indeed for talking to **us**. Thank you for having
h indeed for talking to **us** about that. Thank you
h indeed for talking to **us**. Right you are Marian.
gain for talking to **us**. Alright thank you.
indeed for talking to **us**. Okay thank you. Bye

Figure 2.7 Concordance lines for *us* in a corpus of radio phone-ins.

The benefits of using a corpus in the study of pragmatics are many. However, we also have to acknowledge that not all aspects of pragmatics lend themselves to being studied in a corpus. Rühlemann (2010) looks at how a corpus can be used to study pragmatics but he also deals with how using a corpus can restrict how we study pragmatics. He notes that 'if we take pragmatics as the study of meaning of text in context, it becomes clear that the relationship between pragmatics and corpus linguistics is not unproblematic. The reason is simple: corpora record text not meaning and they record context only crudely' (p. 289). A written text will be devoid of its original textual features such as fonts, layout, photographs, and so on. Transcribed spoken data will usually be devoid of its prosodic features and its non-verbal dimension (e.g. gestures, facial expressions, posture of speakers, proximity of speakers, and so on). Contexts and relationships are usually scantly detailed relative to the reality of any context and the relationship of the speakers. For example, describing a situation as 'two friends chatting in a cafe' gives the outside observer little to go on in terms of how long they have known each other, how close they are as friends, what kind of shared knowledge they have, and so on.

While corpus software allows for rapid retrieval of search items, not everything in pragmatics lends itself to automatic retrieval. For example, it can be difficult to get a range of samples of speech acts, especially those which are face threatening as people generally do not 'perform' these when a recorder is present. Spoken corpora are few, compared to written corpora, and those that are available may not be designed in such a way that suits the study of pragmatic features (e.g. they may have been designed for sociolinguistic or dialect research). Pragmatic tagging is in its early stages, therefore most pragmatics-based work, particularly in relation to speech acts and speech events, has to be conducted manually for the most part. Spoken language corpora are usually not aligned to audio or audio visual files so they lack the detail needed for many pragmatic studies.

Knight and Adolphs (2008) point out that one of the key differences between written and spoken corpus analysis is that the spoken corpus is a mediated record, a textual rendering of an event which is multi-modal in nature. As a result, analyses of pragmatic functions in spoken corpora tend to exclude the exploration of the interplay between gesture and language and therefore neglect a core element in the construction of meaning in interaction. The future of corpus-based pragmatics research lies with more advanced spoken corpora, especially those which are multi-modal. That is where speech and image are simultaneously recorded and where the orthographic transcription is aligned to the image. In multi-modal transcription, non-verbal communication is also transcribed and time-stamped (see Dahlmann and Adolphs, 2009). This allows, for example, for searches of head nods. A concordance of head nods would yield all the places in the transcript where participants nodded and this would be aligned to both the transcript and the audio-visual file for any one occurrence.

All in all, the use of corpora for the study of pragmatics is in its early stages and it is hoped that in coming years more corpora will use pragmatic tagging. Romero-Trillo (2008: 3) notes an increase in the number of empirical studies of pragmatics in areas such as power and politeness, speech acts, and intercultural pragmatics and 'to substantiate the results, studies have *resorted to* corpus linguistics as a methodology' (our emphasis). He notes that likewise, 'many studies in the area of corpus linguistics now use pragmatics as a model for the interpretation of data' (ibid). What Romero-Trillo exposes is a relationship of reciprocating need or, as he puts it, 'a mutualistic entente'.

2.4 CONCLUSION

Research in the area of pragmatics is clearly multi-faceted and this reflects the many directions and applications of the field. In this chapter, we have covered a diverse range of approaches and methods from philosophical debates, literary-based studies, inter-language studies using DCTs, role-plays, questionnaires and corpus-based studies. All of these studies have in common the aim of understanding language use in context, either in theory or practice. There is no right method in the study of pragmatics. Most empirical studies in pragmatics focus on small amounts of data (whether elicited or otherwise) within concentrated parameters of use. All of these in their varied approaches inch us forward in our attempt to better understand language in context. The key guideline for any empirical study in pragmatics is that it is carefully designed.

2.5 FURTHER READING

Adolphs, S. (2008) *Corpus and Context: Investigating Pragmatic Functions in Spoken Discourse.* Amsterdam: John Benjamins.
This book explores the relationship between corpus linguistics and pragmatics. In particular, it discusses possible frameworks for analysing units of language beyond the single word. This involves a close analysis of contextual variables in relation to lexico-grammatical and discoursal patterns that emerge from the corpus data, as well as a wider discussion of the role of context in spoken corpus research.

Boxer, D. and **Cohen, A.** (eds) (2004) *Studying Speaking to Inform Second Language Learning.* Clevedon, England: Multilingual Matters.
This is an excellent collection of papers on how to study speaking in the language classroom. Because it brings together many different approaches and studies it is a very useful starting point for researchers who can look at how empirical studies were carried out in classroom contexts. The editors give an excellent introduction which sets the scene for spoken language research in pedagogical contexts. Many of the methodologies and insights in the volume have applications to studies of speaking outside of the classroom context.

O'Keeffe, A., McCarthy, M. J. and **Carter, R. A.** (2007) *From Corpus to Classroom: Language Use and Language Teaching.* Cambridge: Cambridge University Press.
Chapter 1 of this book provides an introduction to building and using a corpus, as well as providing guidelines on how to look at concordances. Chapter 7 focuses on response tokens and gives a good insight into how a corpus can be used to look at this pragmatic feature. Chapter 8 is entitled 'Relational language' and it covers a range of pragmatic features and their relevance to the language classroom. It may be of use to pragmatics researchers for comparative purposes and it provides a number of examples from corpora.

Rühlemann, C. (2010) 'What can a corpus tell us about pragmatics?', in A. O'Keeffe and M. McCarthy (eds), *The Routledge Handbook of Corpus Linguistics.* London: Routledge.
This chapter gives good coverage of the limitations of corpus linguistics in relation to the study of pragmatics while at the same time providing a solid grounding in what a corpus can address in pragmatics-related research. It provides examples of how a corpus can be

used to look at turn organisation, semantic prosody, discourse markers and speech act expressions. It also addresses the importance of multi-modal corpora to the future of corpus-based pragmatics research.

Schauer, G.A. and **Adolphs, S.** (2006) 'Expressions of gratitude in corpus and DCT data: vocabulary, formulaic sequences and pedagogy', *System* 34(1): 119–34.

This paper looks at the similarities and differences between data drawn from DCTs and a corpus and it discusses potential implications for using the two in a pedagogic context. The authors focus on expressions of gratitude, using both DCTs and corpus data from the five-million word spoken corpus CANCODE. They compare their results with a view to their pedagogic applications but the paper is useful to research students also because it brings insights into the advantages and disadvantages of both approaches to data gathering and it sheds light on their complementarity.

CHAPTER 3

Deixis

3.1 WHAT IS DEIXIS?

As discussed in Chapter 1, the term *pragmatics* is often used in linguistic research to refer to the study of the interpretation of meaning. Although it has proven difficult to determine an exact definition for the term pragmatics (Levinson discusses the issue over more than 50 pages in his influential 1983 work *Pragmatics*), a user-friendly definition is that suggested by Fasold (1990: 119) as 'the study of the use of context to make inferences about meaning'. In this definition, inferences refer to deductions made by participants based on available evidence (Christie, 2000). As we mentioned in Chapter 1, this available evidence is, according to pragmaticists, provided by the context within which the utterance takes place. Therefore, because, according to Levinson (1983: 54), 'the single most obvious way in which the relationship between language and context is reflected in the structures of languages themselves, is through the phenomenon of deixis', deixis is integral to the study of pragmatics. Derived from the Greek word for 'pointing' or 'indicating' (*deiktikos*: 'apt for pointing with the finger'), deixis refers to the way in which speakers orientate both themselves and their listeners in relation to the context of a conversation. Deixis enables interlocutors to refer to entities in context, thereby allowing them to identify people and things in relation to the space they are operating in at the moment at which they are speaking. There are a number of grammatical items that encode deixis, for example, the demonstratives, *this*, *that*; first and second person personal pronouns, *I*, *you*, *we*; adverbs of time such as *now*, *then*; adverbs of space such as *here*, *there*; motion verbs such as *come*, *go*; and a variety of other grammatical features such as tense markers. These grammatical items that encode deixis are commonly referred to as *deictics*.

In this chapter, we aim to provide an analysis of the occurrence and function of deictics in everyday conversation. It is important to note that, in contrast with many of the examples used in other explorations of deixis, the examples used in this chapter are from real-life data and are therefore attested, not invented. Although deixis exists in both the spoken and written domains, this chapter primarily focuses on spoken language. We begin with an exploration of how to recognise when an item has a deictic function and then make the distinction between *gestural* and *symbolic* uses of deictics. This is followed by analysis of traditional and contemporary notions of the *deictic centre*. The classical categories of deixis, *person*, *place* and *time*, are explored and *discourse*, *social* and *empathetic* deixis are also examined. Woven through the chapter is the way in which corpus linguistic techniques can inform our study of deixis. Corpus techniques, such as word frequency lists, allow the researcher to bring into relief the importance of deixis in our everyday speech and writing. It is generally accepted that deixis is extremely prevalent in everyday speech and writing but corpus linguistics allows us to show just how frequent it is in relation to other grammatical features. Corpus linguistics also enables the researcher to conduct comparisons of how deixis is used across different genres (for example, casual conversation, academic discourse, and so on) as well as across different modes (spoken and written language).

3.2 DEICTIC VERSUS NON-DEICTIC EXPRESSION

Personal pronouns, demonstratives (both pronouns and determiners) and adverbs of space and time can be used both deictically and non-deictically, as will be seen in the examples here. As we have already mentioned, to classify something as deictic means that the expression derives part of its meaning from the context. Deictics allow the interlocutors to 'point' to something in the context thereby enabling them to orientate themselves in a variety of ways, be it personally, spatially or temporally.

Personal pronouns

The examples given in 3.1 demonstrate the use of a personal pronoun, in this case *you*, in both deictic and non-deictic senses:

(3.1)

Deictic usage	**Non-deictic usage**
A: I owe **you** a fiver.	A: There's a school that's out there that **you** book in for a week and **you** can learn how to hang-glide.

In the deictic usage of *you*, the speaker identifies a particular person, the addressee. In this example, the addressee is the *referent.* This deictic use of *you* in 3.1 is also likely to be accompanied by some gesture such as eye contact (in this example, a *fiver* refers to Irish and British English slang for a £5 or €5 note). In the non-deictic use, *you* is used to refer to people in general, and therefore does not rely on the context for meaning. In this example it is implied that anyone can learn how to hang-glide in this school, a usage similar to *one* in English, *on* in French or *man* in German. This usage is sometimes referred to as *generic you* (see Tao, 1998; Biber *et al.*, 1999: 353–5; Carter and McCarthy, 2006: 120).

Deictic use of *this, that, these* and *those*

Green (1995) claims that for many linguists and philosophers, demonstratives lie at the heart of deictic issues. The demonstrative *this* and its plural form *these*, when used deictically, often refer to things that are close in space or time whereas *that* (plural *those*) refers to things that are a little more distant (see Section 3.5); however, this is dependent on the speaker's perception. The deictic use of *this* as a determiner in 3.2 is probably accompanied by some kind of pointing gesture, something that indicates that the speaker is referring to one particular bottle (the bottle is the referent):

(3.2)

Deictic usage	Non-deictic usage
A: Will I give him **this** bottle?	A: I mean the post office is one of our meeting places where the people would go along and inquire about **this** and that or another thing.

The non-deictic usage of *this* in 3.2 is classified non-deictic because it is part of a fixed phrase *this and that* which is a marker of vague language, sometimes referred to as a vague category marker (see Chapter 7), here meaning various, unspecified or trivial matters.

Similarly, the deictic use of *that* as a demonstrative pronoun in 3.3 would more than likely contain a gesture on the part of the speaker and so would require some degree of physical monitoring of the context on the part of the addressee in order to correctly interpret the utterance:

(3.3)

Deictic usage	Non-deictic usage
A: **That** one is nice.	A: But I think **that** one of the obvious things in all this affluence there are people who are benefiting from the Celtic Tiger, you know?

On the other hand, the non-deictic use of *that* demonstrates its use as a complementiser.

That

Biber *et al.* (1999: 350) describe *that* as one of the most common and most flexible word forms in English. In addition to its deictic function and that of a complementiser − see extract (3.3) − *that* can also function as:

- A relative pronoun:
  e.g. *Daddy where's the balloon **that** was over the door?*
- A stance adverbial:
  e.g. *He's not **that** heavy.*

Adverbs of time and space

In example 3.4, *there* when used deictically is an adverb of space indicating position. In this case *there* refers to the location of a wedding reception:

(3.4)

Deictic usage   **Non-deictic usage**
A: There was a   A: **There** was a good crowd there.
good crowd **there**.

The non-deictic *there* featured in the above example functions as a dummy subject. Dummy subjects are considered to have no semantic content and 'simply fill the necessary subject slot' (Carter and McCarthy, 2006: 495).

Finally, *now* used deictically is an adverb of time, in this case meaning time 'around now'. However, non-deictically it functions, for example, as a discourse marker that serves to introduce something which contrasts with what has just been said as in 3.5:

(3.5)

Deictic usage   **Non-deictic usage**
A: I had a letter   A: **Now** if after a time they found that that wasn't having
written to her and I'll   making any bite or impact on the company they then
post it **now** maybe.   called for an all out strike.

3.3 GESTURAL VERSUS SYMBOLIC DEIXIS

Once a linguistic item has been determined as deictic, a distinction can be drawn between *gestural* and *symbolic* deixis (see Levinson, 1983: 65–6; Fillmore, 1997: 62–3). Lyons (1977: 10) has suggested that deixis is 'at its purest . . . where the utterance is accompanied by some sort of extra-linguistic gesture'. As the term suggests, *gestural* deixis is frequently accompanied by a gesture such as physically pointing, making eye contact or turning your body to 'face' someone. Therefore, a gestural deictic can only be properly interpreted by a physical monitoring of the speech situation. Extract 3.6 features three female friends getting ready for a night out and contains an example of *this* (marked in bold) used gesturally:

(3.6)

A: Aw it's fab it's gorgeous looking. Look at the state of my elbows. They're all fake tan and Carol always goes 'what's wrong with your elbows Michelle?'

B: Gillian look do I need to iron **this** skirt cos there are creases all down the front?

C: No it's grand they'll fall out.

The use of *this* by Speaker B in *Gillian look do I need to iron* **this** *skirt* in extract 3.6 is classed as gestural as it is easy to imagine the speaker holding up the skirt while asking the question. Similarly, the gestural use of *that* (marked in bold) is illustrated in extract 3.7. In this extract, a mother (B) and daughter (A) are sitting together, discussing what colour to paint the walls of the daughter's house. (The word *shur* in the extract is a discourse marker commonly used in Irish English. It often collocates with *but*, and in this example it is used as a polite way of saying *however*):

(3.7)

A: Oh I know that. But you see the thing is Jean you have to think of your walls.

B: Yeah.

A: I mean if I put ah **that** colour which way then can I go?

B: Yeah I know but shur this doesn't really match this like does it?

A: Yeah I think it does.

B: Do you?

A: I think it's kind of good. I think. I don't know about **that** one. Maybe tis too yellow.

B: Yeah I think it is.

The daughter (Speaker A) refers to *that colour* and *that one* in the course of the conversation. This use of the deictic might be accompanied by a gesture that isolates the colour in question. On the other hand, the *symbolic* use of a deictic item points to context outside the text for meaning, to referents 'in the common cultural background' (Cutting, 2008: 9). Symbolic deixis may also signify entities that are not immediately visible in the immediate speech situation. For example, extract 3.8 features the beginning of a phone call in a radio phone-in show:

(3.8)

A: I think we have Cian O'Donovan on another line.

B: Hello.

A: Cian are you **there**?

B: I am indeed yeah.

A: How're you feeling today?

B: Ah I'm a bit nervous. I'm looking forward to getting it over with though.

The use of *there* in extract 3.8 would typically be considered an example of symbolic deixis as, although a referent is picked out, it is unlikely to be marked by any gesture as *there* is not in the speaker's immediate context. However, because both speaker and addressee understand where they are spatially in relation to one another, *there* can be easily interpreted deictically.

In the gestural and symbolic examples of *you* given in 3.9, *What about* **you** *Jack?* can be interpreted as gestural, since the example comes from a conversation involving multiple parties and, therefore, it is possible that eye-contact is being made between the participants. (However, it is difficult to classify *you* as gestural without either being present in the conversation or having access to a multi-modal corpus.) The symbolic use of *you* is taken from an information technology lecture at university:

(3.9)

Gestural usage	**Symbolic usage**
A: What about **you** Jack?	A: So what **you** want to do is **you** want to type in the first example that I have up here.

Here, the symbolic usage of *you* is much more general – it refers to 'plural *you*', to all the participants at the lecture. This symbolic use identifies a referent – in this case the students present at the lecture – and also delimits *you* to refer to this audience. It is unlikely to be accompanied by any gestural behaviour (contrast this with the non-deictic, *generic you* in 3.1).

In 3.10, the gestural example of *now* comes from a conversation in which the participants are fixing a computer printer. The example of *now* classified as gestural is done so because of contextual information provided by the researcher involved in the recording and transcription of the conversation. *It might work* **now** is immediately followed by the contextual information noted in the transcription that the speaker presses a button on the printer. Therefore, *now* coincides with a gesture:

(3.10)

Gestural usage	**Symbolic usage**
A: It might work **now**.	A: The way I look at it is I can do this again in a year if I want to whereas I want to see where this is going. I don't want to go and say what if? I can go to Cambodia in a year's time. If I go **now** then I risk this and I might say why did I let him go?

On the other hand, in order to interpret the symbolic use of *now*, the addressee does not expect any physical gesture. Provided the addressee knows the time at which the utterance is taking place, he/she can interpret and understand *now* without any great difficulty. In addition to this, Huang (2007) notes that it seems in general if a deictic expression can be used symbolically, it can also be used in a gestural way, but not vice versa.

To summarise, Figure 3.1 illustrates the range of possible uses that a deictic expression may have. As we have shown, the same expression may be used both deictically and non-

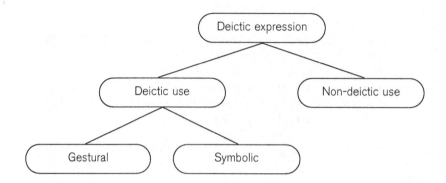

Figure 3.1 Possible uses of a deictic expression.

deictically. In addition, the deictic use can be subdivided into both the gestural use and the symbolic use.

3.4 THE DEICTIC CENTRE

The *deictic centre,* or *origo* (a term coined by Bühler in 1934), refers to a perceived egocentric organisation of the deictic system. Traditionally, this centre is typically organised around an 'I–here–now' axis where 'the speaker casts himself in the role of the ego and relates everything to his viewpoint' (Lyons, 1977: 638). Therefore, in relation to the centre (or anchor point) for the three major categories of deixis – *person, place* and *time* – the centre for person deixis is the speaker (the 'I'), the centre for place deixis is where the speaker produces the utterance (the 'here') and the centre for time deixis is the time at which the utterance is produced (the 'now'). The deictic centre is associated with the current speaker, therefore, when the speaker changes so too does the centre. In extract 3.11, in which four females are getting ready for a night out, the use of the personal pronoun *I* demonstrates this deictic centre switch:

(3.11)

A: What top are **you** wearing?
B: The lemon one.
C: **I** don't have a jacket.
A: **You** have a jacket the denim one.
D: **I** have a jacket cos it matches. Do **you** remember one night out in Dublin **I** brought no jacket?
C: **I** do.
D: And **I** got very cold.

Speakers C and D all use *I* in their speaker turns indicating their acknowledgment that they are now at the deictic centre of the conversation. In addition to this, the personal pronoun *you* moves between several different referents. In Speaker A's first turn, she uses *you* to refer to Speaker B. In her second turn, she uses *you* to refer to Speaker C. Speaker D also uses *you* to refer to Speaker C in *Do you remember one night out in Dublin I brought no jacket?* This constant movement of centre from participant to participant can cause problems for both first and second language acquisition.

However, the notion of an egocentric origo has not gone unchallenged (see, for example, Lyons, 1977; Hanks, 1992; Jones, 1995). According to Jones (1995), theories in favour of the egocentricity of deixis fail to take into account that communication is a social act. He claims that it is inaccurate to call the speaker in conversation the 'central person' just as it would be to call either the husband or wife the 'central person' in a marriage – 'it takes two to tango and two to communicate' (p. 37). This notion of a non-egocentric origo can be seen in the interaction of a father (Speaker A) with his baby son (Speaker B) in extract 3.12 while they are sitting at the breakfast table:

(3.12)

A: Are **you** goin with **daddy**?
B: Yeah.
C: Who's funeral's on now mammy?
A: Eat the breakfast so and **we** go.
D: Jim Smith's.
A: Are **you** goin with **daddy** in the motor car?
B: Oh sorry. I'm goin with daddy.

In this extract, the father clearly aligns his own identity with that of his baby and this is achieved in a number of ways (marked in bold in the extract). First, his utterance *Are you goin with daddy?*, repeated twice, connects *you* with *daddy* thus establishing a shift from a lexical realisation of self for the father to the perspective of his child. The everyday identity the father carries with him is the *I*, however, to his son he is *daddy* and his self-reference of this is evident. Second, in the utterance *Eat the breakfast so and we go*, the father combines his and his son's perspective into one and the same using an inclusive *we* (see Section 3.5). Wales (1996: 56) offers a number of possible reasons for parents' use of kin titles like *daddy* in talking to infants. She suggests that parents use them because they 'recognise the problematic "shifting" nature of speaker/addressee roles, of *I* and *you* reference'. This recognition of the difficulty for children with *I/you* reference is acknowledged by the parents switching the origo from themselves to their children through their use of *you*. This would seem to highlight the flexibility of the deictic centre – an utterance is necessarily centred in the sense that some speaker's viewpoint is inevitably assumed; however, whose viewpoint is assumed, the speaker's or a co-participant's, is a matter of flexibility. In extract 3.12, the father's utterances reflect the close connection that he feels with his son constituted by his use of deictic expressions (see also Tannen, 2007). Although the examples used to illustrate this section are person deictic in nature, the deictic centre is also associated with place and time deixis and this will be discussed later in the chapter.

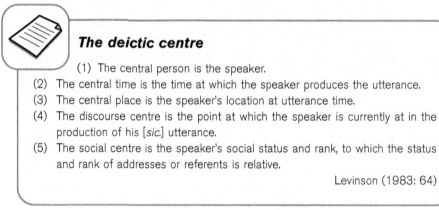

The deictic centre

(1) The central person is the speaker.

(2) The central time is the time at which the speaker produces the utterance.

(3) The central place is the speaker's location at utterance time.

(4) The discourse centre is the point at which the speaker is currently at in the production of his [*sic.*] utterance.

(5) The social centre is the speaker's social status and rank, to which the status and rank of addresses or referents is relative.

Levinson (1983: 64)

3.5 BASIC CATEGORIES OF DEIXIS

Deixis is traditionally subdivided into a number of categories: *person*, *place* and *time* deixis are the most common of these categories. Two additional categories, *discourse* and *social* deixis, are also present in some of the most influential work done in the area (cf. Lyons, 1977; Levinson, 1983; Fillmore, 1997). There is also a sixth deictic category referred to as *empathetic* deixis (see Lyons, 1977).

Person deixis

Person deixis is concerned with 'the identity of the interlocutors in a communication situation' (Fillmore, 1997: 61). Personal pronouns such as *I* and *you* are the most obvious and most frequent manifestations of person deixis. In order to illustrate the frequency and importance of these and other personal pronouns in casual conversation, frequency counts for the top 20 most frequently occurring words were generated for the Limerick Corpus of Irish English (LCIE) using *Wordsmith Tools* (Scott, 2009) and the results are displayed in Table 3.1.

Table 3.1 demonstrates that five personal pronouns – *I*, *you*, *it*, *he* and *they* (marked in bold in Table 3.1) – occur in the top 20 most frequent words in LCIE, which is consistent with many other corpora of spontaneous, face-to-face casual conversation. Similar findings have also been recorded by Biber *et al.* (1999) working with the Longman Spoken and Written English Corpus (LSWE), O'Keeffe *et al.* (2007) working with the CANCODE and CIC corpora, and Rühlemann (2007) working with the BNC. This is in contrast with written corpora. For example, frequency lists based on the written component of the BNC show *I* in 17th position and *you* in 21st (Leech *et al.*, 2001b). Regarding the distribution of these pronouns, Biber *et al.* (1999: 333) have shown that the pronouns *I* and *you* are far more common in casual conversation than in other registers such as academic prose. Rühlemann (2007: 66–9) posits four reasons for the preferred use of *I* and *you* in casual conversation:

(1) *I* is prone to repetition (*I* is repeated at a frequency of about 200 times per million words in conversation: see Biber *et al.*, 1999: 334);

Table 3.1 Top 20 most frequent words in LCIE (personal pronouns in bold)

Rank order	LCIE	Frequency per million words
1	the	35,171
2	**I**	**24,321**
3	and	23,707
4	**you**	**23,011**
5	to	20,140
6	**it**	**18,276**
7	a	17,753
8	that	14,868
9	of	13,948
10	yeah	13,689
11	in	13,401
12	was	10,419
13	is	10,006
14	like	8,667
15	know	8,052
16	**he**	**7,365**
17	on	7,281
18	**they**	**7,264**
19	have	6,831
20	there	6,628

(2) *I* and *you* have a high frequency of collocation especially with verbs of thinking, for example, *I think* and *you know*;

(3) discourse is typically presented in a direct mode, where, for example, a non-present speaker's words are represented as if he/she were actually present;

(4) conversation is co-constructed, with speakers taking turns and each new turn requires the reconstruction of the new speaker's deictic system.

As we have already seen in extract 3.11, the pronouns *I* (and by extension *my* and *mine*) and *you* (also *your, yours*) are typically deictic. However, other personal pronouns such as *he, she, it* and *they*, although on occasion deictic, are typically *anaphoric* in their reference. In order to distinguish between deixis and anaphora (and *cataphora*) it is necessary to briefly explore the notion of *context*. Cutting (2008: 3–11) distinguishes between three different types of spoken context: *situational*, what speakers know about what they can see around them; *background knowledge*, what they know about each other (interpersonal knowledge) and the world (cultural knowledge); and *co-textual*, what they know about what they have been saying. Deixis is associated with context outside the text (text can refer to pieces of both spoken and written discourse), and, therefore, the referent is generally located in the situational or background knowledge context. On the other hand, anaphora and cataphora are associated with the context of the text itself, or the co-textual context. Therefore, the referent is generally located in either the preceding text (anaphora) or the forthcoming text (cataphora). Deixis and anaphora are often considered independently; however, just how independent they are from one another is a subject of debate (see Lyons, 1977; Levinson, 1983; Wales, 1996; Marmaridou, 2000; Rühlemann, 2007). Indeed, Lyons (1977: 676) maintains that a term can be used both deictically and anaphorically. Take the example *I was born in* **New York** *and have lived* **there** *ever since.*

In this example, adapted from Levinson (1983: 67), *there* simultaneously refers backwards to *New York* but also contrasts with *here* in the space deictic dimension, locating the utterance outside of New York. Similarly, in Halliday and Hasan's (1976: 3) example *Wash and core **six cooking apples**. Put **them** into a fireproof dish, them* does not refer to the *six cooking apples* per se but rather to the washed and cored apples, a reference which is constructed on the basis of background contextual knowledge of the genre of recipes (see Wales, 1996). Rühlemann (2007: 63) maintains that 'another difficulty in drawing the line between deixis and anaphora derives from the fact that deictic items may well be used in institutionalised expressions in which only faint, if any, traces of the deictic origins persist'. He cites examples such as the vague expression *this and that* and the discourse marker *there you go*. Anaphora and deixis, therefore, appear to be closely related.

In extract 3.13, a younger sister is talking about her older siblings and using *he* and *she* (marked in bold) anaphorically:

(3.13)

A: My oldest brother is Jimmy and **he**'s [pause] I'm not sure about their ages because there are too many of them but **he**'s in the army and **he**'s a military instructor or something and I've another sister Martina and I don't know her age either and **she**'s a pharmacist and **she** teaches.

As we can see, *he* in the extract refers back to the initial mention of her older brother *Jimmy*, whereas *she* refers to the preceding mention of her sister *Martina*. Similarly, *they* is typically anaphoric in nature, illustrated by the conversation had by two males while watching television in extract 3.14:

(3.14)

A: I saw Pirates of the Caribbean last night, which was very good.
B: I saw the ad for that. It's very good. The pirates are really ghosts.
A: See there was a curse put on them, because **they** are all moody, so when **they** are walking around in the moonlight you can really see them for who **they** are. So **they** need to get back all these coins into the one place, and then **they** need to get the chosen one, and **they**'ve to let his blood pour onto the coins, and then the curse will be lifted. Well **they** think **they** found her but **they** have to bring her back alive so that the curse is lifted.
B: Why are **they** ghosts?
A: **They** want to be alive again.
B: Okay.

Again, *they* (in bold) is used to refer to *the pirates* who are initially mentioned by Speaker B. It is important to note that anaphoric and cataphoric pronouns refer to individual noun phrases in the text (contrast this with the use of *discourse deixis* below).

We have already outlined that deixis enables interlocutors to orient themselves in their immediate context. The first person pronoun *I* allows the person to identify themselves in the 'role' as the speaker, whereas the second person pronoun *you* enables the speaker to refer to the role of the addressee(s). Third person pronouns such as *he*, *she* and *they* most frequently identify people that are neither speakers nor addressees, though on occasion they can be used to refer to the speaker or listener. Therefore, generally, the third person pronoun does not refer to any specific 'participant role' in the immediate context, thereby allowing its classification as typically non-deictic (Lyons, 1977: 638; Levinson, 1983: 69; Huang, 2007: 137).

Finally, there are also two first person pronoun plural *we* pronouns. These are used to create a perspective of:

(1) *I* the speaker + *you* the addressee(s) in the immediate context ('inclusive *we*') and
(2) *I* the speaker + someone else not in the immediate context ('exclusive *we*').

The use of an inclusive *we* (marked in bold) is evident in extract 3.15 from where three siblings are in their living room discussing the origins of the name of their dog:

(3.15)

A: But Goldie's a girl's name like.
B: Yeah but **we** didn't give her the name.
A: What?
B: **We** didn't give her the name.
C: **We** didn't give her the name. Although she was so young she wouldn't notice it.
A: She wouldn't have a clue shur.
C: **We** could've changed it. **We** could call her Alex.

Earlier in the conversation, Speaker A has been complaining about the name of the dog, *Goldie*, and suggesting different names for her. The other siblings, Speakers B and C, use inclusive *we* in the repeated utterance *We didn't give her the name* as a form of 'safety in numbers' defence (*I*, the speaker + *you*, the rest of the family) to deflect the criticism of the dog's name from themselves. Mühlhäusler and Harré (1990: 174) claim that in this use of *we* 'the social bonding aspect and the establishment of solidarity is of importance'. The siblings create an in-group, 'we the family', in opposition to the person who originally named the dog. Further to this, Speaker C adds *We could've changed it. We could call her Alex*, invoking the power that 'we the family' had, and still have, to change the name of the dog should they choose to do so.

On the other hand, exclusive *we* can be used by the speaker to refer to a range of groups that include the speaker but not the addressee(s) in the immediate context. Extract 3.16 is taken from a recording made while a family was putting up their Christmas tree. The extract contains a number of instances of the use of inclusive *we* (marked in bold) and exclusive *we* (marked in bold and underlined):

(3.16)

A: Do **we** need more around there?
B: Yeah a bit more.
A: All right?
B: Yip. **We** might need another bit now but hang on a second and I'll press it down.
C: **We** have them outside too the eighty mini bulbs. Is that what they are? Eighty mini bulbs. Yeah **we**'ve them too.
D: **We** don't need those til tomorrow.
B: Are **we** not putting it up til tomorrow dad no?

The first two instances of *we* (*Do **we** need more around there?* and ***We** might need another bit now . . .*) are examples of inclusive *we*, given that the speaker in both instances is referring to themselves and the other participants assisting them with the task of putting up the tree, the other members of the family. Similarly, ***We** don't need those til tomorrow* and *Are **we** not putting it up til tomorrow dad no?* refer to the participants in the immediate context. However, Speaker C's assertion ***We** have them outside too the eighty mini bulbs* and *Yeah **we**'ve them too* are examples of exclusive *we*. Both *we* and *outside* refer to Speaker C's place of work: *we* referring to her membership of the staff of the organisation; and *outside* referring to the location of the workplace, perhaps in contrast to the 'inside' context of the family home. Speaker C is referring to context outside the immediate conversation and relying on the 'common ground' between the interlocutors to enable them to assign the correct interpretation to the deictic item.

The English language system of person deixis can present many difficulties for the non-native speaker. This is due in part to the issues explored in this section; however, it is also due to the fact that many languages have more complicated systems. In many languages there are three second person pronouns *you* (singular, plural and formal) – *du*, *ihr* and *Sie* in German, for example. These are used as a formal way of addressing someone and, in addition to functioning as person deixis, also function as *social deixis* (see below).

Place deixis

Sometimes called *spatial* or *locational* deixis, place deixis is primarily concerned with the location of people or objects relative to the deictic centre. As has been demonstrated, the deictic centre frequently has the speaker as centre, therefore, these locations are often relative to the speaker's position. Notions of place deixis are commonly expressed using demonstratives (*this, that, these, those*), deictic adverbs of place (*here, there*) or verbs of motion (*come, go, bring, take*). However, locations can also be specified relative to other objects using prepositions of place such as *above, below, left, right, behind* or *from*. In many languages, there exists a fundamental distinction between *proximal* (or relatively close to the speaker) and *distal* (non-proximal, sometimes relatively close to the addressee) deictic expressions of place (Diessel, 1999; Levinson, 2004). For example, *here* and *there* are crucially tied to the deictic field of the speaker, and the addressee(s) determines the spatial coordinates of the utterance in order to assign meaning. The extent to which context is involved in determining the reference of *here* and *there* is evident in the interaction between a grandmother (Speaker A), her daughter (Speaker B) and her grandchild (not speaking but crawling around the room) in extract 3.17:

(3.17)

A: Come over **here** to Nana. Over **here** to Nana.
B: Come on. I'm sitting up **here**. Now I'm **here**. Look at it's down **there** on the floor. Look it's gone out of your hand.
A: Ah you silly billy.
B: She doesn't want that chair. She wants the other one I think **over there**.

In this extract, we can see that both Speakers A and B use *here* (marked in bold) to indicate their own position relative to the child. However, it is obvious that Speaker A's *here* is different to Speaker B's *here*. This use of proximal deixis is in contrast to Speaker B's use of *there* on two occasions (again marked in bold). On the first occasion the distal reference in *It's down there on the floor* refers to the location of something that the child has dropped and is in direct contrast to Speaker B's assertion that *I'm sitting up here*. In addition to this, Speaker B states that *She wants the other one I think over there* which demonstrates how 'over + there' is further away again from the speaker's deictic centre. Similarly, the demonstratives *this* and *that* also display this proximal–distal distinction. In extract 3.18, a mother and daughter, whom we first encountered in extract 3.7, are continuing their discussion of what colour to paint the walls (the demonstratives are marked in bold):

(3.18)

B: Yeah but shur Jean I mean what colour do you want to put on the wall?
                                        [
A: Too pale.
B: I mean you don't want dark walls either.
A: Yeah no. What about **this one**?
B: **That one** isn't bad.
A: 'Sunshine'.
B: Yeah that was the colour of the other one wasn't it?
A: Yeah and it's kinda similar to the other one isn't it? But less flashy.

Extract 3.18 demonstrates that as the deictic centre changes, the demonstrative reference changes from proximal to distal even though it is the same object that both speakers are talking about. The speakers are looking at a colour chart. Speaker A suggests a colour *What about this one?* Speaker B, in her response *That one isn't bad*, acknowledges that the deictic centre has shifted from one speaker to the next (hence Jespersen's (1965) utilisation of the term *shifters* to refer to deictic expressions).

Time deixis

According to Huang (2007: 144), time deixis 'is concerned with the encoding of temporal points and spans relative to the time at which the utterance is produced'. In other words, in order to correctly interpret a time deictic, it needs to be considered in relation to the time at which the communicative act takes place. To do this correctly, we need to distinguish between coding time (CT), the moment of utterance, and receiving time (RT), the moment of reception. Coding time is usually located around the speaker, whereas receiving time is located around the addressee. Because the majority of conversation is face-to-face in nature, CT and RT are considered to be identical. However, there are situations where the CT and RT are different and this can lead to a situation where the utterance becomes *unanchored* (see Fillmore, 1997: 60). For example, Fillmore (ibid.) suggests a 'worst case scenario' for an 'unanchored' sentence: finding a message in a bottle which says *Meet me here at noon tomorrow with a stick about this big*.

Notions of time deixis are expressed using both simple adverbs of time such as *now*, *then*, *today*, *tomorrow*, *yesterday* and complex adverbs of time such as *this month*, *next year* or *last week*. Similarly to place deixis, time deixis also distinguishes between a proximal time *now* (time 'around now' including the CT) and a *distal* time *then* (time 'not now'). *Then* can be used to refer to both a particular past time and a particular future time. In extract 3.19, a workplace discussion about buying a house features *then* (in bold) used to refer to past time:

(3.19)

A: They were to revise loads of figures. I had all those figures done and **then** all the mortgage rates changed again and they were to come back to me with the revised figures and they never did.

B: Jesus you'd better get on get on to them about that.

A: I know.

In contrast, in extract 3.20 a nurse and a student nurse are discussing upcoming exams and *then* (in bold) is used to refer to future time:

(3.20)

A: Are you all ready for Wednesday?

B: I am indeed Mary.

A: Well then how's the study going? You have it all done at this stage anyway I'd say Connor?

B: I'm taking some time off lately. I'm resting.

A: Yeah you'd want to take some time off you'd be wrecked from studying. So when will you be finished? Are you going straight through yeah?

B: Basically the ah it starts on the fourth and I've exams all the way to the tenth and **then** I've a week off and I've economics.

A: And **then** you're finished? So you've nothing done in the economics. You're waiting for your week off.

B: I am yeah.

A: Yeah yeah yeah. So listen best of luck anyway I'm sure you'll be fine.

B: Thanks.

The time deictic adverbials *yesterday*, *today* and *tomorrow* divide time into diurnal spans. These time deictics can be used to refer to a specific time (extract 3.21), a time period within the relevant day (extract 3.22) or to the day in general (extract 3.23):

(3.21) [Context: family at the dinner table]

A: Is there more meat there?

B: Yeah. We'll have bacon and cabbage **tomorrow** like or will we do chicken?

A: You're the cook.

(3.22) [Context: ending sequence in a radio phone-in show]

A: John thank you very much indeed for that. All sorts of other theories on why, when, where, how etc. Anyway that's all from us for **today**, back with you tomorrow at the usual time until then a very good day to you.

(3.23) [Context: friends chatting]

A: Was he in better form **yesterday**?

B: Ah he was in better form **yesterday**.

As we can see, in extract 3.21 *tomorrow* is used to refer to dinner time, in extract 3.22 *today* is used to refer to the time period during which the show is broadcast and *yesterday* in extract 3.23 refers to the entire day.

Corpus linguistic methods also substantiate the assertion that *today*, *tomorrow* and *yesterday* are preferred in spoken discourse over lexicalised names of days like *Monday*, *Tuesday* and so on (see Levinson, 1983; Fillmore, 1997; Grundy, 2008). Table 3.2 illustrates the frequency of occurrence of the time deictics *today*, *yesterday* and *tomorrow* compared to the occurrences of the seven days of the week in LCIE.

Table 3.2 demonstrates that the three time deictics, *today*, *yesterday* and *tomorrow*, occur more frequently than the lexicalised names of the days of the week. The time deictics occur 1,234 times per million words, whereas the days of the week have a frequency of 945 occurrences per million words. Interestingly, *today* is the most frequent time deictic

Table 3.2 Comparison of frequency of occurrence of *yesterday*, *today* and *tomorrow* with the lexicalised names for days of the week

Time deictic	Frequency per million words	Day of the week	Frequency per million words
today	549	Monday	111
yesterday	389	Tuesday	100
tomorrow	296	Wednesday	85
		Thursday	106
		Friday	172
		Saturday	202
		Sunday	169
Total	**1,234**	**Total**	**945**

in Table 3.2, and this, coupled with the high frequency of occurrences of the personal pronoun *I* in Table 3.1, adds credence to the 'I' and 'now' components of the 'here–now–I' deictic centre.

Complex adverbs of time such as *last month*, *next Monday* or *this year* combine a deictic expression such as *this* with a non-deictic such as *year*. In the deictic use of the combination of *this + week/month/year*, on the surface at least, it appears that the referent includes the coding time (the speaker is referring to the present week, month and so forth in which the utterance takes place) and can vary between the non-calendrical measure of, for example, seven days in a week to the calendrical measure of a week beginning, for example, on the 1st of February and ending on the 7th. However, especially in the case of *this year*, as extracts 3.24, 3.25 and 3.26 demonstrate, the interpretation of the referent is not quite so straightforward.

(3.24) [Context: two friends chatting while watching a match]

A: I have to drop three subjects **this year**. I dropped German.
B: That's not right.
A: I need them apparently. I got a C in Technology. And I dropped Home Economics. I was going to keep Home Economics except she got really nasty.

(3.25) [Context: family chatting]

A: Every month has twenty nine days.
B: Well isn't he very knowledgeable? Twenty eight.
A: Twenty nine.
B: But every month has twenty nine days.
A: But February didn't **this year**.
B: Well he was wrong so.

(3.26) [Context: radio interview. The *All Ireland* refers to the All Ireland Senior Football Championship which is a competition in the game of Gaelic Football, played in Ireland.]

A: Am well I at the start of the year I was asked to see to tip who I thought would win the All Ireland and I was torn between Armagh and Tyrone so I'll have to stick with what I said at the start. I'll have to keep going I think Tyrone have a have a brilliant chance of winning the All Ireland **this year**. They're very hungry you know they've been out there and they've playing their hearts out all the time.

As we can see, these utterances containing *this year* are related to the examples shown for *today*, *tomorrow* and *yesterday*. In extract 3.24, which features two friends chatting during a match, in the utterance *I have to drop three subjects this year*, *this year* is used to refer to the school year that runs in Ireland from September to May. In extract 3.25, one of the family members, Speaker A, claims *But February didn't this year* which refers to *this year* as a calendar year, in which February was not a leap year. Finally, in extract 3.26, the interviewee is discussing who he thinks will win the Irish football championship. He maintains that *Tyrone have a brilliant chance of winning the All Ireland this year*. The championship year in Ireland runs from May to September.

The most frequent, and quite possibly the most complex, representation of time deixis is *tense*. According to Levinson (1983: 77), 'tense is one of the main factors ensuring that nearly all sentences when uttered are deictically anchored to a context of utterance' (cf. Lyons, 1977). A brief examination of any extract from spoken corpora (or indeed written ones) illustrates the prevalence of tense in conveying time deixis. Consider the following extract 3.27, tense underlined:

(3.27) [Context: two family members discussing an acquaintance. *Yoke* is a slang term in Irish English, meaning *thing*. It can also be used pejoratively to refer to a person, as is the case here.]

A: Say that yoke <u>was</u> only <u>ringing</u> me to brag about last night.
B: Oh Paddy.
A: Um.
B: <u>Did</u> he <u>ring</u> you or <u>texted</u> you?
A: <u>Rang</u> me.
B: You <u>should ring</u> back for the laugh.
A: No <u>I'm not wasting</u> credit on him because <u>he'll say</u> oh he just <u>can't live</u> without me and oh boy god Paddy I <u>can live</u> without you.
      [Laughter]

As we can see, there are a range of tenses (for example, past simple, present simple, past continuous, *will* future) used in the extract. However, most of these make reference to either the present or around the immediate present time. This 'around the immediate present' time reference is established by the presence of the only one non-tense deictic expression *last night*. Therefore, all the past tense time deictics, for example *was only ringing*, *texted*, *rang* refer to the recent past. In addition, the *will* future *he'll say* refers to immediate future time. This extract demonstrates the importance of the tense system in anchoring speakers in the 'here–now–I' deictic centre.

Discourse deixis

Similar to anaphora or cataphora, discourse deictics can be used to point to elements in the preceding or following discourse. However, there are a number of differences between discourse deictics and anaphoric or cataphoric reference (see Diessel, 1999: 100–3). As we have seen, an anaphoric reference is used to 'track' a preceding noun phrase. Discourse deictics, on the other hand, can be used to 'focus the hearer's attention on aspects of meaning, expressed by a clause, a sentence, a paragraph or an entire idea' (ibid: 101). In extract 3.28, the discourse deictic *this* (in bold) is used by Speaker A while chatting to one of her female friends to refer to an extended narrative, not a single noun phrase:

(3.28)

A: Jeanette's house is the funniest house I've ever been in. Listen to **this**. I remember when I was in first year of college Jeanette's mother was having a surprise eighteenth birthday party for her right. Jacinta and Mandy couldn't go right. They'd invited the three of us to go right. You must have been invited too but I don't know why you didn't go. Anyway and typical me I thought I better go you know and represent like.

B: Represent.

A: So I get the train from Cork to Dublin right. Jeanette's mother is there right and she's such a chatterbox right and she loves my dad and she's always saying tell him to ring me.
      [Laughter]

A: I arrive and I'm kinda nervous like cos I've never met all of her family before. I've met like Linda and that was it and I get to the house anyway and I'm sitting down anyway and they had made so much food like and I was like no I'd just eaten cos I'd eaten on the train like but we had a few sausages and rashers anyway. We were about to have a big dinner within a half an hour of me having these rashers and sausages like. Oh I could have hung on like. Next thing she arrives over with eight sausages on a plate and that was it. Eight sausages and six slices of bread. I was just like 'oh my God'. I was just like ah I have enough. Like on a plate. On a small side plate with just eight sausages. All her brothers and sisters were sitting around me like and asking me was I ok and the eight sausages like.
      [Laughter]

Speaker A's use of *this* in *Listen to* ***this*** anticipates the full story of her journey to a friend's eighteenth birthday party that follows. In addition, discourse deictics can be employed to refer to the underlying intention of the content of an utterance (also known as *illocutionary force*; see Chapter 5). Extract 3.29 exemplifies the use of a demonstrative *that* (in bold) with a focus on the illocutionary force of an utterance:

(3.29) [Context: mother and daughter chatting about an up-coming wedding]

A: Oh look at that the Bay View [hotel] over there. That's the hotel there Anna where Judy is having her reception.
B: Oh right yeah.
A: And if I don't lose enough weight I won't be there.
B: **That**'s a lie.
A: Well I must get dieting fast so won't I and lose some of my eight stone. [Laughter]

In extract 3.29, the interpretation of *that* is more complex than the tracking of a previous noun phrase. The demonstrative *that* does refer to Speaker A's assertion *And if I don't lose enough weight I won't be there*. However, more specifically, *that* refers to the meaning embodied by Speaker A's assertion. Through saying *And if I don't lose enough weight I won't be there*, Speaker A is not commenting on whether or not she will be at the wedding, but is, in fact, claiming that *Right now, I'm fat*. Speaker B's *That's a lie* is a response to Speaker A's intended message and not the literal content of the utterance (also known as *propositional content*). Fillmore (1997) also includes deictic items peculiar to written discourse such as *above* or *below* in discourse deixis. In addition, Levinson (1983) specifies items such as utterance initial *but*, *therefore*, *in conclusion*, *well* and *however* in discourse deixis. Furthermore, Levinson (ibid: 89) contends that 'the scope [of a proper theory of discourse deixis] . . . may be very large, ranging from the borders of anaphora to issues of topic/comment structure'.

Social deixis

Social deixis refers to 'those aspects of language structure that encode the social identities of participants (properly, incumbents of participant-roles) or the social relationship between them, or between one of them and persons or entities referred to' (Levinson, 1983: 89). For example, as already mentioned, many European languages contain the *tu/vous* distinction. Hence, social deixis can contain information about the conversational participants such as age, sex, kin relationship, social class or ethnic group. For this reason, terms of address (see Chapter 4) are often included as a common way of realising social deixis (especially in English, which, in comparison to many other languages, has a relative paucity of linguistic devices which convey social deixis). Extract 3.30 features the use of a kinship term (in bold) by a father:

(3.30)

A: Hurry up **baby son** all the boys is finished their breakfast.

This kinship term *baby son* encodes a range of social information about the conversational participants. Obviously, it points towards the age (baby), sex (male) and kin relationship (son) of the speaker being addressed by the father. However, less obvious is the ethnic identity contained within these kinship terms. Blum-Kulka (1997) has demonstrated how Israeli parents use nicknames in addressing their children, thus emphasising familial involvement and interdependence. In contrast, she observes how Jewish American and Israeli American parents avoid nicknames in order to 'show deference to the child's individuality'. (p. 162). Similarly, in extract 3.30 the father is a member of the community of Irish Travellers and in using child-specific kin titles such as *boy(s)*, *young fella*, *children*, *lads*, *son*, he downplays the value of autonomy evident in a full first name, the emphasis is instead on belonging and interdependence. This is evidence of the close social networks that exist within the Irish Traveller community. These *kinship networks* are based around family and extended family and clearly indicate the presence of the family at the core of the Traveller value system (see Clancy, 2010). (Irish Travellers are a nomadic Irish ethnic group who comprise less than 1 per cent of the population. Although Irish in origin, they maintain a separate identity, culture and history to the mainstream Irish population.)

Empathetic deixis

The notion of empathetic deixis was first posited by Lyons (1977), based on a speaker's choice of *this* rather than *that*, *here* rather than *there* or *now* rather than *then*, 'when the speaker is personally involved with the entity, situation or place to which he is referring or is identifying himself with the attitude or viewpoint of the addressee' (p. 677). Rühlemann (2007: 192) maintains that empathetic deixis 'seems to involve preference of deictics that are characterised by being, literally or metaphorically, *nearer* to the deictic origo (*here* being nearer than *there*, *now* being nearer than *then* etc.)'. Therefore, when a speaker makes a choice of *that* rather than *this*, for example, he/she is signaling his/her emotional relationship with the propositional content of the utterance. In the following extracts 3.31 and 3.32, the use of *that* (in bold) demonstrates the affective implications of the choice of the demonstrative:

(3.31) [Context: family chatting]

A: Yeah exactly. She still has **that bike** of hers.
B: Does she?
A: Yeah.

(3.32) [Context: female friends chatting]

A: And did you see **that dress** she had on that night lately? It was to about here and it had a big piece missing here and there.
B: I saw that yeah.

C: And she's not skinny enough to wear that.

A: Would she not use fake tan? You might as well go out snow white.

In extract 3.31, Speaker A mentions *that bike* and, in extract 3.32, Speaker A mentions *that dress*. On both occasions, these marked uses of the more distal demonstrative *that* seem to signal a sense of disapproval on the speaker's part. Lakoff (1974) calls this use of demonstratives *emotional deixis*. She claims that the emotional-deictic *that*, as in extracts 3.31 and 3.32, where the subject alluded to belongs to neither the speaker nor the addressee, 'appears to establish emotional solidarity between the two by implying that both participants in the conversation share the same views toward the subject of the discussion' (p. 352). Both Argaman (2007) and Rühlemann (2007) note that little study has been devoted to empathetic deixis. Indeed, Rühlemann (ibid: 222) concludes that 'empirical research based on corpus data might potentially advance the already existing knowledge on this intriguing type of deixis substantially'.

3.6 CONCLUSION

In order to illustrate the importance of studying the phenomenon of deixis in speech, a frequency list of the top 20 words in the spoken corpus LCIE was generated and this is presented in Table 3.3. As can be seen, the table contains the personal pronouns whose main use is deictic (*I, you*) and those whose use is predominantly anaphoric (*it, he, they*). In addition, the table features *that* and *there* both of which have the potential to be used deictically (marked in bold).

Table 3.3 Word frequency counts for the 20 most frequent words in LCIE

Rank order	LCIE
1	the
2	**I**
3	and
4	**you**
5	to
6	**it**
7	a
8	**that**
9	of
10	yeah
11	in
12	was
13	is
14	like
15	know
16	**he**
17	on
18	**they**
19	have
20	**there**

As we can see, these items occupy 7 of the top 20 places on the word frequency list, clearly demonstrating their central role in the study of everyday spoken language. As already discussed, *I* and *you* (2nd and 4th on the frequency list respectively) are the most frequent items reflecting, among other things, the alternating nature of the deictic centre between speakers. The top twenty items also contain three pronouns that are predominantly anaphoric – *it* (6th), *he* (16th) and *they* (18th). Rühlemann (2007: 74) describes the prominence of these pronouns as a 'striking finding suggesting that the importance of person deixis and anaphora in conversation can hardly be overstated'. The frequency list also contains a demonstrative and an adverb of space that were explored in the place deixis section – *that* (8th position) and *there* (20th position). Although *that* features, *this* does not. Similarly, although *there* is present on the list, *here* is not. This perhaps represents the greater multi-functionality and flexibility of both *that* and *there*; for example, *that*, as we have seen, has place deictic properties but also featured in our examination of both discourse and emotional deixis. Interestingly, the list contains no time deictic items and this may emphasise just how reliant spoken language is on its tense system in order to construct 'time' between speakers.

3.7 FURTHER READING

Argaman, E. (2007) 'With or without "it": the role of empathetic deixis in mediating educational change', *Journal of Pragmatics* 39: 1591–1607.
A paper that explores the discursive aspect of educational change in an Israeli context, Argaman's corpus-based study offers one of the few insights into the role of empathetic deixis in spoken and written discourse. Argaman maintains that *it* provides researchers interested in language in context with a means of 'unmasking' rhetoric within an institution, illustrating that talk is never without a purpose.

Botley, S. and **McEnery, T.** (2001) 'Demonstratives in English: a corpus-based study', *Journal of English Linguistics* 29(1): 7–33.
This corpus-based study offers an analysis of demonstrative pronouns (*this*, *that*, *these* and *those*) based on an exploration of three 100,000 word corpora. The paper explores a variety of questions commonly associated with demonstratives including their function and distribution across genres.

Rühlemann, C. (2007) *Conversation in Context: A Corpus-Driven Approach*. London: Continuum.
Rühlemann places deixis at the core of his analysis of the spoken component of the British National Corpus. In addition to providing 'traditional' deictic analyses of person, place and time deixis (see in particular Chapter 4), Rühlemann also integrates other features of conversation such as speech-reporting, discourse markers and vocatives and terms of address into the deictic system. His work is also notable for a focus on empathetic deixis.

Strauss, S. (2002) '*This*, *that* and *it* in spoken American English: a demonstrative system of gradient focus', *Language Sciences* 24: 131–52.
This paper provides an alternative model for the analysis of the demonstrative pronouns *it*, *this* and *that*. Strauss moves away from the traditional proximal–distal distinction with a central speaker and instead focuses on aspects of the relationship between speaker and hearer such as degree of shared information between interlocutors.

CHAPTER 4

Politeness in context

4.1 THE LINGUISTIC STUDY OF POLITENESS

In this chapter we set out to explore some of the most influential theories of politeness that are essential reading for those new to the area. However, before doing so, it is worth taking time out to examine your own intuitions about politeness. In her book *Pragmatics and Discourse* (2008), Cutting warns that in pragmatics, when we talk of politeness, 'we do *not* refer to the social rules of behaviour, such as letting people go first through a door . . . We refer to the choices that are made in language use, the linguistic expressions that give people space and show a friendly attitude to them' (pp. 44–5). Therefore, in your reflection on what you consider polite language to be, do you consider terms like *sir* or *madam*, which show respect towards a person, polite? Is using fixed expressions like *please*, *thank you*, *excuse me* or *sorry* polite, socially acceptable behaviour? Or is language which we use to avoid sounding too direct such as *Would you mind awfully if I asked you to move?* an example of language which you consider to be 'distancing' or 'hypocritical'?

Politeness is one of the most researched branches of contemporary pragmatics – Dufon *et al*.'s (1994) bibliography of politeness research extends to 51 pages in small print and claims not to be exhaustive. Watts (2003) noted that his bibliography contained 1,200 titles and was growing weekly!

The question of what constitutes polite and, indeed, impolite, language usage is one of the most researched topics in contemporary linguistics. This chapter examines two distinct seminal theories (or models) of politeness, and demonstrates key features of these models in context. The first, Brown and Levinson's *Politeness: Some Universals in Language Use* (1978, reprinted 1987), is arguably the most influential model to date given that it has dominated the theory of linguistic politeness since it was first published. Brown and Levinson define politeness as a complex system for softening face-threatening behaviour. They view politeness as a phenomenon that can be codified, thereby enabling the linguist to measure politeness quantitatively. This can be done very effectively using corpus software. However, researchers such as Watts (1989; 2003) have shown that cultures have conflicting views as to what constitutes polite language use, particularly when it comes to impoliteness. His model, as outlined in his book *Politeness*, has emerged as perhaps the most prominent alternative for the examination of linguistic politeness. He argues that there is no linguistic structure that can be considered innately polite; rather, politeness arises from a negotiation between individual speakers and the context in which the interaction takes place. In addition to these theories of politeness, we will examine some of the growing literature on impoliteness, for example Culpeper (1996) and Bousfield (2008). Many theorists, such as Watts, now use the term *(im)politeness* to acknowledge that any consideration of linguistic politeness necessarily entails a consideration of impoliteness. We are all aware that impolite or aggressive communication can take place and current approaches to politeness have been unable to account for these occurrences (see Bousfield, 2008 for elaboration on this point).

In order to understand these quite complex theories, it is crucial to explore the foundations upon which they rest. Accordingly, we begin our exploration of Brown and Levinson's model by examining Grice's *Co-operative Principle* and Goffman's concept of *face*. These concepts are also vital in order to understand current theories on impoliteness and, later in the chapter, before our discussion of Watts' theory, we will explore Sperber and Wilson's *relevance theory*.

4.2 PENELOPE BROWN AND STEPHEN LEVINSON

Theoretical models of politeness

Brown and Levinson (1978)
Watts (2003)

The main influences behind these models

For Brown and Levinson
*   Grice's Co-operative Principle
*   Goffman's concept of face

For Watts
*   Sperber and Wilson's relevance theory

The foundations of Brown and Levinson's theory: Grice and Goffman

In his work, Grice (1975) makes a number of observations about conversation, many of which are echoed throughout the work of Brown and Levinson. He claims that conversations are 'characteristically, to some degree at least, cooperative efforts; and each participant recognises in them, to some extent, a common purpose or set of purposes, or at least a mutually accepted direction' (1975: 45). Based on these assumptions, Grice posits his Co-operative Principle (CP): that all people are essentially cooperative in order to achieve the purpose of being 'maximally efficient' (1989: 28) in interaction with others. In order to elaborate on the CP, Grice formulated four maxims: *quantity*, *quality*, *relation* and *manner* (see also Chapters 5 and 6).

Exploring the maxims in context

The first maxim of the CP, *quantity*, requires speakers to be as informative as required for listener comprehension, by ensuring that they are both succinct and explicit. In other words, when talking, we are required to give neither too much nor too little information. Speakers often use a range of signals in conversation that show they are observing this maxim, one of which is illustrated, in bold, in extract 4.1. In this extract, a family is discussing their cousin's personality and the general consensus is that he is *a lovely fellow*:

(4.1)

A: . . . he's a lovely fellow.
B: Oh yeah.
C: And see he would have spent time in Bosnia too as in they do a lot of work over there.
B: Oh.
C: I don't know if he'd actually be there or if he would just do work kind of on behalf of the people there but am so I said it to him in the car down at the church remember the night we+
A: Oh yes indeed.
C: +and couldn't get into the church **that's another story**.

(LCIE)

We can see that, as the conversation progresses, the maxim of quantity is being observed by Speaker C's use of the phrase *that's another story*. This functions to signal a realisation that Speaker C has not provided enough information about the story of not being able to get into the church, but also indicates that further elaboration may perhaps risk, for example, revealing an embarrassing situation or offending a hearer. It may also be the case that the other story is not relevant now and that it can be elaborated on at a later stage.

The second maxim, *quality*, states that speakers should be truthful and not say anything which they cannot provide adequate evidence for or do not believe to be true. An example of this can be seen in extract 4.2, where two friends are discussing the possibility of insuring a car for a period of one month:

(4.2)

A: But I don't think you can get insured for a month.
B: You can yeah.

A: Can you?

B: Yeah you can.

A: Can you?

B: Yeah you can. You can pay your insurance. **I'm not sure** now whether it would mean your mother would have to pay her insurance for the month . . .

(LCIE)

Speaker A seems to be of the opinion that this is not possible but Speaker B disagrees with him. We can see that Speaker B then moves to give his/her reasons for disagreeing and, in doing so, introduces an element of uncertainty to some of what s/he is saying by prefacing with *I'm not sure*, so protecting themselves from correction or contradiction in the future.

The third maxim is that of *relation*, where 'speakers are assumed to be saying something that is relevant to what has been said before' (Cutting, 2008: 35). Extract 4.3 is taken from a university lecture:

(4.3)

A: Now **I mentioned yesterday** that you should look at both sides of the same coin. You should look at those who argue for audiences as guerrilla readers, you know post-modern theorists will see audiences as being involved in interpretative free for all.

(LIBEL)

The lecturer, in beginning this segment of his/her lecture, points to its relevance to what has been said before by using *I mentioned yesterday*.

The last maxim is the maxim of *manner*, which requires speakers to be clear and orderly in order to avoid ambiguity and obscurity. Again, extract 4.4 is taken from an academic setting and the speaker asks his/her audience for confirmation that he/she is adhering to the maxim through the use of an interrogative (marked in bold):

(4.4)

A: If you come across two theorists in the text or in theory in general who you find interesting or attractive or stimulating et cetera use those too. Don't feel that you're aah confined to the ones we have covered. **So I hope that's relatively clear is it?**

(LIBEL)

Grice did not expect rigid adherence to these maxims; indeed he was particularly interested in how the maxims were 'flouted', thus requiring the listener to infer the underlying meaning from clues available in the conversational context, which Grice termed *conversational implicature*.

It is interesting to explore the idiomatic and metaphoric use of *face* in everyday English usage. For example, journalists use the phrase *face-saver* to refer to an action or excuse which prevents damage to your reputation or the loss of people's respect for you. If, for example, you are impolite to someone, you may have to *face up* to the consequences.

Whereas Grice developed his work from a background in the philosophy of language, Goffman (1956, 1959, 1967) employed his background in sociology in order to formulate what has become one of the key notions in politeness research: *face*. Drawing on the work of Durkheim (1915), Goffman echoes the Gricean notion that conversation is essentially co-operative in nature. Goffman developed a concept of face inextricably bound to English idiomatic expressions such as 'to lose face', that is to be embarrassed or humiliated, and 'to save face', that is to prevent damage to one's reputation or the loss of people's respect for the speaker. Goffman (1967: 5) defined face as 'the positive social value a person effectively claims for [him/herself]'. Goffman suggested that in order to maintain this positive self-image, a person invests emotional energy in the face that they present to others which requires a degree of effort on their part, a process Goffman refers to as *face-work*.

Brown and Levinson's theory of politeness

Face

- Brown and Levinson built on the metaphor of *face* from Goffman.
- They define *face* as the public self-image that every member of society wants to claim for himself.
- They divide *face* into *positive* and *negative*:
  - positive face
    the need for enhancement of a positive self-image
  - negative face
    the need for freedom of action and freedom from imposition.

Perhaps the most famous, and most remarked upon (both positively and negatively), study of politeness is Brown and Levinson's ([1978] 1987) study (see also Chapter 6). Following Goffman, Brown and Levinson (1987: 61) maintain that face is 'the public self-image that every member [of society] wants to claim for himself'. For Brown and Levinson, face consists of two related aspects: *positive face* and *negative face*. For both of these aspects of face, our essential needs are the same – we want people to like us – and this impacts on our linguistic behaviour. From the point of view of positive face, we want to receive acknowledgement from others that we are liked, accepted as part of a group and that our wants are understood by them. In the case of negative face, we want to be independent and not have our actions imposed on by others. According to Brown and Levinson, these two basic face needs are satisfied by politeness strategies. In their everyday interaction, people behave as if these face needs will be respected by others, however, despite this assumption, people sometimes engage in actions that threaten these two face needs, what Brown and Levinson refer to as *face threatening acts*.

Face threatening acts (FTAs)

When politeness researchers refer to an FTA, they refer to a communicative act performed by the speaker that does not respect either the hearer's need for space (negative face) or their desire for their self-image to be upheld (positive face) or both. One example of an FTA (marked in bold) can be seen in extract 4.5, which features two colleagues discussing an incident which occurred involving an ex-colleague at a party:

(4.5)

A: ... that was the year that guy was working there and got caught stealing the drink and they thought it was Brendan stealing it.

B: I was there. What about him anyway?

A: Oh you came after.

B: I remember Brendan. I knew him like. I was up in the rooms and he often came up there. I knew Brendan well.

A: **No because the summer I was working there you weren't working there.**

B: Mary I know for a fact I was working there when he was working there.

(LCIE)

Speaker A is telling Speaker B about an incident of mistaken identity involving Brendan, an ex-colleague. Speaker B claims that there is no need to tell her the story as she was in fact at the party, knew Brendan and worked with him. However, Speaker A is apparently unwilling to accept this. Speaker A disagrees with Speaker B with the utterance *No because the summer I was working there you weren't working there*. According to Brown and Levinson, this constitutes an unmitigated FTA on Speaker B's positive face because Speaker A is refusing to satisfy Speaker B's (the hearer) desire to be right (see section on positive politeness) and refusing to agree.

Brown and Levinson view politeness as a complex system for softening FTAs. If an FTA has to be performed, then the speaker has five communicative choices, *bald on record*, *positive politeness*, *negative politeness*, *off record* and *don't perform the FTA* (these choices form the so-called 'superstrategies'), in order to accomplish this, as illustrated in Figure 4.1, where the choices are marked in bold.

The first decision a speaker has to make is *whether or not to perform the FTA*. In other words, do you speak or do you hold your tongue? Should you choose the latter option, communication can be achieved by gestures like pointing a finger (although there may be situations where this may still constitute an FTA!) or nodding your head. On the

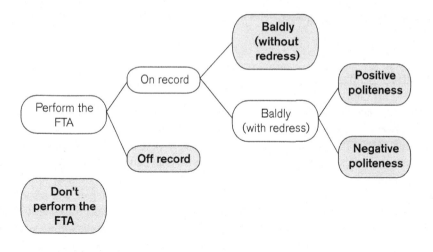

Figure 4.1 Brown and Levinson's (1987) strategies for performing FTAs.

other hand, the speaker can decide to say something, in which case they say something *off record* or *on record*. Performing an FTA off-record involves strategies such as metaphor, irony, rhetorical questions, understatements or hints. Alternatively, the speaker can go on-record, and this requires the speaker to make a strategic choice either to perform the FTA with or without *redress*. Redress, Brown and Levinson maintain, is action a speaker takes by modifying their utterance in some way in order to take the hearer's face into account; in other words, redress involves the use of mitigation (mitigation will be explored further in relation to positive and negative politeness). Another option available to a speaker is to go on-record without downtoning or mitigating their utterance, what Brown and Levinson refer to as a *bald* FTA. In extract 4.6, which features a family chatting around the dinner table, we can see a request performed baldly without redress (in bold):

(4.6)   [Context: *mineral* is a word commonly used in Irish English to refer to a non-alcoholic drink such as lemonade]

A: Does anyone want a mineral?
B: I'll have one.
A: Yeah?
B: **Make me a cup of tea.**

(LCIE)

If we contrast this request with those highlighted in extracts 4.8 or 4.9, a complete absence of mitigation is evident and, in addition to this, the utterance takes the form of an imperative. In this case, Speaker B may be relying on the intimate relationship between family members to mitigate; however, in most cases, in choosing the bald on-record option the speaker is opting for the most face-threatening route.

The final choice is that the speaker chooses to redress the FTA using either a *positive* or a *negative politeness* strategy and in the following sections, we will explore these in more detail.

Positive politeness

As we have already stated, positive face requires that the individual's positive self-image be respected in everyday interaction with others. In order to achieve this, Brown and Levinson claim that conversational participants often work to minimise the social distance between them. Positive face is saved by conversational participants co-constructing a feeling of closeness and fostering the belief that all speakers are working towards a common goal. As we can see Brown and Levinson list fifteen strategies that a speaker can employ in order to avoid threatening the addressee's positive face. Positive politeness behaviour is often compared to that which is characteristic of interaction in an intimate setting such as between husband and wife or within family discourse (see Blum-Kulka, 1997; Clancy, 2005). Brown and Levinson also maintain that because positive politeness can be associated with intimate language use, it can be used as a 'social accelerator' (1987: 103), where, for example, strangers, in using markers of positive politeness, can indicate that they want to form a closer bond. Extract 4.7 features English language teachers in the workplace ruing their lack of status within their organisation, and is a good example of a number of positive politeness strategies in action in that, as we shall see, the teachers exploit these strategies to build on a sense of collegiality.

Fifteen strategies Brown and Levinson list in order to avoid threatening positive face:

- Pay attention to a hearer's interests, wants, needs or goods.
- Exaggerate interest in, approval of or sympathy with a hearer.
- Employ exaggeration and dramatic effect in your speech in order to interest and involve the hearer.
- Use in-group identity markers.
- Seek agreement/make small talk.
- Avoid disagreement.
- Find common ground.
- Joke.
- Assert or imply knowledge of and concern for a hearer's wants.
- Offer, promise.
- Be optimistic.
- Use inclusive 'we' forms.
- Give (or ask for) reasons.
- Assume or assert reciprocity.
- Give gifts.

(4.7)

A: Yes but **we** don't have the power to throw anybody out what I mean is **we** haven't
     been given that kind of clout **we** don't have that status in the university if they fail
     calculus they're out if they fail English they just continue.
B: Yeah.
A: So [laughs] so I think **we** should just accept that our horrible lowly status.
     [General laughter]
C: **We**'re the poor cousins.
A: Yeah and **we** know that.

(C-MELT)

The echoing of the inclusive form *we*, in bold, in the extract creates an 'in-group' and
fosters teachers' feelings of solidarity and common ground. The atmosphere is a joking
one, signalled by the presence of humour, and this adds further to the *we're all in this
together* dynamic (see Vaughan, 2007: 185), strengthening the sense of collegiality. It is
also interesting to note, especially in comparing positive politeness with negative politeness
in the workplace, that the teachers' boss is not present at this meeting.

One of the most common positive politeness strategies, in-group identity markers
such as nicknames, falls under the banner of *terms of address*, which are 'traditionally one
of the central topics in politeness research' (Eelen, 2001: 38). Address terms offer
methodological advantages to researchers of linguistic politeness in that they can be clearly
and unambiguously identified within a text. Address terms can generally be subdivided into
seven semantic categories as outlined in Figure 4.2. However, as Figure 4.2 demonstrates,

Level of formality	Category	Example	Politeness strategy
Informal ↑	*Endearments*	*honey, baby, love*	*Positive politeness* ↑
	Family terms	*Mammy, Daddy, son*	
	Familiarisers	*mate, man, folks*	
	First names familiarised	*Brad, Jen*	
	Full first names	*Bradley, Jennifer*	
	Title and surname	*Mr Holmes, Dr Watson, Professor Moriarty*	↓
Formal ↓	*Honorifics*	*sir, ma'am, your honour*	*Negative politeness*

Figure 4.2 The semantic categorisation of in-group terms of address (adapted from Leech, 1999).

not all address terms function as positive politeness markers – as the categories move from the more informal such as nicknames and first name familiarised to the more formal such as honorifics, the politeness strategy changes from positive to negative politeness.

In positive politeness, some address terms function to mitigate or downtone utterances. *Mitigation* of an FTA, also referred to as *downtoning* or *softening* in some politeness literature, can involve the use of politeness markers such as terms of address in order to reduce the 'force' of an utterance. Take the following extract (4.8); here the speakers on a radio phone-in are discussing marital breakdown when they get into an argument:

(4.8)

Caller:	... but as time goes on it's cool these days ah and pardon me for using that word because it's a slang word I don't like. But as they say it's cool to say 'I'm separated'. It's attractive.
Presenter:	Is it?
Caller:	It's attractive to ah men and women.
Presenter:	Well now I've interviewed a fair number of separated people down through the years and I don't think anybody ever found it cool or a great experience. I mean there was an awful lot of pain and that kind of+
Caller:	How long+
Presenter:	+thing.
Caller:	+ago is that **Marian**?
Presenter:	Well on and off over the years.

(LCIE)

We can see that the presenter contradicts the caller and the caller responds with a challenge. The addition of the term of address in the form of a full first name (in bold) by the caller is crucial in mitigating the FTA posed by the challenge. In using it the caller appeals to the presenter as an equal and, in a sense, reiterates their common goal of discussion rather than argument, thus re-establishing the 'pseudo-intimacy' of the context (O'Keeffe, 2005). Although the address term functions as a marker of positive politeness in extract 4.8, as already mentioned, certain address term categories such as *honorifics* function in the realm of *negative politeness*, the focus of the next section. This illustrates a feature of Brown and Levinson's theory – that strategies such as address terms can be used to soften threats to positive or negative face (we also deal with address terms in relation to language teaching in Chapter 8).

Negative politeness

Negative politeness is action aimed at non-interference and non-imposition on the hearer and so the maintenance of negative face requires the achievement of distance. Brown and Levinson list ten strategies for the linguistic realisation of negative politeness. In the same way that they place positive politeness at the heart of 'intimate' behaviour, they place negative politeness at the heart of external 'respect' behaviour. Traditionally, we are more likely to be aware of negative politeness in conversations where there is a clear difference in factors such as *power relations* (for example, when you are talking to your boss). They claim that 'when we think of Western cultures, it is negative politeness that springs to mind ... it is the stuff that fills the etiquette books' (1987: 129–30).

An example of the negative politeness strategy *be conventionally indirect* can be seen in extract 4.9, where two female friends are chatting:

(4.9)

A: Niamh **would you by any chance** have nail polish remover down in your room?
B: I could have actually.

(LCIE)

Speaker A's utterance is conventionally indirect because she has chosen an interrogative form rather than an imperative for her request. In addition, the pairing of *would* with the expression *by any chance* establishes distance giving the hearer options for interpreting what was said and lessening the face threat associated with saying *no*. The speaker almost creates an 'imaginary' or hypothetical situation, the strategy which Brown and Levinson refer to as *be pessimistic*, which further distances the speaker from the 'real' world, again lessening the threat associated with a refusal.

Ten strategies Brown and Levinson list in order to avoid threatening negative face:

- Be conventionally indirect.
- Question, hedge.
- Be pessimistic.
- Minimise the imposition.
- Give deference.
- Apologise.
- Impersonalise.
- Adopt an inclusive perspective.
- Nominalise.
- Claim or disclaim indebtedness to the hearer.

Similar to terms of address, *hedging* is a much researched negative politeness strategy. There are many definitions of hedges (see Lakoff, 1972; Fraser, 1975; Clemen, 1997; Markkanen and Schröder, 1997; Aijmer, 2002) and hedges come in many forms (see also Biber *et al.*, 1999; Carter and McCarthy, 2006). Hedges are frequently used by speakers to soften face threatening acts such as disagreement, suggestion, advice or criticism.

Generally speaking, a speaker will use hedging to avoid sounding too blunt or assertive, as is illustrated in the following example (taken from Carter and McCarthy, 1997). Hedges are often used in situations where the speaker either cannot or does not want to say something directly:

Hedged utterance	Unhedged utterance
A: **Well, I mean**, I have, **you know** never **actually really** liked her as a teacher.	A: I have never liked her as a teacher.

Speaker A here uses five different hedges *well, I mean, you know, actually* and *really* to avoid giving the blunt assessment presented by the unhedged utterance. This allows the speaker to mitigate any threat that might be presented to the teacher's face.

Extract 4.10 demonstrates the use of the hedge *I think* to mitigate the fact that Speaker B disagrees with his friend, Speaker A, in relation to the positioning of competitors in a sporting event:

(4.10)

A: They're just starting the second circuit I'd say are they?
B: Amm **I think** now but I could be wrong but **I think** that is comin up to the second last.

(LCIE)

In extract (4.10), Speaker B uses *I think* to 'detach' himself from the truth value of his utterance (see also Holmes, 1995). By using the hedge, he acknowledges Speaker A's negative face, the desire to be unimpeded by others, by softening his disagreement.

In addition to this affective function, hedges can also be used to express genuine uncertainty, as in extract 4.11:

(4.11) [Context: two female friends chatting]

A: I've never seen her in the same thing ever. Where did you get that t-shirt?
B: In [name of shop].
A: How much?
B: Thirty euro **I think**. Do you not like it?
A: It's fine.

(LCIE)

In extract 4.11, Speaker A, mindful that her memory might not be accurate, hedges the amount of money the t-shirt cost using *I think*. This conveys her desire to have her opinion accepted by her friend. We discuss hedging further in other chapters of the book, including Chapter 7, where it is looked at in specific contexts, and in Chapter 8, where we try to itemise it in terms of its vocabulary and grammar and address how it might be taught.

Politeness and the notion of social variables

Brown and Levinson claim that our choice of politeness strategy, or lack thereof, is decided by a number of social variables. The first of these is the perceived *social distance* between the speaker and hearer. Social distance is dependent on socio-cultural factors such as age, gender, role, education, class, ethnicity and so forth, all of which contribute towards establishing a degree of familiarity between speaker and hearer. The higher the familiarity, the lower the level of politeness strategies used (see the extracts that we have used from family discourse). The second contextual feature, *power difference*, is similarly dependent on socio-cultural features and these determine who has the dominant role in the conversation: the less dominant the role, the higher the level politeness strategies such as negative politeness. The final feature *cultural ranking*, dependent on a culture-bound evaluation of polite language use, is calculated according to how threatening a particular speech act is perceived to be within a specific culture (see also our discussion of the universality of pragmatic norms in Chapter 6). Once a decision has been made about these variables, the appropriate linguistic strategy is selected by the speaker.

4.3 IMPOLITENESS

As we have seen, Brown and Levinson's theory describes politeness as a complex framework for softening face threatening acts. However, how suitable is their framework when applied to communicative situations in which the speaker's intention is not to soften any threat to face but to instead attack a hearer's face? Culpeper (1996, 2005), Eelen (2001), Culpeper *et al.* (2003) and Bousfield (2008) all argue that, whereas all the leading politeness theories mention the notion of impoliteness, 'their comments on impoliteness are descriptively inadequate and often conceptually biased (i.e. it is assumed that the concepts used to explain politeness can be straightforwardly applied to impoliteness)' (Bousfield, 2008: 71). Taking this into consideration, Culpeper (1996) proposed a comprehensive impoliteness framework which is parallel but opposite to Brown and Levinson's theory of politeness aimed at examining the communication of offence. Impoliteness is characterised by an intentional and purposeful attack on a hearer's face. Bousfield (2008: 72) defines impoliteness as face threatening acts delivered:

(1) unmitigated, in contexts where mitigation is required, and/or,
(2) with deliberate aggression, that is, with the face threat exacerbated, 'boosted', or maximised in some way to heighten the face damage inflicted.

It is important to note here that impoliteness theorists such as Culpeper and Bousfield are concerned with intentional or strategic impoliteness. In order for impoliteness to be 'successful', the intention of the speaker to offend must be understood by the hearer. It is intention that is the key difference between politeness and impoliteness, whether it is the speaker's intention to support face (politeness) or attack face (impoliteness). Linguistically, intention is attributed to speakers through an examination of aspects such as context, activity type, speaker relationship, social roles and so on (see Bousfield, 2008: 74). There are of course situations where speakers can be unintentionally rude, such as in cross-cultural encounters where the potential for pragmatic failure is high (see also Chapters 6 and 8), but these situations would not be considered impolite because it was not the speaker's intention to be rude.

In parallel with Brown and Levinson (see Figure 4.1), Culpeper (1996) developed five impoliteness superstrategies: *bald on record impoliteness*, *positive impoliteness*, *negative impoliteness*, *off record impoliteness* (includes sarcasm) and *withhold politeness*. He also developed a corresponding range of positive and negative impoliteness strategies outlined in Table 4.1.

Bousfield (2008) has also added the strategies *criticise* (dispraise the hearer or some action or inaction by the hearer), *hinder/block* (physically, for example, block passage, or communicatively, for example, interrupt), *enforce role shift* (force hearer out of one social and/or discoursal role into another) and *challenge* (ask the hearer a challenging question, question the hearer's position, stance, beliefs and so on).

The literature on impoliteness distinguishes between two different types of impoliteness; *mock* impoliteness and *inherent* or *genuine* impoliteness. Culpeper (1996: 352) claims that mock impoliteness, or banter, occurs when 'impoliteness remains on the surface, since it is understood that it is not intended to cause offence'. An example of mock impoliteness can be seen in extract 4.12, where work colleagues are in a meeting.

Table 4.1 Culpeper's (1996) impoliteness strategies

Positive impoliteness strategies	Negative impoliteness strategies
• *Ignore, snub – fail to acknowledge the other's presence* • *Exclude the other from activity* • *Disassociate from the other – deny common ground or association; avoid sitting together* • *Be disinterested, unconcerned, unsympathetic* • *Use inappropriate identity markers – for example, use title and surname when a close relationship pertains* • *Use obscure or secretive language* • *Seek disagreement – select a sensitive topic* • *Make the other feel uncomfortable – do not joke or use small talk* • *Use taboo language – swear, be abusive* • *Call the hearer names – use derogatory nominations* • *Etc.*	• *Frighten – instil a belief that action detrimental to other will occur* • *Condescend, scorn or ridicule – emphasise own power, use diminutives, be contemptuous, belittle, do not take the hearer seriously* • *Invade the other's space – literally, position yourself closer than the relationship permits, or metaphorically (ask for information too intimate given the relationship)* • *Explicitly associate the hearer with a negative aspect – personalise, use the pronouns 'I' and 'you'* • *Put the other's indebtedness on record* • *Etc.*

(4.12)

A: Do you feel like we solved anything?
B: Does that mean me or everyone?
C: What?
A: Generally. Have we achieved what we came to achieve?
C: **Got a date or something?**
   [General laughter]

(C-MELT)

Speaker A is trying to bring the meeting to a close and wants to know if her colleagues have found it fruitful, demonstrated by the utterances *Do you feel like we solved anything?* and *Have we achieved what we came to achieve?* Speaker C seems bemused by Speaker A's hurry to finish and the utterance *Got a date or something?* appears, on the surface, to represent the negative politeness strategy *invade the other's space.* Speaker C is asking for information that is personal and this is inappropriate in a work context. However, Speaker C has designed her comment to draw laughter from her colleagues and she succeeds in doing so. The presence of laughter indicates that the impoliteness is indeed 'surface' and the utterance, far from designed to be impolite, actually serves to re-enforce group harmony at the end of the meeting process (see Vaughan, 2008).

The existence of mock politeness or banter suggests that there are speech situations in which an apparently impolite speech act will be judged as polite, or at least as not impolite, because of the particular interaction of act and context. On the other hand, there are situations where the combination of act and context do give rise to impoliteness. This has been labelled 'genuine' or 'inherent' impoliteness. Culpeper (1996) claims that inherent impoliteness occurs when an act (such as a request) cannot be completely mitigated either by a politeness strategy or the context or a combination of the two. He uses the utterance *Do you think you could possibly not pick your nose?* as an example of a situation where it is difficult to see how any amount of politeness work or contextual factors could remove impoliteness from the utterance. Extract 4.13, which features four siblings in conversation, provides an example of genuine impoliteness in an intimate context. The siblings are discussing how they cannot sleep at night and Speaker A suggests a herbal tea that he thinks would help. The conversation is interrupted by the arrival of Speaker D with food for the group which he begins to distribute.

(4.13)

A: Yeah I've a herbal tea inside that'll do you wonders now.
B: [unintelligible]
A: I've a herbal tea that'll knock you out like.
B: Yeah? What is it?
C: The smell alone could knock you out.

A: It's [name of herbal tea].
      [Speaker D enters room]
D: **You're fat. You'll eat them all.**
A: Ah Jimmy that's stupid.
C: Thank you.
A: **You do that now and I'll kick the face off you.**
      [Pause]
B: Connor?
A: Hm?
B: What did he do now?
A: He was throwin in the big packet of [name of product].

                                                                              (LCIE)

As we can see the first highlighted FTA (in bold), *You're fat. You'll eat them all*, contains a reference to a person's physical appearance, perhaps Western society's most insulting attack on self-image, demonstrating how Speaker D opts for the impoliteness strategy *call the hearer names* (although this use of the word 'fat' is also be considered taboo in some cultures) in order to threaten Speaker C's positive face. In addition, Speaker A employs negative politeness strategies in his utterance *You do that now and I'll kick the face off you*. This is intimidating and unfriendly in the extreme, and can be classified as an attempt to *frighten* Speaker D. This is all the more apparent due to the pause that follows the negative politeness strategy and the absence of extralinguistic mitigation such as laughter.

Similar to Watts' notion of politeness below, the interpretation of impoliteness relies heavily on the context of the conversation. A feature of much of the work done on impoliteness, as outlined here, is a move away from the focus on individual lexical or grammatical strategies which characterises much of Brown and Levinson's work. Impolite utterances can often cause a reaction from the hearer, especially in relationships where the power differential is small (such as between friends), and this, in turn, can quickly lead to an escalation in the situation. Therefore, impoliteness theorists are interested in the response to an impolite utterance and also in how confrontational encounters are resolved. This marks another important shift in any consideration of impoliteness (or politeness) – the move to incorporate hearer perceptions as well as those of the speaker. Finally, impoliteness studies such as Culpeper *et al.* (2003) and Culpeper (2005) have shown the importance of understanding aspects of interactants' behaviour such as prosody, lending weight to the adage *It's not what you say but how you say it*.

4.4 RICHARD WATTS

We now switch the focus of the chapter to Watts' theory of politeness, perhaps the most prominent alternative to Brown and Levinson for an examination of linguistic politeness. We begin the exploration of Watts' theory with a look at Sperber and Wilson's *relevance theory*.

Relevance theory

Context is everything

Sperber and Wilson's (1995) *relevance theory* (RT) is an attempt to provide a cognitive account of how we understand what we hear. The origins of their theory derive from a dissatisfaction with the Gricean model of co-operation. Sperber and Wilson maintain that the four Gricean maxims can be subsumed under the one overriding super-maxim of *relation* – a speaker's utterance should be relevant to previous utterances in the conversation. Therefore, the maxim of quantity can be expressed as *provide the right amount of relevant information*, that of quality as *provide truthful relevant information*, and manner as *provide unobscured or unambiguous relevant information*. According to Sperber and Wilson, an utterance is relevant when a hearer's background knowledge enables him/her to interpret, in a meaningful way, what a speaker says. In other words, an utterance is relevant to us as hearers when it does something for us, for example, answers a question, settles a doubt, confirms a suspicion and so forth. Sperber and Wilson (2006: 608) call this *positive cognitive effect* because it makes a 'worthwhile difference to an individual's representation of the world'. They claim that input (a sight, a sound, an utterance, a memory) and context combine to create the most important type of cognitive effect, that of *contextual implication*. Consider the following example (taken from Wilson, 1994: 45):

A:	It will rain in Paris tomorrow.
Previous context:	The hearer is going to Paris tomorrow and has thought about bringing a coat just in case.
Cognitive effect:	The utterance is combined with previous knowledge to create the contextual implication that it is necessary to pack the coat.

This processing, whereby new information combines with already stored information, which in turn results in the production of the cognitive effect of packing the coat, makes the utterance *It will rain in Paris tomorrow* relevant. However, it should be noted that it is not just the cognitive effects that make an utterance relevant, but also the *processing effort*. Processing effort is the time a hearer has to devote in order to interpret an utterance and involves cognitive processes such as perception, memory and inference. According to Yus Ramos (1998: 318), 'effective processing … does not demand an excessive effort [on the part of the hearer]. Everybody aims at the economy of their mental efforts.' Therefore, a quick summary of the relevance of an utterance to a hearer reads: *The greater the cognitive effect, the more relevant the utterance; the lower the processing effort, the more relevant the utterance.* To put it more simply, to understand an utterance is to prove its relevance (Grundy, 2008).

In relation to politeness theory, RT allows us to account for the large range of assumptions that a hearer can derive from a single utterance. Take, for example, the following extract, 4.14 (from Watts, 2003: 210-11):

(4.14)

A: Where's Margaret this evening?
B: Sorry, I don't know.

In this exchange, if Speaker A accepts Speaker B's utterance as maximally relevant, then he/she formulates the assumption that Speaker B does not know where Margaret is. However, if we assume that Speaker A is aware that Speaker B generally knows Margaret's movements, then Speaker A may formulate a range of different assumptions such as *Speaker B is lying*. As the exchange stands here, Speaker A is free to determine which of these assumptions is true and, by extension, how polite he/she considers Speaker B to be. Here we see the importance of the notion of context — Speaker A uses his/her background knowledge, in combination with the immediate exchange and his/her anticipation of what is to come in the conversation, in order to formulate what is genuinely relevant, so arriving at the correct assumption. This allows relevance theorists to see politeness not just as a series of strategies designed to protect a hearer's face, but as a complex, ongoing process of negotiation and renegotiation within verbal interaction.

Watts' theory of politeness

According to Watts, politeness is a dynamic process by which 'being polite' is not connected to the linguistic structures we use, but to the individual's interpretation of these structures as polite or impolite in instances of ongoing verbal interaction. In order to fully understand, explore and apply Watt's model, we need to make a clear distinction between the concepts of *politeness1* and *politeness2* and also his notions of *politic* and *polite* behaviour.

Politeness1 versus politeness2

Researchers in politeness theory frequently make a distinction between the concepts of *politeness1* and *politeness2*. For Watts, politeness1 refers to folk, lay or commonsense interpretations of politeness. He maintains that when people are asked to characterise polite language usage, they inevitably mention expressions like *please*, *thank you* or *sorry*, linguistic expressions that they regard as 'considerate' or 'respectful'. However, he also claims that we encounter people who consider polite language to be 'hypocritical' or 'dishonest' or 'unfeeling' (2003: 2); a case in point is the expression *Have a nice day*, apparently an integral part of polite language usage in the US but viewed as 'unfeeling' in other countries (it should be stressed that this reflects a cross-cultural situation). Therefore, as Watts suggests, these interpretations are inherently evaluative and differ from one culture to another, one group of speakers to another and even at the level of individual speaker to individual speaker. Watts argues that our own interpretation of what constitutes polite language forms the basis for our evaluation of how polite, or impolite, we consider other people to be.

On the other hand, politeness2 is concerned with 'politeness' as a technical term used in both the pragmatic and sociolinguistic study of spoken and written language, such as in Brown and Levinson's model. We can illustrate this distinction by examining the following extract (4.15) of family talk:

(4.15) [Context: the family is talking about Christmas. *Feck off* is often used in Irish English
as a polite expletive.]

A: It's religious it's the birth of Jesus and we all should be aware of that.
B: [laughs]
A: It's nothing got to do with presents.
         [
C: **Shut up**.
D: [laughs] Come here Connor. **Shut up**.
A: It's nothing to do with presents and happiness it's got to do with celebrating the
birth of Jesus.
B: Okay so we won't give you any presents.
                  [
A: We're not allowed be happy because we are Catholic.
                  [
C: Connor **shut up**.
                    [
D: You're having no presents so are you?
B: I'll say a prayer for you.
A: We are Catholic. We are not allowed be happy. It's all about the birth of Jesus.
C: [laughs]
B: That's okay so I'll get you a novena said for Christmas.
A: **[shouts] Good. Feck off.**

                                (LCIE)

An example of politeness1

How to be polite at a dinner. This is an example from a web page of
politeness1, our common understanding politeness, verbally and non-verbally within
a certain culture.

- Eat only what you can handle.
- Wait for some signal that the meal is beginning, such as the hostess lifting her
fork.
- Ask politely (by name if possible) and smile when you need a utensil or other
item. Be sure to thank the person who fetches it for you.
- Talk, but try to keep your voice peaceful and polite. Importantly, try not to
interrupt others; let them talk and show them that you are listening to them
with respectful eye contact.
- Smile at other guests and treat them all well – be polite, peaceful, calm and
classy.

- Practice basic table manners. Keep your elbows off the table, chew with your lips closed, don't scrape your teeth on your fork or spoon, never talk with food in your mouth, always say please and thank you, and use your napkin.
- Thank your host: they will have worked hard to pull it off.
- Uncomfortable silences are the bane of all dinner parties. Suggest new conversation topics, or compliment the dish.
- If you drop or break something simply laugh at yourself then clean it up.
- Avoid touchy conversation topics like religion, politics and sex.
- Excuse yourself politely if you need to use the bathroom, or if you burp.
- Some people consider it very rude if you use 'Can I?' instead of 'May I?' To be safe, always use 'may'.
- Chew in small bites if you want to be polite.

Adapted from wikiHow: http://www.wikihow.com/Be-Polite-at-a-Dinner

When we examine this extract closely, we can see that Speaker A, Connor, is told to *Shut up* three times (marked in bold) and Speaker B, who happens to be Connor's mother, is shouted at (marked in bold), all of which constitute bald on-record face threatening acts. There are also four speaker overlaps (marked by [ ) as the participants attempt to seize control of the speaker turn. None of these features would be considered traditionally polite; indeed, in many contexts, telling someone to *Shut up* or talking over a speaker would be considered impolite or rude. However, if we further explore the extract, we can see the presence of laughter and that the conversation appears to proceed without any notable arguments taking place, indicating that the speakers remain unaffected by the apparent impoliteness. This raises a key question for us as researchers of linguistic politeness: do we label the family *polite* or *impolite*? In terms of politeness2, theoretically or objectively at least, according to Brown and Levinson's terms, the speakers are being impolite and this is signalled by the presence of unmitigated face threatening acts, but also by the absence of other politeness strategies such as indirectness or hedging. However, politeness1, due to its evaluative nature, allows the researcher to consider that this family represent an example of negotiated politeness, where one family have constructed a level of politeness which they have evaluated as acceptable for use in this particular context.

Politic behaviour versus polite behaviour

The distinction between our individual interpretation of politeness and the theoretical interpretation forms the basis for the difference between Watts' model of politeness and Brown and Levinson's. As we have seen, Watts contends that politeness1 is argumentative and evaluative in nature. He considers a range of linguistic structures traditionally associated with politeness and distinguishes between *formulaic, ritualised utterances* such as terms of address (*sir, Bill, Dr McGrath*) or expressions of speech acts such as thanking (*thanks, thank you very much*) and *semi-formulaic utterances*, for example, hedges (*I think, I mean, actually*) or boosters (*of course, clearly*). His aim is to demonstrate that these structures are not stand-alone markers of politeness, rather open to interpretation as polite in ongoing verbal interaction, therefore, no linguistic structure can be considered inherently polite. According to Watts (2003: 20), *politic behaviour* is 'that behaviour, linguistic and non-linguistic, which the participants construct as being appropriate to the on-going social interaction'. Therefore, politic behaviour can be equated with appropriate social behaviour (Meier, 1995). *Polite behaviour*, on the other hand, refers to a marked version of politic behaviour in that the use of linguistic structures such as those outlined here exceed a level of linguistic behaviour that is expected in the context, thereby leaving them open to interpretation by the participants as polite. In order to determine which linguistic expressions can be classified as 'polite', Watts claims that the researcher 'needs to carry out a fine-grained, sensitive analysis of verbal interaction relying heavily on features of the context' (2003: 170). We again turn to extract 4.16 from family discourse and look at more of the interaction in order to exemplify the difference between these behaviours:

(4.16) [Context: speaker A = mother, B = son, C = father]

A: Does anyone want a mineral?

B: I'll have one

A: Yeah?

B: **Make me a cup of tea.**

C: The kettle is boiled. He's dehydrated.

A: Do you want a cup of tea?

C: Does anyone want the cup before she goes?

D: Ok I will so.

C: Kettle is boiled anyway. Oh I'll have a cup too . . .

A: . . . do you take sugar?

B: Yes **please**.

A: How many?

B: One and a half.

A: Do you want [some chocolate]?

B: **Please** yeah.

C: **You shouldn't give him anything.**

(LCIE)

In extract 4.16, we have already shown that Speaker B performs a bald face threatening request that is unmitigated and takes the form of an imperative *Make me a cup of tea* (marked in bold). This is likely to be evaluated negatively, or as 'impolite', by the conversational participants. This negative evaluation can also be seen in Speaker C's utterance *You shouldn't give him anything* (marked in bold) which is interpretable as a response to Speaker B's perceived impoliteness in that Speaker C appears to be saying *He doesn't deserve a cup of tea because he has been rude*. In addition to this, the two instances of the word *please* (in bold) may imply that Speaker B is aware of the negative force of his request and is attempting to repair his breach of politic behaviour. This, of course, is our evaluation of the behaviour of the participants, however, it can be supported by an analysis of the family sub-corpus of LCIE.

Table 4.2 shows the frequency count for the word *please* in the family sub-corpus of LCIE (comprising 28,500 words) in contrast to a selection of more frequent items. As we

Table 4.2 Frequency of *please* in family sub-corpus (LCIE), (not normalised)

Word	Frequency of occurrence
the	944
he	362
so	164
lovely	39
stuff	17
please	2

can see, when normalised per 10,000 words, *please* has a frequency of 1 occurrence every 10,000 words, which is considerably less frequent than the most frequent item *the* (332 occurrences per 10,000 words) or *lovely* (14 occurrences per 10,000 words) or *stuff* (6 occurrences per 10,000 words). Returning to extract 4.16, *please* is used twice by Speaker B over the course of the extract, giving it a frequency rate much higher than once every 10,000 words. This demonstrates that Speaker B has 'exceeded' what is expected in the context in order to attempt to repair the possible damage caused by his impoliteness and, thus, *please* is likely to be open to interpretation as polite behaviour by the conversational participants.

4.5 CONCLUSION

This chapter has focused on theories of politeness and impoliteness and applied them to corpus data drawn from a range of different contexts. It is hoped that researchers with an interest in linguistic politeness (or impoliteness) will have a firm base from which further study can begin. We conclude with the following points in relation to the area:

(1) No consideration of theories of linguistic politeness or impoliteness, or indeed pragmatics in general, can proceed without a full understanding of the building blocks used to construct it. Accordingly, we have seen how insights from different disciplines such as the philosophy of language (the *Co-operative Principle* and corresponding maxims of *quantity, quality, relation* and *manner*), sociology (the notion of *face*) and cognitive linguistics (*relevance theory*) have all made a significant contribution to the formulation of distinct models of politeness.

(2) We have used corpus extracts wherever possible to illustrate some of the key features of (im)politeness in context. Context has a crucial role to play within pragmatics and its importance in interpreting meaning cannot be overstated. As Culpeper *et al.* (2003: 1576) state, 'it is the response to the utterance, and indeed the construction of the whole speech activity, that may determine how the utterance is to be taken, including whether it be polite, impolite or somewhere in between'.

(3) In relation to context, many of the examples we have used in this chapter are taken from small sub-corpora or specialised corpora (academic lectures, English language teacher meetings, radio phone-ins). These small-scale corpora are ideally suited to the fine-grained analysis of polite behaviour posited by Watts. Corpus linguistics allows the researcher to move beyond the level of utterance in order to consider the full

context in which polite behaviour occurs. This interpretation of (im)politeness at a micro-level allows us to gain insights that might be overlooked in present quantitative analysis of mega-corpora. The notion of a mega-corpus is associated with corpora such as the Bank of English (500+ million words) or the British National Corpus (100 million words).

(4) The models of politeness and impoliteness presented in this chapter are by no means the only influential studies of linguistic politeness. The models we have examined were chosen on the basis that Brown and Levinson's model represents probably remarked upon study of linguistic politeness, whereas it is hoped that the views of Culpeper and Watts offer the reader a sufficient contrast to illustrate the different aspects and variables associated with the phenomenon of politeness. There are many other influential theories of linguistic politeness such as Lakoff (1973), Leech (1983), Ide (1989) or Fraser (1990) which space constraints restrict us from examining. Nonetheless, they should form an integral part of any researcher's grounding in the area of linguistic politeness.

4.6 FURTHER READING

Bargiela-Chappini, F. (2003) 'Face and politeness: new (insights) for old (concepts)', *Journal of Pragmatics* 35: 1453–69.

Spencer-Oatey, H. (2002) 'Managing rapport in talk: using rapport sensitive incidents to explore the motivational concerns underlying the management of relations', *Journal of Pragmatics* 34: 529–45.

Both papers offer a thorough critique of face. Bargiela-Chappini claims that '"face" has become a term with a great deal of theoretical and cultural baggage' (p. 1465). She suggests instead the term 'polite behaviour' (*à la* Watts) that is understood through a system of rules, conventions and expectations that govern social encounters. Spencer-Oatey reconceptualises face by suggesting that it has another dimension. She argues that many politeness theorists equate face with personal or individual needs or wants. However, she claims that any consideration of face must also account for our *social identity face* – that which is concerned with people's acknowledgement of our social identities or roles, for example, as a close friend, group leader, valued customer.

Goffman, E. (1967) 'On face work', in *Interaction Ritual: Essays in Face-to-Face Behaviour*. Chicago: Aldine Publishing.

'Every person lives in a world of social encounters, involving him in either face-to-face or mediated contact with participants. In each of these contacts, he tends to act out what is sometimes called a line – that is, a pattern of verbal and non-verbal acts by which he expresses his view of the situation and through this his evaluation of the participants, especially himself.' So begins Goffman's seminal essay on face, which constitutes essential reading for any researcher interested in the study of linguistic politeness.

Mills, S. (2003) *Gender and Politeness*. Cambridge: Cambridge University Press.

As well as offering a thorough analysis of politeness research to date, Mills draws on the notion of community of practice to examine the complex relationship between gender and politeness in order to challenge traditional claims that women are necessarily more polite than men.

Watts R., Ide S. and **Ehlich, K.** (eds) (2005) *Politeness in Language*, 2nd edn. Berlin: Mouton de Gruyter.
This book, which was first published in 1992, provides a comprehensive introduction to both the history of the theory of linguistic politeness and its application in empirical studies. The 2005 introduction affords a thorough examination of current debates in linguistic politeness.

CHAPTER 5

Speech acts in context

5.1 INTRODUCTION

Consider the following extract from a telephone conversation between a health advisor and a female patient. The exchange takes place at the end of the phone consultation.

(5.1)

Advisor: Lovely. I Just need to ask you a couple of questions if I may?
Caller: Eh ha
Advisor: Can I ask you how you heard about our service please?
Caller: From on the Internet I think it was.
Advisor: Ah yeah.
Caller: Yeah.
Advisor: And if you hadn't called us today what would've you done instead?
Caller: [in an emotional way] I don't know.
Advisor: That's fine. That's fine [laughs]

The health advisor asks a standard question which forms part of a protocol of the particular service and the patient answers his questions. In asking the questions, the health advisor is performing the (speech) action of a request for information. The patient complies with this request and provides the appropriate answers. In this highly institutionalised context, the way in which the request is being made is very explicit so as to avoid any confusion or miscommunication. There are other situations where speech acts are performed in a less explicit way and participants to a conversation have to infer the meaning of what is said through reference to contextual information.

Examples often used to illustrate this point include the use of statements or observations such as *It is late* or *It is cold* (see Chapter 1). Depending on the context in which such utterances are used, they may carry different functions. The former may be a suggestion to leave a party while the latter may be a request to shut the window. When we consider examples like this in language corpora or other sources of naturally-occurring discourse, such utterances are hardly ever ambiguous as the surrounding context and co-text often point to the intended meaning.

The notion of directness and indirectness and of literal and intended meaning have been a chief concern dealt with in Speech Act Theory. At the heart of Speech Act Theory lies the assumption that utterances can be described in terms of the actions they perform, as highlighted by J. L. Austin in his book *How to Do Things with Words* (1962). Speech Act Theory provides a taxonomy of the different functions that utterances might perform, and it also offers an approach to understanding the apparent discrepancy between what we say and what we mean. Speech Act Theory has since played a key role in linguistics and philosophy, and has enjoyed applications in a range of other disciplines, such as in the modelling of speech acts for computational linguistics, and the study of pragmatic competence in cross-cultural and cross-linguistic contexts (see Chapters 6, 7 and 8).

In this chapter we will provide an overview of Speech Act Theory. We will discuss and illustrate the main arguments advanced within Speech Act Theory and introduce some of the underlying assumptions on which this theory is based. We will also highlight the importance of context, both at the level of discourse and at the wider level of situation, in the analysis of speech acts. We will draw on examples from a number of different corpora in this chapter.

5.2 SPEECH ACT THEORY

Speech Act Theory emerged in the 1960s against the backdrop of theories focused on language structure and individual sentences which were mainly analysed according to their descriptive qualities. Such 'sentences' were seen to have a truth value, i.e. they could be either true or false, and were also referred to as 'constatives'. Examples of constatives are sentences like 'The sky is blue' or 'The cat is in the house'. In his initial work Austin (1962) suggested a division between 'constatives' and 'performatives' to reflect the fact that the former could be analysed as either being 'true' or 'false' while the latter could be described in terms of the act that they perform when uttered in a given context.

The type of performative utterance that Austin initially focuses on is the 'explicit performative' which carries a number of qualities that set it apart from other utterances. It is marked by the use of a performative verb which names the action that is being performed by the utterance. Examples of explicit performatives are 'I hereby declare the ceremony open', 'I name this ship . . .'. In addition to the use of a performative verb, the initial definition of explicit performative acts also required that they include a first person pronoun and indicative form. Institutionally recognised contexts in which performatives occur include a variety of processes, such as conferring degrees, appointing someone to a job or role, or placing a bet. However, performatives also occur in less institutionally recognised contexts, such as the utterances 'I apologise', 'I suggest we meet at 5pm', and so on.

Austin recognised the difficulty with analysing performatives in terms of them being true or false, a dichotomy applied to constatives; instead he proposes that performatives are rated in terms of their validity when used under specific conditions. We will return to a description of such conditions later on in this chapter. For now, we note that performatives are assessed according to whether they are successful in a specific situation. The example of 'I declare the ceremony open' can be used to illustrate this point. This speech act is only performed successfully if the context in which it is used is appropriate, i.e. at the beginning of a ceremony, delivered by a speaker who has authority to open the ceremony, and in the presence of an audience which recognises the intent of the speaker.

Austin's revised theory

Following the initial distinction between performatives and constatives, Austin realised that the basis on which the two were differentiated was flawed. This can be illustrated with reference to the following example:

(5.2)

A: Is Sally still in hospital?
B: No she's home.

(LCIE)

The utterance *No she's home* can be analysed in terms of being either true, if Sally was at home, or false, if she was not at home. We could thus argue that it fits the definition of a 'constative'. However, we might also imagine contexts in which this utterance could be used in a performative way. The utterance might function as a response to a request for information, or it may even function as a threat or a warning, depending on the relationship between Sally and Speaker A. Thus, if Speaker A had an argument with Sally and did not want to see her, the reference to her being at home could function as a warning if Speaker A was about to visit the house.

It follows that most utterances, regardless of whether they include a performative verb, are used to perform speech acts, and in doing so to convey the intention of the speaker. Austin thus shifts the focus of his theory from the distinction between constatives and performatives to the different types of procedures that play a key role in the performance of speech acts.

Felicity conditions

In his revised theory, Austin distinguishes three kinds of action within each utterance:

(1) Locutionary Act: this is the actual utterance itself, i.e. the physical act of producing an utterance and its apparent meaning;
(2) Illocutionary Act: this is the intended meaning of the utterance. The illocutionary act tends to be the focus of analysis in Speech Act Theory and is often referred to as the 'illocutionary force' of an utterance;
(3) Perlocutionary Act: the effect that is achieved through the locution and illocution. Examples include *persuading, inspiring, convincing* and so forth.

We have already mentioned the shift in Austin's theory from distinguishing between constatives and performatives to regarding all utterances as potentially performing a speech action, the success of which relies on a number of conditions to be met. These conditions are also referred to as 'felicity conditions' and they can be broken down into the following four categories: propositional, preparatory, sincerity and essential (Searle 1969).

Using the speech act 'request' as an example, the condition related to propositional content would be that what is being requested is a future act to be carried out by the hearer. Preparatory conditions relate to the broader context in which the speech act is being performed, and include the situational context, whether the speaker has the authority to make a specific speech act, and the assumptions a speaker makes in relation to the hearer. Thus, the preparatory condition for a request would involve that the speaker believes in the hearer's ability to carry out the requested action and that the hearer would not carry out the requested action anyway. The speaker must also occupy a role in which he or she can make requests of a hearer. Sincerity conditions involve the speaker being genuine about the speech act he or she is performing. The sincerity condition of a request is that the speaker genuinely wants the hearer to do the action that is being requested. Finally, to meet the essential condition, an utterance must count as performing a particular speech act. By saying 'Pass me the water please' the essential condition is met when this utterance is seen to count as an attempt to get the hearer to pass the water.

Felicity conditions for requests (adapted from Levinson, 1983: 240):

(A = act, H = hearer and S = speaker)

Propositional content:	Future act A of H
Preparatory:	1. S believes H can do A
	2. It is not obvious that H would do A without being asked
Sincerity:	S wants H to do A
Essential:	Counts as an attempt to get H to do A

Speech act classification

Following the early revisions in his theory, Austin, and later Searle (1976), turned their attention to the identification of different kinds of speech act function in language. Searle's taxonomy of speech acts is based entirely on felicity conditions. He establishes a number of meta-categories of speech acts that follow patterns of felicity conditions, and suggests the following classification of basic acts (as outlined in Levinson, 1983: 240):

(1) Representatives, which commit the speaker to the truth of the expressed proposition (paradigm cases: asserting, concluding, etc.);
(2) Directives, which are attempts by the speaker to get the addressee to do something (requesting, questioning);
(3) Commissives, which commit the speaker to some future course of action (paradigm cases: promising, threatening, offering);
(4) Expressives, which express a psychological state (paradigm cases: thanking, apologising, welcoming, congratulating);

(5) Declarations, which effect immediate changes in the institutional state of affairs and which tend to rely on elaborate extralinguistic institutions (paradigm cases: excommunicating, declaring war, christening, firing from employment).

There are a number of issues that arise from the classification model outlined by Searle. For example, there is a degree of overlap between different meta-categories. We will explain this in more detail with the example of directives and commissives when it comes to the speech act of making suggestions. It is also not clear how we might identify different types of speech acts if they are not linked to any surface features. Again, we will return to this aspect later on in the chapter.

Direct and indirect speech acts

The notion of 'indirectness' of a speech act is often related to the grammatical form of a sentence. It occurs when the 'locution' is apparently at odds with the 'illocution' of an utterance. When the illocutionary force is in line with the linguistic form, we can expect the following patterns:

declarative = assertion
imperative = order/request
interrogative = question

Both Austin and Searle, however, note that many utterances are indirect, that is, the illocutionary force of many utterances is not reflected in the sentence form. Nattinger and DeCarrico (1992) distinguish between 'non-conventional indirect speech acts' and 'conventional indirect speech acts'.

While conventionalised indirect speech acts can be described in terms of the recurrent phrases that are used to introduce them, there is no such correspondence between form and function with non-conventionalised indirect speech acts. Conventionalised indirect speech acts such as 'Can you pass me the water' are immediately recognised as being a request rather than a question about the ability of the hearer to pass the water. This is not the case with non-conventionalised indirect speech acts. Searle (1975: 61) gives the often quoted example:

X: Let's go to the movies tonight.
Y: I have to study for an exam.

Searle argues that the meaning of Y's response is understood on the basis of non-linguistic, extrinsic factors. It can potentially fulfil a range of different functions depending on the situational context and the immediate discourse co-text. Thus, the hearer infers the meaning of an utterance with reference to a set of inference procedures relating to his or her knowledge of the context in which an utterance is made.

Searle also refers to primary and secondary illocutionary acts where in the example above the primary act is an indirect act functioning as a rejection of X's suggestion. The secondary act is a direct act which provides information about Y's planned activities which prevent him or her from taking X up on his or her suggestion of going to the movies.

Indirect speech acts and the Co-operative Principle → *Refer* to p. 105

Indirectness in speech acts occurs when the locution, i.e. the words that are being used, does not fully determine the illocutionary force of the same utterance. The question of how we 'disambiguate' this type of indirectness, or how we know what a speaker means when they are not saying it in a direct way, has led scholars to consider the processes we use to 'infer' meaning of indirect utterances. Such processes are often linked to a set of 'principles' that form part of the background knowledge of the speaker and hearer (Grice, 1975; Leech, 1983; Levinson, 1983). Grice (1975) argues that a speaker's words often convey more than the literal meaning of the words uttered. To interpret another speaker's utterance, or to arrive from the surface meaning at the implied meaning, he puts forward the concept of 'conversational implicature'. This process can only be successful if the listener co-operates. Hence Grice develops the 'Co-operative Principle' (see also Chapter 6, Figure 6.1)

As demonstrated in Chapter 4, Grice distinguishes four categories within this general principle which he calls 'maxims'. These are the maxims of quantity ('say only as much as is necessary'), quality ('try to make your contributions one that is true'), relation ('be relevant') and manner ('be brief and avoid ambiguity') (1975: 46).

In conversation, however, these maxims are often flouted, which is where the notion of implicature comes in. If we say something that apparently has no relation to the previous utterance, one or more of the maxims is flouted. However, since the Co-operative Principle works as a background guide for hearers and speakers, the hearer attaches meaning to the utterance in relation to obvious divergence from the maxims. Levinson (1983:102) gives the following example:

A: Where's Bill?
B: There's a yellow VW outside Sue's house. → *Bill's yellow V.W. would allow an inference*

Could offer relevant info depending on context

Speaker B's response seems to be unrelated to Speaker A's utterance and at a literal level, flouts the maxim of relation and quantity. According to Grice, a hearer will interpret an utterance according to the Co-operative Principle at some level and infer 'meaning' from the divergence from it. The hearer will thus infer that the fact that a yellow VW is outside Sue's house must be relevant to the question that he or she has asked, that Bill might drive a VW, and that he might therefore be in Sue's house.

In terms of conventionalised indirect speech acts, similar inference processes are proposed. The utterance 'Can you pass the salt?', then, will flout the maxim of relation if it is taken literally as the speaker is unlikely to be interested in the ability of the hearer to pass the salt. Therefore, an interpretation of a 'directive' is inferred. However, it is more likely in the case of conventionalised indirect speech acts that they are not subject to the same elaborate inference procedures as non-conventionalised speech acts. We will return to this issue in the next section.

There have been several criticisms levelled against this theory (see Levinson, 1983). First, there are other possible maxims than the four maxims that form the basis of the Co-operative Principle (see for example Leech's politeness maxims in Chapter 6). Since the Co-operative Principle is mainly based on language that is informative, the more inter-personal side of interaction remains underrepresented by the maxims in the Co-operative Principle (see also Kasper, 1990). The Gricean maxims might also be considered to be rather vague in that it is difficult to determine the point at which a maxim is flouted, for example, because of lack of information or relevance. The level of information that a speaker must provide before flouting the maxim of quantity, for example, is highly context specific. It is also specific to the culture in which the exchange takes place. A court hearing might require the speaker to provide more, and more relevant, information than a casual conversation between friends. The point at which maxims are seen to be flouted thus depends on the context in which the interaction takes place. The following example taken from a telephone call to the UK National Health Service (NHS Direct) illustrates this point:

(5.3)

Advisor:	Okay. How can I help then [name removed]?
Caller:	Right. I went to see the doctor yesterday.
Advisor:	Mm.
Caller:	I've got erm what they're calling a middle ear infection.
Advisor:	Yeah.
Caller:	Erm it's a new doctor cos I've erm recently moved into the area.
Advisor:	Mhm.
Caller:	Erm when I've been before I've been prescribed something different. This time she's given me antibiotics and basically the problem is that I've collected them I'm a bit worried about taking them cos I'm not actually sure if I might be pregnant and erm obviously I I know about you know not taking medication when you're pregnant. So I just wanted to really check what I could do and really whether I should be taking antibiotics anyway with you know all these things about you're not supposed to take them unless you really need them.

The context of the extract above is highly institutionalised and the quantity of information that is being provided is therefore extensive. The caller is not flouting the maxim of quantity in this context. However, if the context was a casual conversation between friends or colleagues, this maxim might have been flouted.

In the extract below taken from the same corpus, we find that the caller is flouting the maxim of relation to achieve a humorous effect. The reason for her call to the health service relates to her concern about taking a particular medication and the effects of that medication on a possible pregnancy.

(5.4)

Advisor:	Right. And are you allergic to anything?
Caller:	Only cats. [laughs] If that's any help.
Advisor:	Yeah. So what's happened tonight? Why haven't you started taking the [name of medication]?

The advisor's question relates to possible allergies to prescription medications but the caller takes her question literally, and provides an answer that is not directly relevant ('only cats'). Flouting of maxims for humorous effects is not something that the advisor would expect in this context and she quickly returns to the main topic of the consultation.

The dependency on context when it comes to assessing the degree to which speakers adhere to individual maxims, or flout them as the case may be, adds to the difficulty of using Gricean maxims as a descriptive tool for unpacking indirectness in language. In addition, the maxims are again quite culture-specific.

Indirectness: semantics and pragmatics

The processes underlying our understanding of indirectness discussed in this chapter so far rely on inference procedures which are part of the hearer's knowledge, i.e. the hearer infers the meaning of indirect utterances through reference to what is expected in different contexts.

However, there are other points of departure to explain indirectness which relate particularly to conventionalised indirect speech acts. Morgan (1978) points out for example that a sentence such as 'Can you pass the salt?' can be calculated according to inference procedures such as those outlined above, but this might not be what the hearer does when he or she hears this utterance. Instead, it triggers what he calls a 'short-circuited' implicature. A short-circuited implicature refers to the process of recognising a specific utterance as one that has acquired a separate meaning, or in this case function, from the literal meaning of the sentence. In this sense, it is similar to how we understand an idiom or other forms of formulaic language:

→ generation/culturally (teacher) marked

Conventionalised Indirect Speech Act	'Can you pass the water please?'	'Can' implies that the speaker is interested in the hearer's ability when instead the speaker is making a request for action.
Idiom	'at the end of the day'	The literal meaning is a time reference while the idiomatic meaning is used to express that everything has been taken into consideration.

↳ into argument

Sadock (1974) suggests that we may claim an idiomatic expression whenever the intended meaning is at odds with the literal meaning of an utterance. 'Can you x' is thus regarded as an idiomatic expression for 'do x'. A similar example is the phrase 'why don't you x' which often stands for 'do x'. As such it is not a question which the individual words and grammatical form would suggest, but a suggestion to follow a proposed line of action. The status of these 'idioms' 'stems from their discourse uses, since their surface meanings can be readily decoded' (Moon, 1997: 47).

Many indirect speech acts can thus be considered as examples of 'routinised language' (Aijmer, 1996), where there is an 'entrenchment' of meaning in certain lexico-grammatical strings as a result of extended usage.

A number of studies have tried to account for the use and processing of routinised language in terms of semi-fixed functional phrases (Fernando,1996; Moon, 1994, 1998;

Pawley and Syder, 1983; Cowie, 1988). Nattinger and DeCarrico (1992) discuss examples of indirect speech act frames, such as 'Can you . . . X?'. They describe such pre-assembled formulaic chunks of language as existing 'somewhere between the traditional poles of lexicon and syntax, conventionalised form/function composites that occur more frequently and have more idiomatically determined meaning than language that is put together each time' (1992: 57). Assuming that the realisation of (indirect) speech acts relies heavily on some sort of routine formula, they suggest a model of syntactic frames for language teaching purposes, which in the example above would read something like this: 'modal + you + verb phrase'. Research into routinised speech act formulas in a corpus has highlighted the ubiquitous use of such formulaic language related to a specific speech act force (Adolphs, 2008) which lends further weight to the argument that the hearer's understanding of indirect speech acts does not necessarily rely on inference procedures alone. This is particularly true for more conventionalised forms of indirect speech acts, such as indirect requests.

5.3 IDENTIFYING AND ANALYSING SPEECH ACTS

While the early discussions of speech acts by Austin and Searle have relied mainly on invented examples, more recently speech acts have been studied in role-play situations (House and Kasper, 1981) or Discourse Completion Tasks (Blum-Kulka, 1989). Both of these types of elicited data are discussed in detail in Chapter 2. Here is an example of a scenario presented in a Discourse Completion Task (from Schauer and Adolphs, 2006):

You have not been feeling well and have not attended a lecture. A friend who lives nearby and takes the same module is coming over and is bringing you the handouts. The doorbell rings. You open the door. After the two of you have said hello, your friend gives you the handouts.

You: _____

_____

The Discourse Completion Task was first used to examine pragmatic speech act realisations by Blum-Kulka (1982). Since then it has become one of the most frequently used data elicitation instruments in interlanguage pragmatic research (Kasper and Rose, 2002). Although they are one of the most popular instruments in interlanguage pragmatics, DCTs have also been criticised for not providing the same variety of linguistic elements, such as repetitions, inversions and omissions that can be observed in naturally-occurring data (Yuan, 2001). In addition, studies comparing naturally-occurring compliments (Golato, 2003) and rejections (Hartford and Bardovi-Harlig, 1992) with DCT data have shown that the utterance length and the participants' preference for certain strategies can vary. Researchers investigating the strategies and lexical items gathered by DCTs and other data collection methods found, however, that the same words and expressions were used in written DCTs, role-plays and naturally-occurring data (Eisenstein and Bodman, 1986; Sasaki, 1998).

While this type of methodology allows for a more controlled environment, which in turn makes comparisons more feasible, the discrepancies between the language used in role-play and discourse completion exercises, on the one hand, and authentic spoken language, on the other, are considerable, and therefore a cause for concern (Hinkel, 1997). Role-plays and Discourse Completion Tasks (DCTs) tend to highlight a particular function and analyse how this function is realised linguistically. Studying speech acts in a corpus requires a different approach in that the starting point has to be a common linguistic realisation, such as utterances starting with 'Can you...' to identify requests or suggestions. This approach makes it difficult to identify all of the different forms of speech act realisations that might perform a specific function. The latter can only be achieved by a close reading of corpus material and subsequent annotation with speech act functions which is often the method of choice in the tagging of dialogue acts for computational modelling.

The example of 'suggestions'

The question of how many speech acts there are, and in what way meta-categories such as 'directives' and 'commissives' can be broken down into more delicate levels of description, has been one of the issues addressed in Speech Act Theory. Related questions are whether lexico-grammar or speech act verbs should be taken into account as guides to illocutionary forces, or whether the classification of speech acts should be based solely on pragmatic criteria, such as felicity conditions. The speech act 'suggest' is used here to serve as an example to highlight some of the issues that arise from such an analysis using corpus data.

'Suggestives' come closest to Searle's (1969) category of 'Advisement', a subcategory of directives, which the speaker believes will benefit the hearer (1969: 67). Suggestions can take a number of different forms and are often introduced with either a speech act verb or a set of prefabricated units (prefabs) that make their function easily identifiable. This is illustrated in the examples below taken from the MICASE and Nottingham Multi-Modal Corpus (NMMC):

(1) Why don't you take some notes? (MICASE)
(2) Why don't you write this up? (MICASE)
(3) Let's just pass this over for first reads ... (MICASE)
(4) Let's look at a population ... (MICASE)
(5) Let's just have a look at this. (NMMC)
(6) So I'd suggest that you might want to begin by ... (NMMC)
(7) How about, if we start with Erin ... (MICASE)
(8) Well, you should take chemistry, you should take, French ... (MICASE)

These examples illustrate some of the issues that arise when we try to classify speech acts. Examples 6 and 8 are relatively straightforward in that they meet the felicity conditions for a suggestion and example 6 even includes the speech act verb 'suggest'. Examples 1 and 2 are indirect speech acts as they take the form of a question but the intended meaning is a suggestion. Examples 3, 4, 5 and, to a certain extent, 7 are problematic for a different reason. Examples 3, 4 and 5 include the speaker, at least at a semantic level, in the proposed line of action. This presents a problem with Searle's classification. If the speaker commits himself or herself to an action, then these utterances should count as 'commissives'. However, since they also include the hearer, they should be 'directives'. The relationship between the speakers is important in this context as a directive force might be implied if the utterance is produced by the speaker who is institutionally recognised to have more power, i.e. the lecturer in this case.

Thus, a distinction has been made between prefabs which at a semantic level include the speaker, such as 'why don't we' and 'let's', and those which only include the hearer, such as 'why don't you' or 'maybe you should' (Tsui, 1994). The rationale for making such a distinction lies in the 'rate of the imposition' (Brown and Levinson, 1987) which is higher when the 'burden' of the suggestion is on the hearer rather than on both hearer and speaker.

However, an 'inclusive' prefab such as 'let's' does not necessarily realise an 'inclusive' suggestion. The suggestion 'Let's close the door' usually only involves either the hearer or the speaker, rather than both, in carrying out the suggested action. Yet the speech act prefab 'let's' suggests that both are involved. However, it seems that this ambiguity is not important for the participants in the interaction, otherwise there would be more emphasis on clearly articulating who is supposed to take responsibility for the proposed action. It is likely that extended usage can override the semantics of such an utterance, which comes to acquire a meaning in its own right as argued above. In the case of 'let's' the meaning is closely related to the function as a discourse structuring device which becomes more prominent than the illocutionary force of the suggestion.

5.4 WHAT IS A SPEECH ACT CONTEXT?

At the beginning of this chapter we have seen that the illocutionary force of an utterance can depend to a large extent on the context in which it is used. In this section we will look in more detail at possible ways in which we may describe such contexts and how those descriptions can help us in the analysis of speech acts.

Searle (1969) argues thus:

> ... suppose at a party a wife says 'It's quite late'. That utterance may be at one level a statement of fact; to her interlocutor who has just remarked on how early it was, it may be (and be intended as) an objection; to her husband it may be (and be intended as) a suggestion or even request ...

(1969: 70)

The interpretation of the speech act that Searle describes depends both on its place in the ongoing discourse as well as on situational factors. Hymes (1972) proposes a distinction between speech situation, speech events and speech acts. Speech situations are activities that are recognised by a community, such as 'birthday parties' or 'dinners'. In a way, they form a wider category for 'speech events' which are describable by rules of speech, while speech situations are broader constructs which relate to specific activities rather than rules for speaking. A 'speech event' could be a lecture, for example, which is marked by a particular structural organisation as well as a specific distribution of speaker roles. Speech acts occur within speech events and speech situations, and are to some extent determined by them. We have discussed earlier how highly ritualised speech situations, such as hiring and firing from a job, or christening at church can only be performed felicitously if the speakers have the authority to carry out the speech act and are in the right place to do so.

According to Hymes (1972), the speech act encodes social norms in linguistic form. The interpretation of speech acts thus leads to an analysis of the sequential organisation in discourse as well as to an analysis of the social roles of the speakers in the particular context they are engaged in at the time. In order to delineate criteria for analysing different contexts, various approaches have been developed, especially in the field of genre theory. The underlying arguments will be reviewed in the following section.

Speech acts, frames and genres

While the types of inference procedures proposed by Leech (1983) and Brown and Levinson (1987) rely predominantly on the (shared) internal knowledge of the speaker and hearer, they make little reference to the knowledge of the participants about the context of the situation. Yet, since speech acts occur within speech events, speakers must have some idea of the constraints that the situation puts on possible contributions to the conversation. Speakers and hearers have what has been called a 'frame' or a 'schema' around which they orient themselves when they speak (Coulmas, 1979; Goffman, 1981; Brown and Yule, 1983; Cook, 1994; Aijmer, 1996). Aijmer argues that the 'frame should be regarded as a hypothesis about speakers' stereotypic knowledge of a situation and how this knowledge is organised in the long-term memory' (1996: 27). A frame includes criteria such as the identity of the participants, the setting and the reason for the interaction (see Coulmas, 1979). As situations recur, certain ways to perform speech acts recur and become conventionalised, such as greetings and goodbyes at a party for example.

One area that has focused on establishing 'categories' that account for the relationship between language and situation is 'genre theory' (Mitchell, 1957; Hasan, 1985, 1999; Ventola, 1987; Hammond and Derewianka, 2001). Many accounts within genre theory are based on the assumption that speech events are describable in terms of 'stages' that are either optional or compulsory in the completion of the event. A service encounter, for example, will have an opening, possibly a hand-over of goods phase, and an ending. In the following example of a service encounter in a shop we see evidence of all three stages. In addition, there is a shift in focus from the exchange of goods to an episode of small talk about the weather.

(5.5)

Customer 1:	How we doing?
Shop assistant:	Hi there how are you?. <$E> sound of till <\$E> That's one seventy seven please.
Customer 1:	Alright seventy seven give it to you now.
Shop assistant:	Not a bad day shur it's not?
Customer 1:	Naw it's cold though.
Shop assistant:	Cold.

Customer 1:	'Twas nice earlier on the sun was shining.
Customer 2:	Turning cold out there now is it?
Customer 1:	It is yeah.
Customer 2:	I'd say we'll get a right cold spell of it.
Customer 1:	I'll give you twenty seven there if you don't mind.
Shop assistant:	Grand no problem.
Customer 1:	Sound yeah. I d= I agree with you I don't mind the cold you know as long as it's not raining.
Shop assistant:	As long as tis not raining is the main thing. Thank you very much.
Customer 1:	That's right. Thanks good luck.

Hymes (1972) argues that genres and speech events are not identical but that different genres can occur in one speech event. Hence, in an office meeting, participants may follow the items for discussion on the agenda, and then 'drift into' a conversation about the weekend plans of one of the participants. The dynamic character of genres, the fact that speakers can themselves change the 'frame' they orient to from one minute to the next, means that in order to understand the 'context' of speech acts we need to consider smaller units of discourse.

In the following example from the Nottingham Multi-Modal Corpus, the PhD supervisor asks the part-time student to talk about their recent move to another place of work. The supervisor signals clearly in the first turn that this part of the discourse does not relate to the thesis. The latter is the accepted and expected topic for a PhD supervision session. However, by shifting the frame of discourse, albeit only slightly, to a personal matter, the supervisor introduces a different context for the interaction and this is reflected in both the content and the turn structure of this part of the supervision session. Following this digression from the main topic, the supervisor resumes his primary role and brings the conversation back to discussing the student's research.

(5.6)

Supervisor:	Okay. Alright go on then tell me where you've got to. I d= not thesis wise I mean+
Student:	Oh right.
Supervisor:	+we'll come on to thesis in the moment.
Student:	Right okay. But er New York wise+
Supervisor:	Yes.
Student:	+oh God. It's so full on it's unbelievable +
Supervisor:	Yeah.
Student:	+but but I'm I'm okay I'm keeping it+
Supervisor:	Hm.
Student:	+you know all together. I think the er you know the main the main aspect of it is just this massive learning curve . . .

This leads us to look at the different ways in which speech acts have been considered within a discourse framework which will be further explored in the next section.

5.5 SPEECH ACT CLASSIFICATION IN DISCOURSE ANALYSIS

There are a number of discourse level models which involve speech acts as core units of analysis. Sinclair and Coulthard (1975), for example, incorporate situational factors, as well as some lexico-grammatical features into their classification scheme and define acts by their interactive function. The discourse model developed by Sinclair and Coulthard involves a 'rank-scale' which is used in the description of classroom discourse. Each of the ranks has its own structure which can be analysed with reference to the rank below. The highest rank is the 'lesson'; this is made up of various 'exchanges' which in turn consist of 'moves'. A typical move structure consists of an opening move in the form of a question by the teacher, an answering move by the student, and a follow-up move by the teacher evaluating the student's answer. The lowest rank consists of 'acts', which are more general than the speech acts in Searle's categorisation scheme but can be further classified at the level of 'sub-act'. Sinclair and Coulthard differentiate between meta-discursive, interactive and turn-taking acts. Their three initiating (interactive) acts at the exchange level are:

(1) informative
(2) directive
(3) elicitation.

An informative act is realised through a statement that provides information relevant to the lesson while a directive act requests a non-verbal response (e.g. 'Open your books'). An elicitation act requests a linguistic response. The following is an example of an elicitation by a lecturer in an academic supervision session:

(5.7)

| Supervisor: | Can it be made to work institutionally though? |
| Student: | I don't know but I think I I've got to just work systemically. |

Sinclair and Coulthard's model is based on classroom data and many adaptations have since emerged which apply the model to conversational and other types of data (Burton, 1981; Tsui, 1994). Tsui (1994) differentiates three primary classes of acts based on the three moves of an exchange: initiating acts, responding acts and follow-up acts. Her classification criteria for the different speech act classes are based on intended speaker response. As initiating acts she names the following:

Speech act	Discourse function
Elicitations	To elicit an obligatory verbal response or its non-verbal surrogate.
Requestives	To solicit non-verbal action with the option to carry out this action.
Directives	To solicit non-verbal action with no option of whether or not the addressee will carry out solicited action.
Informatives	To provide information and to report events and states of affairs, recount personal experience, etc.

Tsui contends that 'requestives subsume utterances which have been referred to in the speech act literature, as requests, invite, ask for permission, and offer. They do not subsume those which have been referred to as order, command, and instruct. The latter are subsumed under a different subclass: directives' (1994: 91).

According to Tsui's classification, suggestions are therefore a subcategory of directives. She distinguishes between *mandatives*, which direct the addressee to perform an action for the benefit of the speaker, and *advisives*, which direct the addressee to perform an action for his/her own benefit.

Tsui's model cannot easily accommodate suggestions such as those in the examples above either. Utterances such as 'I would suggest that we take your bag inside' (Adolphs, 2008) are neither mandatives nor advisives. She therefore creates a further category, which she calls 'proposals'. A 'proposal' or 'suggestion', according to Tsui, 'prospect both speaker action and addressee action and is typically realised by "Can/Could/Shall we do X?"' (1994: 100). It is beneficial to both, speaker and hearer. Her matrix for requestives is as follows:

Requestives:

	Speaker action	**Addressee action**	**S+A action**
Speaker benefit	Request for permission	Request for action	
Addressee benefit	Offer	Invitation	
S+A benefit			Proposal

Tsui (1994: 104)

The problem with classifying utterances in the abstract, i.e. detached from their discourse context, is that it is difficult to think about cost and benefit to the speakers and hearers when they are abstracted from their social roles. Role relationships are of major importance (Levinson, 1983; Leech, 1983); however, in real data it is not always easy to determine how they affect the cost-benefit scale. An utterance such as 'Let's look at a population' does not seem to have immediate benefit to anybody. When it is placed into its academic context, however, where it is used by a lecturer and its discourse context is starting a new transaction in the discourse, thus sign-posting a change in the structure of the lesson, cost and benefit scales become secondary.

The difficulties in analysing suggestions as outlined above are related partly to the grounds on which a directive is differentiated from a requestive. Corpus data seems to suggest that, apart from speaker and hearer benefit, there is a type of benefit which is related to completing a particular task. There can be tensions then between speech act classifications and taxonomies which were developed on the basis of invented examples, and the analysis of speech acts in corpus data. In the examples taken from the corpus the relevance of speaker or hearer benefit is reduced while the goal-oriented nature of the interaction is foregrounded.

Finally, when we draw on transcribed corpus data as the basis of analysis of speech acts and discourse structure, one of the issues that arises is that our analysis is necessarily limited to the data types that have been collected. In terms of spoken corpora, this is often still limited to transcripts rather than audio-visual data. However, in everyday conversation, some of the discourse functions are performed through non-verbal acts and some of the categories of discourse acts are predicated on the effect of non-verbal action (see for example the discourse function of 'directives' in Tsui's framework above). A transcript can therefore only provide part of the picture of the overall interaction that has taken place. Recent developments in multi-modal spoken corpus analysis are trying to address this issue, and advances are being made in the analysis of language and gesture within a corpus linguistic framework (see Knight *et al.*, 2009). These developments are likely to have a significant impact on the way in which we are able to describe systematically speech acts and discourse structure, and may even challenge some of the more traditional taxonomies of discourse function.

5.6 CONCLUSION

In this chapter we have introduced some of the terms and concepts which have been developed in the area of Speech Act Theory. We have covered the underlying arguments for regarding language as action, as well as looked at different ways of classifying speech acts in context. We have shown that the use of real data changes the way in which we might approach both the identification of speech acts and their classification. In particular, we have looked at studying speech acts in the extended discourse context in which they occur, and we have discussed related models for analysing speech acts in discourse. As such, this chapter has covered theory and practice that traditionally is seen as belonging to the area of pragmatics, as well as theory and practice related to the area of discourse analysis. Speech acts are a key unit for both of those disciplines, and once we start to look at real language in use, it is often advantageous to bridge those traditional boundaries in order to enhance our description and understanding of discourse.

5.7 FURTHER READING

Adolphs, S. (2008) *Corpus and Context: Investigating Pragmatic Functions in Spoken Discourse*. Amsterdam: John Benjamins.
This book uses a five-million word corpus of everyday interaction to study the relationship between context and the use of conventionalised speech acts. The current chapter is based to some extent on the research reported in this book which provides a much more detailed account of the issues at hand. The book also discusses how a shift from mainly textual data to audio-visual corpora can impact on our analysis of functional units in discourse.

Aijmer, K. (1996) *Conversational Routines in English*. London: Longman.
Drawing on data taken from the London-Lund Corpus of Spoken English, this book analyses recurrent speech act expressions, such as 'thank you' or 'can you x . . '. A range of speech act functions are covered, including indirect requests, thanking and apologising. The book offers an in-depth analysis of pragmatic functions and also takes into account the discourse context in which they occur.

Green, M. (2007) 'Speech acts', *The Stanford Encyclopedia of Philosophy (Spring 2009 Edition)*, Edward N. Zalta (ed.). Available online: <http://plato.stanford.edu/archives/spr2009/entries/speech-acts/>
This is an excellent and highly accessible introduction to speech acts and the relationship between speaker meaning, context and illocutionary force. The entry also touches on the

analysis and classification of speech acts in relation to their discourse environment, and on the notion of logical relations among speech acts.

Jucker, A. H. and **Taavitsainen, I.** (eds) (2008) *Speech Acts in the History of English.*
    Amsterdam: John Benjamins.
This edited volume takes a historical perspective to the study of speech acts, and includes a set of articles that explore the theoretical and methodological underpinnings of the use of speech acts. The volume is divided into three parts: directives and commissives, expressives and assertives, and methods of speech act retrieval. It is a particularly useful book for those interested in studying speech acts on the basis of corpus data.

Levinson, S. (1983) *Pragmatics.* Cambridge: Cambridge University Press.
The chapter on speech acts (Chapter 5) of this volume is essential reading for anybody who is doing research in this broad area. Levinson provides a thorough overview of the history of Speech Act Theory, its challenges and criticisms, and the interface with related disciplines. A detailed account of the semantic/pragmatics divide and the resulting issues that arise in the analysis of speech acts make this chapter an invaluable piece of further reading.

CHAPTER 6

Pragmatics across languages and cultures

6.1 INTRODUCTION

According to Thomas (1983: 97), 'while grammatical errors may reveal a [non-native] speaker to be a less than proficient language user, pragmatic failure reflects badly on him/her as a person'. This can work both ways. Consider this testimony from a teacher of English as a Foreign Language at an Irish university:

> Every year I teach university students from around Europe who come to our university to take courses in their subject areas. They come to me for English classes. Once they have settled in, I always spend some time teasing out the cultural differences which they have become aware of. Invariably, they comment on the insincerity of their Irish counterparts. When I delve deeper, the same scenario is used to exemplify insincerity each time. They explain that when they walk around the campus, Irish classmates seem very friendly. They smile and say, '"Hello, how are you?" but as I stop to tell them how I am, they have kept walking.' I have to explain to them that 'How are you?' in the context of a greeting is actually not meant as a question as to one's welfare, it is simply a greeting, best replied to with 'How are you?' or a short reply, like 'Great, see you around.'

When we move between languages, we also move between pragmatic norms and this can be a minefield for learners of a language. As the example above illustrates, what ostensibly looks like an inquiry as to state of health and welfare is in fact intended as a greeting. Without this pragmatic information, the non-native speaker is left feeling that the people who keep asking this question are grossly insincere. Thomas's quip comes to mind: 'every instance of national or ethnic stereotyping should be seen as a reason for calling in the pragmaticist and discourse analyst!' (Thomas, 1983: 107).

As Bardovi-Harlig (2001: 13) points out, everyone who works in language teaching 'knows a funny story about cross-cultural pragmatics ... From the perspective of the speaker, they may be about feeling silly, helpless, or rude; from the perspective of the listener, they may be about feeling confused, insulted, or angry'; but, as she points out, it is these stories and anecdotes that inspire us to say that we ought to teach, to quote a learner, the 'secret rules' of language.

Socio-pragmatic mismatches occur when:

(1) In different cultures, different pragmatic 'ground rules' are invoked.
(2) Relative values, such as 'politeness', are ranked in different order by different cultures.

Thomas (1983: 106)

Boxer (2002: 150) states that the study of cross-cultural discourse represents an especially important endeavour because of the great potential, in modern times, 'for miscommunication and misperceptions based on differing norms of interaction across societies and speech communities'. This chapter will take a look at this important area of study, in which pragmatics is looked at across languages and cultures and the impact of differing pragmatic norms can lead to cultural misrepresentations, stereotyping and misunderstandings. More and more, it is being seen as an area which needs to be integrated into language learning (as discussed further in Chapter 8). Our overarching concern in this chapter is an attempt to gather together the different frameworks under which this area has been studied. This is quite a challenge as there is a myriad of definitions and models to contend with and they are sometimes in conflict with each other.

In the early 1980s, Leech referred to 'cross-linguistic comparisons of communicative behaviour' as a fascinating area of study in which much research needs to be done (see Leech, 1983: 231). Around the same time, Thomas (1983) provided a seminal justification for the need not only to compare how the pragmatic norms of languages differ but also to make learners of a language aware of the pragmatic norms of the target language and culture. Thomas' essential point is that the transfer of pragmatic norms of one language onto another may lead to what she termed *pragmatic failure*. For instance, for native speakers of English, politeness norms intuitively suggest that the hedged interrogative, *Could I have a cup of coffee, please?*, is more appropriate in a café than the more direct declarative form, *I want a cup of coffee*. The latter would be interpreted as rude in most cafés in English-speaking countries. However, in many languages, *I want a cup of coffee*, a direct form of request, would be much more common; indeed, the polite English equivalent when transferred into some languages could even sound obsequious.

There has been much research, especially since the 1980s, into the pragmatic differences between the different manifestations of speech acts across cultures. However, there seems to be a relative lack of theoretical discussion regarding the area in general. That is to say, while there is a boom in empirical research into pragmatics across languages and cultures, there is a dearth of theoretical reflection on the implications of such research for second language acquisition, applied linguistics, language teaching, sociolinguistics, and so on. New studies continually add more and more to our understanding of how different languages and cultures compare and contrast pragmatically but their weight is perhaps not felt theoretically as much as it should.

What is striking from the literature is how often the points of cultural difference occur in core social situations as manifested in common speech acts such as apologising, requesting, refusing, suggesting, and so on. An even more 'basic' example is the area of expressing gratitude, something we often do in daily life. This is widely accepted to be one of the most important social acts because of its key role in establishing and maintaining good relations and feelings of solidarity between speakers (see Cohen, 1996; Eisenstein and Bodman, 1986 and 1993) and yet it poses a lot of difficulty for non-native speakers of English. Aijmer (1996) notes that even advanced learners of English have problems with *thanking*, partly because of the idiomatic nature of the phrases used, and partly because of 'the socio-pragmatic constraints on their use ... when one compares English with other languages, there are differences in whom one says *thank you* to, when one says *thank you*, the setting in which thanking is expected', and so on. Compared with other speech acts, expressions of gratitude have received a low level of attention. Lin (2007) further notes that most research into expressions of gratitude focuses only on the main strategies, without looking at sub-strategies or the semantic content of the strategies. In addition, Hymes (1972) and Eisenstein and Bodman (1993) note that *thank you* is used differently within English, for example in American English, it is more common as an expression of gratitude while in British English it is more a formal marker. Jautz (2008) also looks at markers of gratitude comparatively in British and New Zealand radio programmes. We also look at *thank you* in Chapter 2 and *please* in Chapter 4.

At a time when every year millions of people cross the borders, not only between countries but also between languages, and when more and more people of many different cultural backgrounds have to live together in modern multi-ethnic and multi-cultural societies, it is increasingly evident that research into differences between cultural norms associated with different languages is essential for peaceful co-existence, mutual tolerance, necessary understanding in the workplace and in other walks of life in the increasingly 'global' and yet in many places increasingly diversified world.

(Weirzbicka, 2003: viii)

6.2 DEFINING THE AREA: A TRICKY TASK

Newcomers to this area could be forgiven for feeling that there is a mire of confusion, and even contradiction, at the level of terminology. Boxer, in her state-of-the-art paper on the area, stakes out a distinction between cross-cultural pragmatics (CCP) and interlanguage pragmatics (IP). She delineates these two 'research foci' in the following ways (2002:151):

Interlanguage pragmatics: (Speaker or nearer)

- is an application of Second Language Acquisition;
- sees the non-native speaker as progressing along an interlanguage continuum, ultimately leading to target language norms;
- sees the language learner as the newcomer whose task it is to acquire the norms of the target language community. That is, they learn the target language (phonology, syntax, semantics) and the norms of its culture;

- looks predominantly at how specific speech acts are realised using elicited data, usually in the form of role-plays and Discourse Completion Tasks (DCTs) (see Chapter 2), as opposed to real spontaneous interactions.

Cross-cultural pragmatics:

- is an application of Sociolinguistics;
- does not see the non-native speaker as progressing along a non-native speaker continuum to target language norms;
- takes the view that individuals from different societies or communities interact according to their own pragmatic norms often resulting in a clash of expectations and ultimately misrepresentation;
- predominantly employs an ethnographic approach or interactional sociolinguistic approach to empirical research, where recorded interactions are analysed in micro-detail. Interviews with participants and getting them to review and reflect on the miscommunications within the recorded interactions are often used as a means of triangulation (see Erickson and Schultz, 1982).

Boxer

The essential difference between IP and CCP, according to Boxer (2002), lies in how they view cross-cultural communication:

Interlanguage pragmatics views cross-cultural communication from a one-way perspective.	Cross-cultural pragmatics views cross-cultural communication from a two-way perspective.
language/ culture 1 → language/ culture 2	language/ culture 1 → ← language/ culture 2

Though Boxer's overview of the area seems to make perfect sense, in reality however, one finds that it is difficult to operationalise when one looks at the array of studies and literature. In other words, authors do not appear to adhere to the nomenclatures as outlined in Boxer (2002). The term cross-cultural pragmatics seems to be used in a generic manner regardless of whether the study relates to a one-way or a two-way perspective on communication. Many studies which fall under Boxer's definition of 'intercultural' use DCTs, rather than recordings, as their methodology (a point which Boxer acknowledges). Therefore, though Boxer's neat distinction is very attractive, it does not always fit the body of literature that one finds. Nonetheless, it is worth keeping in mind as it raises important distinctions that one should use when looking at various studies.

Grundy (2008: 232) makes a more basic distinction which is easier to apply:

Cross-cultural communication occurs when a non-native member operates in someone else's culture.

Intercultural communication occurs when interactants communicate outside their own cultures, often using a lingua franca that isn't the first language of either.

(Grundy, 2008: 232)

↳ Creole ?, English
Greek
Latin
French

Grundy notes that this is an important distinction that is not always scrupulously maintained in the literature, where the terms are sometimes used interchangeably. Grundy goes on to give a very clear and operationalisable set of definitions (see Grundy, 2008: 232–3). In summary, in addition to *cross-cultural* and *intercultural communication* as detailed above, he poses the following definitions of *intracultural communication* and *trans-cultural communication*:

> *Intracultural communication* occurs when interactants share a common culture and (first) language.

> *Trans-cultural communication* [a term coined by Grundy] refers to any communication that is not intracultural. Hence it subsumes cross-cultural and intercultural communication.
>
> (Grundy, 2008: 232–3).

Grundy's 'trans-cultural' category gets around the trickiness of scenarios such as: A business meeting conducted in English, comprising a Hong Kong Chinese speaker and a native English speaker, born in Hong Kong, a Japanese person and an American native speaker of English. Clearly, in such a scenario the distinction between cross-cultural and intercultural is too complicated to apply. Hence, it comes under the heading of 'trans-cultural'.

6.3 THE ISSUE OF *UNIVERSALITY* OF PRAGMATIC NORMS

As we have discussed in Chapter 4, certain universals have been put forward about pragmatic norms of politeness across all languages. Grice (1975) formulated a set of maxims of conversation, and Leech (1983) proposed six politeness maxims which he says work in tandem with Grice's maxims and notes that they may vary in relative importance from culture to culture. Brown and Levinson (1987) put forward the notion of *face* as a universal human need, based on Goffman (1967) (see Chapter 4). This theory, they claimed, was based on the 'extraordinary parallelism in the linguistic minutiae of the utterances with which people choose to express themselves in quite unrelated languages and cultures' (Brown and Levinson, 1987: 60). These three universals are summarised in Figure 6.1.

The concept of underlying universal pragmatic norms for all languages and cultures is a very attractive one. While there is little dispute that norms exist, it is the universality of these norms which causes a degree of polarisation. For instance, Wierzbicka (2003), a forerunner in the field of cross-cultural pragmatics (CCP), gives a very insightful view on how studies in CCP challenged the notion of dominant paradigms of universal pragmatic norms. According to Wierzbicka, from the early to mid-1990s more and more people challenged the notion that these norms, or 'misguided orthodoxies of the time' (2003: vi), were universally applicable to all languages. Wierzbicka and others, argued strongly that in fact these notions were ethnocentric viewpoints with a strong Anglocentric bias (see, for example, Kochman, 1981; Sohn, 1983; Matsumoto, 1988; Ide, 1989; Mao, 1994). In an early paper directly challenging the notion of universality, Wierzbicka (1985) looked at speech acts in Polish and English, arguing that the notion of 'freedom from imposition' (i.e. negative face: Brown and Levinson, 1987: 66) was an Anglocentric value and that the avoidance of flat imperative sentences, which Searle (1975: 69) attributed to 'ordinary

Didn't take into account how White English is

Grice's Co-operative Principle

The conversational maxims of quantity, quality, relation and manner:

Quantity: Make your contribution as informative as is required (for the current purpose of the exchange). Do not make your contribution more informative than is required.

Quality: Do not say what you believe to be false. Do not say that for which you lack adequate evidence.

Relation: Be relevant.

Manner: Avoid obscurity of expression. Avoid ambiguity. Be brief. Be orderly.

By breaking these rules, you can cause somewhat at a shady meaning "implicature".

Leech's politeness maxims

1 Tact Maxim
a. minimise cost to *other.*
b. maximise benefit to *other.*

2 Generosity Maxim
a. minimise benefit to *self.*
b. maximise cost to *self.*

3 Approbation Maxim
a. minimise dispraise of *other.*
b. maximise praise of *other.*

4 Modesty Maxim
a. minimise praise of *self.*
b. maximise dispraise of *self.*

5 Agreement Maxim
a. minimise disagreement between *self* and *other.*
b. maximise agreement between *self* and *other.*

6 Sympathy Maxim
a. minimise antipathy between *self* and *other.*
b. maximise sympathy between *self* and *other.*

↳ Based solely on what the other person needs.
Do unto others as you would have them do unto

Brown and Levinson's politeness theory

- Regardless of superficial diversities that might exist, there are underlying universal principles of politeness across all languages and cultures.
- These are based on the notion of *face. Face* is one's public self-image and is divided into *positive* and *negative* face, both of which need to be protected against *face threatening acts*. In any social interactions, cooperation is needed between participants to *maintain* each others' positive and negative face needs.
- *Positive face* refers to one's self-esteem. It relates to the want for positive self-image, the want to be liked, admired, ratified, and related to positively.
- *Negative face* refers to the desire not to be imposed upon. It relates to one's freedom to act.

Figure 6.1 Summary of Grice's Co-operative Principle, Leech's politeness maxims and Brown and Levinson's politeness theory.

conversational requirements of politeness', did not reflect universal principles of politeness but rather 'expressed special concerns of modern Anglo culture' (Wierzbicka, 2003: vi).

It can be helpful to look at this issue of universality from an Eastern rather than a Western perspective. Many have noted the more collective notion of face or identity in Eastern cultures; see, for example the work of Matsumoto (1988), Ide (1989) and Mao

(1994) on the importance of 'social identity' in Japanese and Chinese societies. They note that this is something which is not accommodated within Brown and Levinson's notion of *face*.

Cheng (2003), in the introduction to her book on 'intercultural communication' (based on Hong Kong-based interactions between Hong Kong Chinese and native English speakers), gives a very good insight into the conflict between the Western and Asian notion of 'politeness' (see in particular Cheng, 2003: 5ff). While she notes that the concepts of face and self-image are considered universal characteristics, she clearly illustrates how they are 'conceptualized differently from one culture to another, depending on the underlying cultural values and beliefs' (p. 5). Cheng looks separately at the notions of *face* and *self* in relation to how they compare between Asian and Western cultures (2003: 6; see also Scollon and Scollon, 1995).

Self in Western versus Asian cultures

In Western culture, *self* is a very individualistic notion. Asian *self* is a more collectivistic notion, connected with membership of basic groups such as family, social circle, workplace. The Asian *self*, as part of a larger social group is more conscious of the consequences of actions on the addressee. In Asian culture, there is an interdependence of *self* (after Markus and Kitayama, 1991 and 1994). Essential to the development of *self* (in Chinese culture) is the orientation to the needs, wishes and expectations of others (see White and Chan, 1983; Gao, 1996). The self's orientation to 'other' in Chinese culture, Cheng (2003) explains, is reflected in the norms of modesty and humility, reserve and formality and restraint and inhibition of strong feeling. This is in contrast to the Western independent notion of self. In Western cultures, this manifests in norms where it is more acceptable to be openly critical, confrontational, competitive or generally expressive.

Face in Western versus Asian cultures

Chinese *face* has two facets: *miànzi* and *lian*. *Miànzi* refers to 'one's need to conform to social conventions and to express one's desire to be part of the community'; *lian* is defined as the 'need to show a moral sense of place and role' (Cheng, 2003: 7). The Western notion of *face* comes from the work of Goffman (1967) which is linked to the losing and keeping of face. It is something which is constantly maintained and nurtured within an interaction. Within Brown and Levinson's elaboration of *face*, it is seen as a public self-image comprising the wants of positive and negative face (see Chapter 4). Essentially, as Cheng puts it, Westerners respect individual rights to autonomy and freedom of choice. In this context, language is considered central to the negotiation of ongoing speaker relationships. As a result negative face strategies are of key importance in redressing imposition and so on. In contrast, for Asians, particular care is taken to affirm and ratify existing relationships. Asians, therefore, usually place greater emphasis on the harmony of the interactions and, as a result, use more positive politeness strategies.

6.4 STUDIES OF PRAGMATICS ACROSS LANGUAGES AND CULTURES

As we have already pointed out, the research associated with cross-cultural and inter-language pragmatics is large (see Kasper and Rose, 1999; Bardovi-Harlig, 2001; and Barron, 2003 for an overview of cross-cultural and interlanguage studies). As the studies reviewed here will show, much of the research has focused on the production of speech acts (to such an extent that Ellis (1994) limits the use of the term interlanguage pragmatics to speech act research). The majority of these studies have focused on intermediate to advanced learners from a variety of first language backgrounds and have used a variety of data collected from, for example, recorded casual conversation, DCTs and role-play (see Chapter 2).

Many publications have acknowledged the fact that second language pragmatics is receiving more attention than ever before (see, for example, Barron, 2003; Rose, 2005; Belz, 2007; Cohen, 2008; and Vásquez and Sharpless, 2009). The study of pragmatics across languages and cultures provides important information on interactive norms in different languages and cultures. The best-known research project in this area is the Cross-Cultural Speech Act Realisation Project (CCSARP; see Blum-Kulka *et al.*, 1989 for a full description of the project). This project was established in 1982 to investigate cross-cultural variation in two speech acts – requests and apologies – and has led to numerous publications and insights (see Chapter 5 for an exploration of speech acts). DCTs were typically used to examine both native and non-native speakers' cross-cultural and intralanguage use of these speech acts in American English, Australian English, British English, Canadian French, Danish, German, Hebrew and Argentinean Spanish (see Chapter 2 for a detailed treatment of DCTs). In addition, a coding scheme was developed within the project in order to standardise the terminology used across the research (see Blum-Kulka and Olshtain, 1984).

As evidenced by the array of research, we can say that speech acts such as greetings, apologies, suggestions, requests, expressions of gratitude, and so on, appear to be available to most cultures. Indeed, Kasper and Rose (1999) maintain that an impressively stable result of the research into interlanguage pragmatics is that second language (L2) learners have access to the same range of speech act realisation strategies as native speakers, irrespective of proficiency level. Studies on apologising by Danish English as a Foreign Language (EFL) learners (Trosborg, 1987 and 1995) and Japanese English as a Second Language (ESL) learners (Maeshiba *et al.*, 1996) demonstrate that learners can use the full range of apology strategies given in the taxonomy provided by Blum-Kulka *et al.* (1989). However, L2 learners do not always capitalise on the knowledge they have. Bardovi-Harlig and Griffin (2005) conducted a study where students were taught apologies, requests, suggestions and refusals through recordings of 20 scenarios. As part of the task, learners were asked to appraise the appropriateness of the speech act and to make repairs to the dialogues. Bardovi-Harlig and Griffin (2005) found that repairs made by the learners illustrated that while they were generally able to identify the source of pragmatic break-downs, they were less successful in coming up with how to improve the interactions. We argue, as does so much of the research, that pragmatic instruction in the classroom has a clear role to play, not just in imparting information that the students may be unaware of in terms of how speech acts manifest differently in the target language, but also in making them aware of what they already know and encouraging them to use transferable native language knowledge in appropriate L2 contexts (Kasper and Rose, 2001).

Bardovi-Harlig (2001) addresses how native speakers (NSs) and non-native speakers (NNSs) differ in how they produce speech acts; she uses three headings but she points out that these are not exhaustive: *choice*, *content* and *form*.

Choice

In terms of speech act *choice*, according to Bardovi-Harlig (2001: 14), 'NNSs may perform different speech acts than NSs in the same contexts, or, alternatively, they may elect not to perform any speech act at all'. Bardovi-Harlig and Hartford (1993) looked at the suggestions and rejections made by both NSs and NNSs of English in academic advisory sessions. Although they found that NSs and NNSs made approximately the same number of suggestions in this context (1.5 and 1.3 per interview respectively), they found that in the early sessions NNSs had a 1:1 rejection to suggestion ratio, meaning they rejected as often as they suggested. On the other hand, NSs had a 1:9 rejection to suggestion ratio. This tendency of NNSs to produce more rejections than NSs resulted in them being less successful than NSs in this context.

Content

The *content* of the speech acts refers to the specific information given by a speaker. Beebe *et al.* (1990) examined explanations offered by Americans in contrast to those offered by Japanese speakers of English. They characterised American explanations as being more definite and Japanese as more vague in comparison. In one classic example, a Japanese speaker declined an invitation saying *I have to go to a wedding*. While this explanation did not appear initially to be vague, the researchers subsequently discovered that the speaker was referring to her *own* wedding. It has also been noted by a number of studies (see for example, House, 1988; Bergman and Kasper, 1993; Olshtain and Weinbach, 1993) that intermediate to advanced learners of a second language tend to be more verbose than NSs in performing certain speech acts. This appears to be a result of overcompensation.

Form

The third way in which NNSs can differ from NSs is in the *form* of the speech act; although NSs and NNSs may produce the same speech act, the form can be markedly different. For example, Félix-Brasdefer (2003) examined English speakers of Spanish and found that in situations of unequal status (for example, teacher–student and employer–employee), when declining an invitation, NNSs were more direct in refusing than NSs, who preferred to mitigate their refusals. He observes that 'even some very advanced NNSs speakers of Spanish did not know how to decline an invitation appropriately, nor did they know how NSs of Spanish would typically decline an invitation' (p. 248).

NSs and NNSs can also differ in their responses to certain speech acts and this can also lead to the establishment of negative stereotypes. Boxer (1993) examined the use of indirect complaints between Japanese ESL learners and their English-speaking peers. She found that indirect complaints, expressions of dissatisfaction about oneself or someone/something that is not present, are frequently used by NSs to build solidarity between speakers. However, she notes that when responding to indirect complaints, the NNSs used only backchannels or contradictions, both of which work against the establishment of solidarity in this case. She claims that 'by merely changing an *um hmn* to an *oh no!*, learners can change their response from an insufficient one to a commiserative one and thus redirect the course of the interaction' (p. 294). This is a result of the different orientations towards talk evident in the two cultures.

NNSs' perception of speech acts has also been shown to differ from NSs'. Bergman and Kasper (1993) examined perceptions related to apologies in two groups of university students – Thai speakers of English and speakers of American English. They found that out of 20 scenarios, on 12 occasions, the NSs of English ranked the obligation to apologise higher than the NNSs did. This means that if the speaker does not feel obliged to perform a speech act, they may opt out, leaving other conversational participants feeling confused or upset. Also focusing on the speech act of apologising, Kotani (2002) analysed the use of *I'm sorry* in a conversation between a native speaker of English and a Japanese speaker of English. She found that both the English- and Japanese-speaking informants recognised at least two actions with regard to the use of *I'm sorry*: (1) offered when the speaker feels sorry for the offence; and (2) offered when the speaker does not feel responsible for their actions. The informants differed with regard to the second action, especially in conflict situations. The NS perceived someone saying *I'm sorry* but not meaning it as insincere, whereas the NNS, due to cultural expectations as discussed above, thought it appropriate to say *I'm sorry* in some situations even if they did not mean it. Kotani maintains that this may result in cultural misunderstandings, with English speakers viewing Japanese speakers as over-polite and Japanese speakers interpreting English speakers' limited use of *I'm sorry* as a lack of goodwill towards them.

6.5 PRAGMATIC VARIATION WITHIN THE SAME LANGUAGE

In looking at frameworks for the study of cross-cultural and intercultural pragmatics earlier in this chapter, we referred to the broad and easily applicable distinctions that Grundy (2008) makes (see section 6.2). One of his categories which we have not yet addressed is *intracultural communication*, which occurs when interactants share a common culture and (first) language. There is an ever-growing body of work on intracultural communication, for example, studies which look at aspects of Peninsular (or Iberian) Spanish versus Latin American Spanish or British English versus American English, and so on.

Many of these studies fall under the category of sociolinguistics and language variation studies but many also come under pragmatics. Márquez Reiter and Placencia (2005), for example, look at the pragmatics of Spanish, focusing on the relationship between language use and socio-cultural contexts and their uptake by speakers of different varieties of Spanish. They draw on a wide range of Spanishes, using data from different Spanish corpora. Their publication is a good example of the nexus of sociolinguistic variation and pragmatics. They use the term 'socio-pragmatic variation' to package the area that they cover. The book includes a chapter on empirical studies of socio-pragmatic variation in different varieties of Spanish across speech act realisation, conversational organisation and politeness. While they compare Peninsular Spanish to Latin American, they are careful to point out that there is also much variation within these broad categories. Within Latin American Spanish, there is variation across countries and even within the same country, for example, the differing politeness norms between two varieties of Peruvian Spanish spoken in Cuzco and Lima. Placencia and García (2007) have produced an edited volume dedicated to research on politeness in the Spanish-speaking world which contrasts politeness in Peninsular Spanish, Argentinean versus Uruguayan Spanish, Colombian, Ecuadorian and Peruvian Spanish, Venezuelan versus Cuban Spanish, Mexican Spanish and Spanish in the United States. It also contains sections on Spanish used in institutional settings (e.g. talking with a doctor). The volume brings to light immense pragmatic variation within the same language.

Another framework which merits mention here in relation to the intersection of sociolinguistics and pragmatics is *variational pragmatics*, a concept coined by Schneider and Barron (see Barron and Schneider, 2005) in order to address research gaps that existed in both modern dialectology and pragmatics. According to Schneider and Barron (2008: 1), variational pragmatics 'investigates pragmatic variation in (geographical and social) space'. In this sense, variational pragmatics represents the interface between pragmatics and variational linguistics, a subset of modern sociolinguistics. Variational pragmatics has as its primary concern how the choice of one pragmatic strategy over another encodes macro-social indices of region, socio-economic status, ethnicity, gender or age in everyday language use. These five types are not a closed set: the impact of other macro-social factors such as education and religion can also form part of this research framework. In addition, various micro-social factors, for example, power and social distance or register which impact on pragmatic language variation may also be relevant factors.

The impact of both macro- and micro-social factors on pragmatic choice is essential to our understanding of language-use differences. Wolfram and Schilling-Estes (2006: 93) state that 'knowledge of when and how to use certain forms is just as important for communication as the literal understanding of structures and words'. However, they acknowledge that the study of how language is used in context is a relatively recent development in dialectology, especially when compared to the traditional focus on language form (pronunciation, vocabulary and grammar). This general lack of focus on the pragmatic features of a language in modern dialectology is noted as a 'serious shortcoming' by Schneider and Barron (2008: 3). In addition, in terms of the study of pragmatics, two criticisms of contemporary cross-cultural pragmatics are made by Schneider and Barron (2008). The first is that these studies are based on the assumption that language communities of native speakers are homogenous wholes when language variation is considered, thus, in a sense, negating any suggestion of an impact of social variables on language communities. They also claim that many researchers in this area employ participants from student communities, often from their own courses, thereby compromising representativeness.

In general, Schneider and Barron maintain that studies into pragmatic variation can be criticised in relation to both their scope and representativeness; however, as exceptions they cite two studies that concentrate on regional language variation in English. These studies, Tottie (1991) and McCarthy (2002), are corpus-based studies. Both of these studies focus on the differences between backchannels (or response tokens) in British and American English. Tottie employs the London Lund Corpus (LLC) and the Santa Barbara Corpus (CSAE), and McCarthy the Cambridge and Nottingham Corpus of Discourse in English (CANCODE) in addition to a similar-sized sample of the Cambridge North American Spoken Corpus (CNASC). McCarthy (2002) maintains that cross-corpora comparisons of different varieties of the same language are useful for a number of reasons. Crucially for the study of variational pragmatics, he notes that they provide safer ground for generalisations.

Schneider and Barron (2008: 19–21) identify five levels of pragmatic variation: *formal*, *actional*, *interactional*, *topic* and *organisational*. They maintain that 'these distinctions are based on an integrative model of spoken discourse which incorporates approaches to pragmatics from different disciplines, including speech act theory, discourse analysis and conversation analysis' (p. 19). A brief description of each of these levels of analysis is presented in Table 6.1.

Variational pragmatics is undoubtedly of value to the researcher seeking to account for the relationship between social differentiation and pragmatic variation. O'Keeffe and Adolphs (2008) used variational pragmatics in a study focusing on response tokens (or backchannels) in British and Irish English. This falls under the *organisational* level of pragmatic analysis according to Schneider and Barron's (2008) framework but as detailed below, differences at *formal* level often led to pragmatic differences. Ostensibly, given how close England and Ireland are geographically, one might not expect to find much variation at this level between British and Irish English. O'Keeffe and Adolphs (2008) looked at data drawn from two corpora, the Cambridge and Nottingham Corpus of Discourse in English (CANCODE) and the Limerick Corpus of Irish English (LCIE). First, they noted at a *formal* level a broader range of response tokens was used by British English speakers. British speakers, overall, appear to use more response tokens in conversation than Irish English speakers do.

Difference in response token forms, such as *yes* and *quite* in British English, also led to pragmatic insights. These forms were found to have no corresponding occurrence in the Irish data. O'Keeffe and Adolphs posited that such forms index a higher level of formality in British English. This may also correlate with the higher frequency of response token use in British English. They found that religious references and swearwords (used as response tokens) appear in both the British and Irish data. However, their use in the British data is limited to *God* and *oh God*, while the Irish data comprise *God, oh God* and *oh my God* and the swear words *Jesus* and *Jesus Christ* (in bold in extract 6.1).

Table 6.1 Schneider and Barron's (2008) levels of pragmatic analysis

Level	Description
Formal	This level concerns the analysis of linguistic forms such as discourse markers or hedges.
Actional	This level focuses on the realisation and modification of speech acts.
Interactional	The focus here is on sequential patterns such as adjacency pairs, exchanges or phases (for example, openings and closings).
Topic	The focus is on how conversational topics are selected, addressed, developed etc.
Organisational	This level deals with turn-taking phenomena such as pauses, overlaps, interruptions or backchannels.

(6.1)   [Context: friends are looking at an old school team photo and are trying to identify the people in it]

A: Ryan the oldest guy Tom Hartnett John Rodgers+
B: Oh yeah.
A: +Brian Fitz.
B: Paul Regan.
     [General laughter].
A: **Jesus Christ.**
B: What year is this?
A: The late nineties

(LCIE)

The differing use and frequency of religious references, according to O'Keeffe and Adolphs, points to pragmatic variation at the level of social formality. It supports the notion that there is a greater level of informality within the Irish data. The Irish speakers of English seem to accept the use of religious swear words as a normal and frequent response token in casual conversation. It seems to have reached semantic neutrality according to the authors.

6.6 CONCLUSION

In conclusion, it is fair to say that because every aspect of pragmatics could be compared and contrasted within and across languages, there are endless possibilities for further study in this area. Indeed, it could be argued that studies to date have largely limited themselves to the contrastive study of certain aspects of pragmatics over others, especially politeness and speech act realisation. Most studies have been synchronic and most have been based on elicited data. While many interesting findings have been amassed, the often fragmented nature of how pragmatics is studied across cultures means that the bigger picture is frequently obscured by the wonder of the latest finding. As a whole, it is fair to say that this is an area with many small-scale and interesting studies but it lacks a clear theoretical paradigm to guide it.

The greatest potential for the development of a cogent framework for the study of pragmatics across languages is likely to be within applied linguistics in the context of language learning, in that the findings from studies of pragmatic difference between languages and cultures ultimately need to feed into language learning syllabi. Therefore, more attention needs to be given to the definition of pragmatic competencies and description of their acquisition. Learners have overt competency targets in terms of areas such as vocabulary, grammar, listening, writing skills, oral fluency, and so on. What are the competency markers for different levels of pragmatic attainment? This is not an easy question to answer (see Roever, 2004, for a detailed treatment). Barron (2003), for example, conducted a longitudinal study of 33 advanced-level learners of German, over a 10-month period, while they were on a study-abroad placement in Germany as part of their university studies. One of her research questions was the following: is there evidence of changes in learners' L2 pragmatic competence toward or away from the L2 norm over time spent in the target speech community? While Barron (2003: 238) found some evidence of the development of pragmatic competences 'towards' the L2 pragmatic norm, she notes that the actual L2 norm was rarely reached. What is very interesting about her study is the length she goes to itemise developmental markers of pragmatics, or 'pragmatic learning'. Barron's study also adds weight to the suggestion that there may be stages of development in target language pragmatic competence.

The use of corpus analysis tools would greatly benefit such a study of pragmatic competence over time. This approach would allow for a more dynamic view of pragmatics, whereby actual language in interaction could be recorded and analysed in detail. One would need to tag and code all pragmatic items, as well as errors, so as to appraise at which stage of language competence learners can competently use certain pragmatic features, such as speech acts, hedging, pragmatic markers, and so forth. One would need to look at language in different contexts of use and one would need to do so in a multi-modal manner. This is a complex undertaking but without some such approach one disparate study will pile upon another and it will remain difficult to gain a clear view of whether new ground is being gained in terms of our greater understanding of the interface of pragmatics, culture and society. We will explore the teaching of pragmatics further in Chapter 8.

6.7 FURTHER READING

Bardovi-Harlig, K. (2001) 'Evaluating the empirical evidence: grounds for instruction in pragmatics?', in K. Rose and G. Kasper (eds), *Pragmatics in Language Teaching.* London: Routledge.
A very accessible paper which looks at the case for teaching pragmatics. The paper provides a framework for the pragmatic differences between learners and native speakers in terms of production. It also addresses the lesser studied area of perception and judgement in relation to pragmatic differences for both native and non-native speakers, for example, the impact of differences found between degrees of implicature, or differing speech act strategies. At a basic level of perception, she notes that sometimes non-native speakers may have difficulty in identifying the intent of a speech act. The chapter puts a very useful frame on many of the key studies in the area.

Cheng, W. (2003) *Intercultural Conversation.* Amsterdam: John Benjamins.
This book provides an insightful look at real data, from a corpus, in the context of intercultural conversations in Hong Kong, which is a rich site for such an investigation. The introduction is especially valuable for readers who want to know more about the basic assumptions of Chinese and Western cultures, with a particular focus on the context of Hong Kong.

Grundy, P. (2008) 'Intercultural pragmatics', Chapter 11 in *Doing Pragmatics* (3rd edn). London: Hodder Education.
This chapter gives a very useful overview of the different configurations and terminologies in relation to cross-cultural, intercultural, intracultural and trans-cultural communication. Grundy's model is very clear and easy to apply. It also contains a very interesting section on lingua franca pragmatics.

Placencia, M. E. and **García, C.** (eds) (2007) *Research on Politeness in the Spanish-Speaking World.* Mahwah, NJ: Lawrence Erlbaum.

Even if one is studying politeness in a context other than Spanish, we recommend that you look at this book. It has an excellent range of studies across many varieties of Spanish. It will be useful to examine the empirical studies in the volume and it may be useful for those looking for ideas for a study in cross-cultural pragmatics.

Schneider, K. P. and **Barron, A.** (2008) 'Where pragmatics and dialectology meet: introducing variational pragmatics', in K. P. Schneider and A. Barron (eds), *Variational Pragmatics: A Focus on Regional Varieties in Pluricentric Languages.* Amsterdam: John Benjamins.

This introduction is recommended if you are looking at pragmatic variation within the same language. The authors elucidate their variational pragmatics framework, which is an intersection between pragmatics and sociolinguistics, where pragmatic choices encode indices of region, socio-economic status, ethnicity, gender or age in everyday language use.

CHAPTER 7

Pragmatics in specific discourse domains

7.1 INTRODUCTION

In this chapter, we explore the notion that specific domains of discourse involve the use of language in pragmatically-specialised ways. To support this idea, we draw on real language from different specialised contexts such as casual conversation, healthcare communication, the classroom, service encounters (shops) and soap operas.

First, let us consider the notion of 'specific discourse domains'. What are the aspects that we need to consider in order to delineate a certain type of language use as 'specific'? When we talk about specialised use of language, we are really talking about 'variation'. However, terms such as 'variation' and 'specialised language' only have meaning by reference to something else and so the concept of *comparability* is core to this chapter. That is to say, one can only gauge that something is different, or special, by comparing it. We can compare Kenyan and Singapore English (without using American or British English); we can compare lectures with casual conversation, and so on.

In looking at variation in spoken language, we also need to consider that variation in how we interact in specific situations is not only a by-product of place and history, it is also integral to context. The term *register,* from Halliday (1978: 31–2), refers to the 'very simple and very powerful . . . fact that the language we speak or write varies according to the type of situation'. This term is also strongly associated with Biber's research over the years (see especially Biber, 1988 and 1995; Biber and Conrad, 2009). Finegan and Biber (1994) and latterly Biber *et al.* (1999: 15–17) provide a useful matrix for the major distinctions between the situational characteristics which distinguish registers from each other (see Table 7.1). When looking at variation in any context, it is worth attempting to complete this matrix.

We have also added *spoken genre range,* which refers to the Bakhtinian notion of relatively stable units of talk where 'each separate utterance is individual . . . but each sphere in which language is used develops its own *relatively stable types* of utterances' (Bakhtin, 1986: 60; italics from original source). The term *spoken genre range* within the framework of Biber *et al.* (1999: 16) refers to the finite range of expected generic talk units within each register. We use the examples of two specific discourse domains, a radio phone-in call and a post-observation teaching training observation meeting, by way of illustration (based on Biber *et al.*, 1999: 15–17 and Farr and O'Keeffe, 2002: 30). The matrix in Biber *et al.* (1999), with the addition of the category of 'spoken genre range' (see Farr and O'Keeffe, 2002), illustrates at least some of the characteristics of a spoken discourse domain which, in aggregate, lead to variation. By examining a discourse domain

Table 7.1 Identifying characteristics of situational variation based on Biber *et al.* (1999: 15–17)

		Radio phone-in	Post-observation teacher training interaction
Register characteristics	**Mode**	Spoken: voice only	Spoken: face to face
	Interactive online production	With a degree of advanced planning	With a degree of advanced planning
	Shared immediate situation	Shared within a virtual community/ society	A university office
	Main communicative purpose/content	Good radio disclosure, entertainment	Instructive/directive/gatekeeping
	Audience	Public within broadcast range, mainly Irish	Individual, mainly Irish
	Dialect domain	Local	Local
	Spoken genre range	(Diverse but finite) narrative, argumentative, expository, directive, opinion-giving/ seeking	(Less diverse than radio phone-in): directive, observation-comment, expository, reflection/self-direction, motivational

under these headings, it soon becomes clear that there are many reasons why context of use brings about specialised use of language.

7.2 COMPARABILITY AT THE LEVEL OF TURNS

In exploring the pragmatics of language in specific contexts, we can compare variation in a number of ways. At the level of turns, it is worth looking at the work of conversation analysts. The conversation analysis (CA) tradition of establishing the 'canonical turn sequence' of an interaction (i.e. the most typical sequence of turns) and then using this as a means of comparison for other types of interaction is also very fruitful from a pragmatics perspective. By way of background, CA is a research tradition that has grown out of ethnomethodology, an area within sociology rather than linguistics. Researchers such as Sacks, Schegloff and Jefferson have, since the 1970s, contributed to, and strongly influenced, research into conversation in specific contexts (for example Schegloff, 1968; Sacks *et al.*, 1974; Schegloff *et al.*, 1977; Sacks 1992).

Notably CA takes a 'bottom-up' approach to the study of the social organisation of conversation, or 'talk-in-interaction'. It does this by means of a detailed inspection of transcribed recordings of specific situations. Essentially, it focuses in on how conversations are structured and organised locally by looking at them in micro-detail, turn by turn, and from this inductive process comments are made about social organisation in a given domain of interaction. McCarthy (1998) notes that CA offers the possibility of fine-grain descriptions of how participants orient themselves towards mutual goals and negotiate their way forward in highly specific situations. Such highly specific situations are usually socially-defined, such as the beauty salon (LeBaron and Jones, 2002), the hairdresser, the driving lesson

(McCarthy, 2002) or institutional settings such as courtroom interaction (Atkinson, 1979; Atkinson and Drew 1979), doctor–patient interactions (Maynard, 1997 and 2003; Maynard and Heritage, 2005), radio phone-in calls (Hutchby, 1991) or emergency phone calls (Whalen and Zimmerman, 1987; Tracy, 1997; Tracy and Anderson, 1999).

As we noted, the turn-by-turn focus of CA has application to pragmatics. For example, in order to examine a telephone call opening, a conversation analyst will always begin by looking at the canonical turn sequence for call openings (see below). Let us take as a case study, CA work focusing on telephone call openings (see Schegloff, 1968; Godard, 1977; Schegloff, 1986; Whalen and Zimmerman, 1987; Hopper, 1989 and 1992; Sifianou, 1989; Cameron and Hills, 1990; Hopper *et al.*, 1991; Hutchby, 1991, 1996a, 1996b and 1999; Halmari, 1993; Drew and Chilton, 2000, among others). Essentially, telephone openings in different settings can be compared in terms of their turn sequences. First a norm had to be established, that is, a sequence of turns which is seen as the norm or the canonical structure. Schegloff (1986), for example, characterised the canonical structure for a phone call opening between 'unmarked forms of relationships' (that is those who are not particularly intimate, but who are not strangers) as having the following structural organisation:

(7.1) Schegloff (1986) Canonical call opening between 'unmarked forms of relationships' (Drew and Chilton, 2000)

Summons-answer:	0		Phone rings
	1	Answerer:	Hello
Identification-recognition:	2	Caller:	Hello Jim?
	3	Answerer:	Yeah
	4	Caller:	's Bonnie
Greetings:	5	Answerer:	Hi
	6	Caller:	Hi
'How are you?' sequences:	7	Caller:	How are yuh
	8	Answerer:	Fine, how're you
	9	Caller:	Oh, okay I guess
	10	Answerer:	Oh okay
First topic:	11	Caller:	What are you doing New Year's Eve?

Based on this as the canonical sequence, we can then compare other call opening sequences. For example, Whalen and Zimmerman (1987) present the following as the typical sequence of call openings between strangers on an emergency phone line.

(7.2) Call openings between strangers – Whalen and Zimmerman, 1987 (after Hopper and Drummond, 1992: 191)

Summons-answer:	0		Phone rings
	1	Answerer:	Mid-city Emergency

Business of Call:	2	Caller:	Um yeah. Somebody jus' vandalized my car.

We see by comparing this institutional interaction with the canonical baseline from Schegloff (1986) that there is an attenuation (a cutting short) of the stages because the relationship and setting are different. There is no identification-recognition phase, nor do caller and answerer engage in 'how are you?' sequences. In CA terms, we can then say that this reflects the institutional organisation of talk in this context of interaction. In pragmatic terms, we could say:

- Because of the institutional nature of the interaction, the imperative of politeness norms is not as strong;
- The pragmatic norms of the situation do not call for the reciprocation of greetings and first names, nor the 'how are you?' small talk, as would be the norm for positive politeness between people who know each other in English-speaking cultural norms;
- The institutional context of the call is initiated by the call answerer's use of an institutional identity at the identification stage. The answerer is defining the pragmatic space between the caller and the answerer as institutional (compare '*Mid-city Emergency*' with something like 'This is John, Mid-city Emergency, how can I help?');
- The highly institutional nature of the opening turn appears to be face-threatening to the caller who is unsure of how to begin his/her account to this unnamed, ungreeted person on the other end of the line (the caller begins his/her turn with the hesitation, *Um yeah*).

Another comparison is provided by Drew and Chilton (2000) who look at call openings between intimates, drawing on a corpus of calls made between a mother and daughter over a two-month period. Most of these calls are for the purpose of 'keeping in touch'; in other words there is normally no express purpose for calling other than to maintain contact:

(7.3)   Call openings between intimates after Drew and Chilton (2000)

Summons	0	Phone rings	
Answer + identification-recognition +	1	Answerer:	Hello
greetings ('How are you?' also possible)	2	Caller:	Hello
	3	Answerer:	Oh hello
First topic:	4	Answerer:	I've been waiting for you

Here again we see attenuation of call stages when compared with Schegloff's canonical or baseline sequence in extract 7.1. It is similar to the pattern for emergency calls between strangers though for different reasons. As Drew and Chilton point out in CA terms, the relationship of the callers allows for the attenuation of the canonical stages because the callers are intimates (they know each other well), and because they are expecting the call. The voice sample provided by *Hello* is immediately recognised by the answerer and achieves all Schegloff's stages of answering, identification/recognition and greeting in this interaction. From a pragmatic perspective we could say that:

- The intimate relationship of the family members is a given, to such a degree that it obviates the need for norms of positive politeness such as name and greeting reciprocation;

- Unlike the emergency call interaction in extract 7.2, the lack of first name and greeting reciprocation does not create any face threat for the caller or answerer. This is a pragmatically-specialised norm in this routine interaction between intimates.

One further example comes from the NHS Direct corpus (see Adolphs *et al.*, 2004). This comprises recordings of phone calls made to the British National Health Service in Nottingham. The corpus comprises 61,981 words from 17 calls. As you read the extract from the opening of a call to the helpline, consider the CA interactions that you have just examined and think about it from a pragmatic perspective in comparison with extract 7.2 to the Mid-city Emergency, to which it has institutional parallels:

(7.4)

1		phone ringing
2	NHS advisor:	Good evening. This is NHS Direct. My name's [name]. I'm a health advisor here. Could I just start by taking your telephone number please?
3	Caller:	[personal details removed]
4	NHS advisor:	Okay. How can I help then [name removed]?
5	Caller:	Right. I went to see the doctor yesterday.
6	NHS advisor:	Mm.
7	Caller:	I've got erm what they're calling a middle ear infection.
8	NHS advisor:	Yeah.
9	Caller:	Erm it's a new doctor cos I've erm recently moved into the area.
10	NHS advisor:	Mhm.
11	Caller:	Erm when I've been before [pause 0.5 sec] I've been prescribed something different. This time she's given me antibiotics and basically the problem is that I've collected them. I'm a bit worried about taking them cos I'm not actually Sure if I might be pregnant and erm obviously I I know about [inhales] you know not taking medication when you're pregnant. So I just wanted to really check what I could do and really whether I should be taking antibiotics anyway with [inhales] you know all these things about you're not supposed to take them unless you really need them.
12	NHS advisor:	Yeah. Okay. Erm [pause 1 sec] okay. Best off that you talk to a nurse about this.
13	Caller:	Right.
14	NHS advisor:	Er so you've got a middle ear infection.
15	Caller:	Yeah.
16	NHS advisor:	What you been prescribed then?
17	Caller:	Augmen= Aug=

18	NHS advisor:	Augmentin?
19	Caller:	Something. Yeah.
20	NHS advisor:	Yeah.
21	Caller:	Yeah. Something like that. [laughs]
22	NHS advisor:	Yeah. It's Augmentin.
23	Caller:	That sounds about right yeah.

(NHS Direct)

From a CA perspective, looking at the opening sequence (lines 1 to 5), this differs greatly from extract 7.2. There is no attenuation of turn sequences and it more resembles the turn sequences of the canonical in extract 7.1, with identification and greeting sequences, and so on. From a pragmatic perspective, we can see that there is an attempt by the NHS advisor to replicate a call opening that is closer to that of extract 7.1. We can observe that:

- At a positive politeness level, we can see a strong attempt to simulate a close relationship through name exchanging and greeting;
- At the level of negative politeness, the advisor deferentially asks *How can I help then [name removed]?*;
- The use of discourse markers (*okay, so*) and response tokens (*yeah, mhm*) by the health advisor is an attempt to downplay his/her institutional role through positive politeness. The result, one could argue, is to allow the caller to feel closer to the advisor and to calmly explain the issue at hand.

Consider how the interaction might have gone differently had it paralleled extract (7.2), in the following way:

| 1 | | phone ringing |
| 2 | NHS advisor: | NHS Direct. |

It is unlikely to have led to a similar interaction as we find in extract 7.4.

We see from this brief CA case study the usefulness of using a canonical pattern as a baseline for identifying variation in specialise contexts of use, in this case telephone calls. On a more general level of comparison, the norms of the turn-taking structure of casual conversation are also well-documented and form the basis for many studies based on the influential Sacks *et al.* (1974) study. This notion of using a canonical or norm as a baseline for comparison is a very powerful one and it can also be used in conjunction with pragmatics.

7.3 COMPARABILITY USING A CORPUS

A corpus is a very useful means of identifying how language differs across discourse domains. To begin with, you need to establish a baseline to which you can compare the data you are examining. For example, if you are looking at a corpus of academic discourse, you might use a corpus of casual conversation as your 'reference corpus'. The reference corpus is the baseline to which you compare word frequencies, patterns and upon which keywords are statistically calculated, using the corpus software (see Chapter 1). Here are some examples of how a corpus can be used for comparison.

Again let us look at the NHS Direct corpus. Table 7.2 compares its 40 most frequent words with those of the BNC spoken corpus (from Leech *et al.*, 2001a). What is immediately striking is the high number of pragmatic markers (response tokens *yeah, right, okay,* and discourse markers *right, okay, well*) in the NHS Direct data when compared with the BNC wordlist. This reflects the institutional nature of the helpline interaction and as well as the mode (see Table 7.1), that is telephone. Also, because there is a high degree of information-seeking and information-giving, there is, as a result, a high number of response tokens. In particular, we see a high number of 'information receipt' response tokens (see O'Keeffe and Adolphs, 2008), typically *right,* which acknowledge the receipt of information from the institutional power-role holder.

Table 7.2 Comparison of NHS and BNC 1–40 wordlists

	NHS corpus	BNC		NHS corpus	BNC
1	you	the	22	but	have
2	I	I	23	your	what
3	the	you	24	if	he
4	yeah	and	25	so	that
6	and	it	26	well	to
7	right	a	27	not	but
8	it	's	28	in	for
9	to	to	29	have	erm
10	a	of	30	on	be
11	okay	that	31	with	on
12	erm	n't	32	or	this
13	it's	in	33	for	know
14	of	we	34	I'm	well
15	know	is	35	do	so
16	that	do	36	can	got
18	er	they	37	like	've
19	just	er	38	be	not
20	is	was	39	then	are
21	no	yeah	40	oh	if

The fact that the mode of communication is 'audio only' means a higher reliance on response tokens so as to keep the channel of communication open and to work through the caller's problem as smoothly as possible by incrementing from identifying the problem through symptoms to giving appropriate advice to the caller, as seen in extracts 7.5 and 7.6:

(7.5)

Advisor:	. . . And I understand you've got a rash?
Caller:	**Yeah**. Yes. Erm [0.5 second pause] and first noticed it really quite how bad it had got last night when I came round my friend's house for a shower.
Advisor:	**Right**.
Caller:	And erm it's sort of round my waist round about the waistband of my trousers and it's kind of worked its way up the sides erm [1 second pause] er sort of towards my armpits on on both side. [inhales]

Advisor: **Right**
Caller: Erm and erm I'm wondering what could be wrong. [exhales]
Advisor: **Right. Okay.**

(7.6)

Advisor: **Right.** What I'm gonna do [name] is ask you some questions about your past medical history+
Caller: **Okay.**
Advisor: +and some more questions about your symptoms now.
Caller: **Right.**
Advisor: Then advise you what I think you ought to do. Is that okay?
Caller: That's fine yeah.
Advisor: **Right. Okay.** Do you have any health problems at all [name] that I ought to be aware of?
Caller: [inhales] Erm no but I had to see the doctor last week erm about an ear infection.
Advisor: **Okay.** Are you taking any antibiotics for that?
Caller: **Yeah. Yeah.** That's er cos I rang up on Saturday night cos I'd got the antibiotics and I wasn't sure whether to take them cos I didn't know at that time whether I might be pregnant but it's turned out that I'm not so that was okay. [inhales]

Central to the process of successfully expediting the call through its phases is the very careful monitoring of new information between advisor and caller. The advisor is careful to orient the caller to what he/she needs to know or do: *what I'm gonna do*; *what I think you ought to do* and the caller marks understanding of new information through frequent use of response tokens. We also see that the caller is careful to present the new information to the advisor in a clear and organised way, using discourse markers such as *okay* and *well*.

When we look at the keywords (see Chapter 1) for the NHS Direct corpus, using LCIE as a reference corpus, we find the words in Table 7.3 used with unusually high frequency and the results here consolidate the high use of pragmatic markers, *right* and *okay*.

Another item that is worth exploring is the keyword *sort*. On searching the corpus using a concordancer, we find it used frequently by callers when describing their symptoms. They use the two-word chunk or multi-word unit *sort of* as a vagueness marker (see Prodromou, 2008 for a detailed treatment of *sort of*; see also Chapter 1) to downtone or hedge the directness of presenting a fact about how their symptom, as shown in Figure 7.1. We also find *just* used as a vagueness marker in the same way and the two are often found to co-occur – marked in bold in extract 7.7:

(7.7)

Advisor: Right. Okay. Right. So you're getting pain or discomfort. Whereabouts? Is it below your belly button?

Caller: Yeah.

Advisor: Right. Is it in the centre or to one side or right across?

Caller: Mm. It's **sort of** m= more central but a bit across if you know what I mean. It's **just sort of**. It's not just directly in a line down+

Advisor: Okay.

Caller: +the middle it's **just sort of** the general if you stick your hand on the middle of your tummy and that area that's **sort of** where it is.

Advisor: Right. Does the pain move around?

Caller: No. It's **just** that **just** that area. It doesn't+

Advisor: Right.

Caller: +you know.

Advisor: Is it like a contraction or is it a stabbing pain? How would you describe it?

Caller: Erm [blows out air] well when it's gonna come it **sort of** it feels a little bit like a contraction when it's gonna come I suppose. You know+

Advisor: Right.

Caller: +that **sort of** ooh you know ... But the rest of the time it's **just sort of** like a dull.

The vagueness marker *bit* also appears on the keyword list and we find through concordance searches that it clusters with another keyword *it's* (the software treats contracted words as single items). *It's* and *sort of* also co-occur with vagueness items *little* and *kind of* in the description of caller symptoms. We can say that this is a pragmatically-specialised usage – when callers are talking about their health problems and symptoms to health professionals, they frequently do so using vague language markers as hedges.

Table 7.3 Keywords of NHS Direct corpus

1	right	21	following
2	okay	22	calling
3	mm	23	you
4	antibiotics	24	advisors
5	sort	25	you've
6	diarrhoea	26	anything
7	it's	27	mhm
8	nurse	28	itchy
9	bye	29	doctor
10	any	30	ear
11	I've	31	please
12	rash	32	taking
13	bit	33	bear
14	your	34	mean
15	just	35	itching
16	teeth	36	I'm
17	help	37	symptoms
18	infection	38	yeah
19	augmentin	39	cos
20	advisor	40	swelling

window in a minute. I mean I **sort** of feel like I could probably manage
I should you know cos I **sort** of er said "Well I can't ring the
ll it er no because I'd **sort** of I'd hadn't the doctor didn't ask
know the girls at work I mean I've **sort** of started a new job and they're all sort
nch time laughs dose he **sort** of sort of s= half spat back and half
n it's gonna come it **sort** of it feels a little bit like a
+but as soon as I've been it **sort** of goes. So it's just sort of inhales
you know it **sort** of feels a little bit +
r ear although it's **sort** of like in your ear+ Mm.
mean in some bits of the rash it's **sort** of slightly raised but er aside from that+
ut as soon as I've been it **sort** of goes. So it's just sort of inhales
ah. But it's it's red. It's **sort** of you know itchy red. Yeah.
tends following syllable Mm. It's **sort** of m= more central but a bit across if
iarrhoea look like? It's just **sort** of watery and runny and you know.

Figure 7.1 Concordance extracts of *sort* in the NHS Direct corpus.

It's kind of <\$=> Although **It's a bit** painful
It's a bit inflamed? Are they red and+
It's a bit like nettle rash. <$3> Is it? Okay. <$=> <$H> Are you <\$H>
It's a bit more difficult. <$4> Right. Yeah. <$2> <$E> inhales <\$E>
Mm. Well **It's** angry. **It's a bit** red yeah. <$3> It is **a bit** red.
It's a bit itchy. <$3> **It's** itchy. <$2> Yeah.
It's a bit <\$=> **It's a bit** embarrassing really. <$4> Yeah. <$2> <$=>
It's quite <$H> big and raised <\$H>? <$2> Yeah. **It's a little bit** but **It's** blobby.
It's a little bit but **It's** not not **sort of** too bad. I found some zinc and castor
It's a little bit embarrassing. And they're they're a bit funny about+ <$3
It's a little bit sore where the rash is rubbing but_erm <$E> 0.5 sec <\$E

Figure 7.2 Concordance line extracts for search item *it's*.

Taking a different context of use, namely English Language Teacher meetings, we look at another small corpus, the Corpus of Meetings of English Language Teachers (C-MELT). This comprises approximately 3.5 hours of data, circa 40,000 words of English Language Teacher meetings, recorded in Mexico and Ireland (see Vaughan, 2010). When we do a keyword analysis, using LCIE as the reference corpus, we find the results as displayed in Table 7.4.

As one would expect, there are many words relating to the business of English Language teaching, such as reference to the international English Language exams KET (Key English Test), PET (Preliminary English Test) and TOEFL (Test of English as a Foreign Language), references to students, semester, class, exam, certificate, book, grammar and so on. When we take away all of the content words relating to the ongoing work, we are left with those in Table 7.5.

Table 7.4 Keywords of C-MELT

1	KET	21	so
2	PET	22	kind
3	students	23	laughter[1]
4	semester	24	mean
5	class	25	maybe
6	exam	26	sufficient[2]
7	we	27	grammar
8	English	28	insufficient
9	classes	29	weak
10	think	30	level
11	certificate	31	university
12	elementary	32	if
13	book	33	materials
14	pass	34	move[3]
15	semesters	35	module
16	they	36	inter[4]
17	intermediate	37	could
18	okay	38	student
19	Pre	39	yeah
20	TOEFL	40	post

Table 7.5 Keywords, minus content items, of C-MELT corpus of teacher meetings using LCIE as a reference corpus

1	we
2	think
3	they
4	okay
5	so
6	kind
7	mean
8	maybe
9	if
10	could
11	yeah

Notes:
1 *Laughter* refers to where laughter has been noted as an extralingustic feature.
2 *Sufficient, insufficient, level* and *weak* relate to the context of level of attainment and exam results.
3 *Move* relates to moving students to higher or lower level classes, i.e. student placement.
4 *Inter* and *post* refer to *inter*mediate and *post* PET level, respectively.

It is these words then that will give most insight into the pragmatics specific to this discourse domain. The high use of *we* indexes a predictable sense of team identity among the teachers but when the concordance lines are examined, we find that *we* has some specialised uses and patterns that relate to the pragmatics of this discourse domain. *We* can be used as a means of proffering opinion in the meeting in a way that does not threaten the cohesion and harmony of the team (see the work of McCarthy and Handford, 2004) on the Cambridge and Nottingham Business English Corpus in which they found *we* to be used to project a team identity, sometimes coercively, e.g. the company boss's use of *we need* when he/she means *you need*. Here is an example from the teachers' meetings:

(7.8)

Teacher 1:   All I'm saying is that **we** are you know **we** are going a lot slower than than they have recommended for this book. And I'm not saying that's that that's wrong because maybe within our context it might be what **we** have to do when you consider that three weeks at least out of each semester.
Teacher 2:   Is lost.
Teacher 1:   Are lost . . .

As we can see in extract 7.8, a colleague is making a critical point which might be face threatening to colleagues. She uses *we* (and *our*) to present this in a collaborative way to express it as *our* problem. The near repetition of Teacher 2's turn (*is lost*) indicates convergence and agreement rather than disagreement on the part of her colleague.

Suggestions and opinions are presented with differing degrees of hedging. For example, a strong pattern of *we* is *we can* where teachers suggest courses of action which are uncontroversial and uncontested, shown in extracts 7.9 and 7.10 and Figure 7.3.

(7.9)

Teacher 1:   Yeah I think we need to give them a better more pre-information so that they can really.
Teacher 2:   Now **we can** certainly do that better than the last time.
Teacher 3:   Yeah.
Teacher 5:   Yeah.
Teacher 1:   Yeah yeah and...

(7.10)

Teacher 1:   ... if they're stuck in KET, it's more of an aptitude rather than attitude. Probably it+
Teacher 3:   Don't know if **we can** assume that to be honest.
Teacher 4:   I don't have any students with attitude problems to tell you the truth
              . . .

Yeah I mean **maybe we can** we can get some more
er elementary. **Maybe we can** put her in the. Yeah.
ing like that. Yeah am **maybe we could** incorporate all of that into the
ative as possible then **maybe we have** to think about something
ew students in a. And **maybe we might** want to make it that the
why and the what and then **maybe we might** come up with some proposals
s been in. Yeah. **Maybe we should** wait and see. Instead of
finitely. And I mean **maybe we should** give them also+ But
ainst it. laughter **Maybe we should** start with one two and
eah I don't know I. **Maybe we should** learn from experience that
e little sister. **Maybe we shouldn't** open that can of worms.
e done. Right. **Maybe we'll have to** move over to that next a

---

Figure 7.3 Extract of concordance lines for *maybe* + we + modal/semi-modal verb in C-MELT.

Most often, uncontentious issues such as student levels, curriculum, scheduling and student-related matters are presented and discussed with a low degree of hedging compared to more sensitive and face-threatening matters relating to the teachers as individuals or as a group (especially when referred to by their Director of Studies).

On looking at the keywords in detail through concordance lines, we find that they all relate to politeness strategies, buffering the difficult moments of the teacher meetings. When we look at the patterns with the keyword *maybe*, for example, we see how it works with *we* and modal and semi-modal verbs *can, could, might, should, have to*, which evinces the careful presentation of suggestions and solutions within the teaching team.

7.4 OTHER WAYS OF INVESTIGATING PRAGMATICS IN SPECIFIC DISCOURSE DOMAINS USING A CORPUS

One of the many useful aspects of a spoken corpus is that it will contain 'extralinguistic' information about the context, such as sounds, laughter, crying, pauses, hesitations, overt inhalations, and so on. This can prove very useful when looking at pragmatics in context. One of the typical extralinguistic items in a corpus of shop counter recordings (from LCIE) is the sound of the till opening or closing. By searching for this item, we can investigate patterns of use around this. In the concordance lines for <$E> *sound of till* <\$E>, we can see that the high frequency discourse marker *now* frequently follows the item (Figure 7.4). This allows us to see the contextual pattern whereby the shop attendant rings up the price of the customer's item on the till (hence <$E> *sound of till* <\$E>), and the attendant announces the price of the item to the customer. The shop attendant consistently precedes the announcement of the price with the discourse marker *now* and uses the discourse marker *so* followed by *please* usually after the price (see Binchy, 2000).

When we look at extralinguistic information in the NHS Direct helpline corpus, we find a lot of caller inhalations noted by transcribers. We therefore treat these as important to this discourse domain. When we look at the concordance lines for <$E> *inhales* <\$E>, we find the following as displayed in Figure 7.5.

<$E> sound of till <\$E> **Now** two fourteen thanks. <$1> Two fourteen so he
<$E> sound of till <\$E> **Now** two fifteen so please <$E> pause <\$E>. <$E>
<$E> sound of till <\$E> **Now** two sixty seven so please. <$2> Now I have the
<$E> sound of till <\$E> **Now** three twenty so please <$E> sound of coins
<$E> sound of till <\$E> **Now** sixty eight please <$E> pause <\$E>. Thanks.
<$E> sound of till <\$E> **Now** one twenty please. Thanks. <$2> Thank you.
<$E> sound of till <\$E> **Now** eight twenty eight so please. <$E> sound of
<$E> sound of till <\$E> **Now** two forty please. <$E> sound of coins <\$E>
<$E> sound of till <\$E> **Now** a pound please. <$1> <$E> sound of till
<$E> sound of till <\$E> **Now** six eighty please thank you. <$2> Thank you.
<$E> sound of till <\$E> **Now** seventy eight so please. <$E> pause <\$E>

Figure 7.4 Extract from concordance lines for *now* in shop recordings from LCIE.

a that you know of? <$2> <$E> **inhales** <\$E> Erm no. His stools were a little
h ones are you on? <$2> <$E> **inhales** <\$E> Oh. Er erm Amoxycillin? <$3>
about painkillers? <$2> <$E> **inhales** <\$E> Er well I had some sort of on
health problems? <$2> <$E> **inhales** <\$E> Erm I've been ill. <$=> Er s=
colour is the rash? <$2> <$E> **inhales** <\$E> Erm <$E> 1 sec <\$E> well
been scratching? <$2> <$E> **inhales** <\$E> Oh yeah. Oh ye. <$3> <$=>
is he with that? <$2> <$E> **inhales** <\$E> I mean he's not complained
blisters are they? <$2> <$E> **inhales** <\$E> Well they look like them a bit
water than usual? <$2> <$E> **inhales** <\$E> <$E> extends follow syllable
can I help you? <$2> <$E> **inhales** <\$E> Well I've come to babysit for

Figure 7.5 Examples of concordance lines of <$E> inhales <\$E>.

On exploring these in more detail by going back to the source files, we find that there
is a pattern of the NHS Health Advisor asking a question followed by the caller inhaling
and then hesitating before answering. The hesitation is marked by the inhalation and by
a hesitation device such as *erm*. We also find that the discourse marker *well* can also
function as a hesitation device here. The discourse marker *oh* also figures and it seems
unusual to find a surprise marker uttered by the caller when describing his/her symptoms.
It seems that the caller is using *oh* as a response to the question rather than a marker of
the answer, which suggests an unease or nervousness on the part of the caller as
exemplified by extract 7.11:

(7.11)

Advisor: Let's go through some specific questions then we can ema= eliminate a
           few things.
Caller: Right.
Advisor: How does that sound?
Caller: Yeah.
Advisor: All right? Are you normally well? Do you have any health problems?
Caller: <$E> **inhales** <\$E> **Erm** I've been ill... **Erm** I had a very bad throat
           infection last week and I was on antibiotics. . . .
Advisor: Which ones are you on?
Caller: <$E> **inhales** <\$E> Oh. **Er erm** Amoxycillin?
Advisor: Yeah. Okay. And the the rash has just come up today?
Caller: Yeah.
Advisor: And you've got how many more tablets to take? <$=> Or <\$=>
Caller: <$E> **inhales** <\$E> **Oh** I've nearly finished.
Advisor: You've nearly finished.
Caller: <$2> Yeah.

This pattern of health advisor *question + caller inhalation + hesitation/surprise marker + response* is indexical of the power semantic in this context, where the health professional is the 'primary knower' (after Labov, 1972; see also Berry, 1981) and the caller is unsure as a discourse participant in this specialised context of talking about health with a professional (even though, ironically, the caller is actually the primary knower in terms of what his or her own symptoms and health issues are). The caller's uncertainty in the role of non-expert is indexed by the use of hesitation devices and vagueness markers (in bold) and ellipsis (the leaving out of words that can be guessed from context, marked with [^]), shown in 7.12, 7.13, 7.14 and 7.15:

(7.12)

Advisor: He's not had any diarrhoea that you know of?
Caller: <$E> inhales <\$E> **Erm no**. His stools were **a little bit** loose but nothing [^] you know.

(7.13)

Advisor: What about painkillers?
Caller: <$E> inhales <\$E> **Er well** I had **some sort of** [^] on the Saturday but I've not not really had any since. . .

(7.14)

Advisor: . . .They are blisters are they?
Caller: <$E> inhales <\$E> **Well** they look like them **a bit** yeah.

(7.15)

Advisor: How many times did you have diarrhoea yesterday?
Caller: <$E> inhales <\$E> **Oh** it was more yesterday. **I'd say about** <$=> f= [pause =1 sec] three or four.

Multi-word units

Another avenue of exploration when looking at the pragmatics of language in specific discourse domains is to look at how words combine and form fixed semantic and pragmatic units. These are variously referred to in the literature using terms such as *multi-word units* (Greaves and Warren, 2010), *routine formulae* (Coulmas, 1979), *lexicalised stems* (Pawley and Syder, 1983), *formulaic sequences* (Wray, 2002; Schmitt, 2004), *chunks* (O'Keeffe *et al.*, 2007) and *lexical bundles* (Biber *et al.*, 1999; Biber and Conrad, 1999), *pattern grammar* (Hunston and Francis, 2000), as well as *n-grams, clusters, skipgrams* (these include a limited number of intervening words), *phrase-frames, and phrasal constructions* (see Greaves and Warren, 2010 for a summary).

For example, looking at a very small corpus of English language classes from the LIBEL corpus (30,000 words), we generated a list of all of the three-word items. In Table 7.6, we illustrate the first 30 items (all occurring at least 10 times). From this, we can see that some multi-word units appear fragmented, such as *what do you, look at the* or *you to do*. While others are more recognisable chunks, such as *use a comma, a little bit* or *at the end.*

The more complete or recognisable chunks have more obvious pragmatic unity and in the context of discourse in specific domains, they have often acquired some more obvious pragmatic specialisation. In this case, for the most part, these pragmatic specialisations relate to the teacher's managerial talk (Walsh, 2006), where she signals to the students what she or they will do next (we note that the teacher most frequently refers to the class as *we* so as to downtone the face threat of the imperative being issued), as in extracts (7.16) and (7.17).

(7.16)

Teacher: Am. Alright. **I'm going to** put three things on the board here . . .

Table 7.6 30 most frequent three-word units in ELT classes from LIBEL

1	I'm going to	16	do you want
2	what do you	17	look at the
3	We're going to	18	this is a
4	you want to	19	use a comma
3	going to do	20	what are you
5	I don't know	21	would like to
6	going to be	22	you have to
7	do you think	23	if you want
8	what did you	24	is going to
9	a lot of	25	not going to
10	I want you	26	we have a
11	did you do	27	you to do
13	want you to	28	you're going to
14	brother lives in	29	a little bit
15	are you going	30	at the end

(7.17)

Teacher: **We're going to** talk about this subject and **we're going to** talk about it from three different aspects. Okay? **We're going to** look at three ways that this that Chinese should be replaced by English . . .

The 'incomplete', or fragmented, recurring units act as frames for building other patterns and even in such a small corpus, we see strong patterns around the activity of the classroom, for example when we look at some of the patterns of the fragmented unit *what do you*:

What do you call someone who stays there all the time?
call that what they're wearing?
call that when you're not afraid to talk to new people?
call the people who go to a nightclub?
do when you're embarrassed?
have for number two?
hope will happen?
like cooking for your friends?
like cooking?
like doing with your friends?
think group A?
think it might mean?
think that is?
think that should be?
think that the article might be about?
think they might mean by a healthy lunch then?
think?
want to do when you finish in the language centre?

Hence, these fragments should not be dismissed when looking at recurring strings in specific context of use as they are indicative of pervasive interactional patterns.

Let us look at another example from the context of media scripts. When we generate the top 30 three-word items for a 24,000 word corpus of soap opera scripts (taken from a TV soap opera called *Fair City*, based in Dublin, see Palma Fahey, 2005), we find the following list. By comparing it with Table 7.6, we can see how patterns vary considerably even across such small amounts of data.

In the dramatic structure of a soap opera, confrontation and argumentation are often key to driving the plot. This is reflected in the three-word list results as illustrated in the examples below. In this specific context of use, we find many more face-threatening acts and moments of crisis than we would expect in everyday casual conversation between family and friends:

Table 7.7 30 most frequent three-word units in corpus of soap opera scripts

1	I don't know	16	you know I
2	I don't think	17	do you mean
3	I'm going to	18	don't want to
4	what do you	19	I don't want
5	no no no	20	do you know
6	I'll see you	21	I told you
7	a lot of	22	not going to
8	I have to	23	well you know
9	what are you	24	do you think
10	you have to	25	how do you
11	you know what	26	I know that
12	you want to	27	what did you
13	do you want	28	why did you
14	going to be	29	yeah well I
15	is going to	30	a bit of

(7.18)

A: . . .Things still aren't going well between you? How do you feel?

B: Not good Kay. You don't want to know. I feel like I'm in a fog. I **I don't know** how I feel and I **I don't know** what to do.

A: Well there have been a lot of big changes in your life.

B: I guess except we're suddenly strangers to each other. It's like I look at Paul and I **I don't know** him any more.

(7.19) [Context: talking about a murder]

A: . . . I'm so scared Tracey <$E> crying <\$E> if anybody finds out what happened to Billy I'm going to be blamed.

B: No one is going to find out Carol.

A: Promise me you won't tell anyone.

B: I promise.

A: <$E> sighs<\$E> No one knows about this not even Lorcan.

B: Sure what would I say anything. We're all better off without Billy.

A: If anything happened to Lorcan I think I'd kill myself.

B: <$E> sighs <\$E> what did they do with the body?

A: **I don't know.**

B: It must've been terrible Carol.

A: <$E> crying <\$E> I'm so scared Tracy it was like a nightmare . . .

We also see the unusually high frequency of the reduplication of *no*. While it occurs as a three word chunk, a concordance search shows that it occurs in up to six-word units. This again reflects the conflict-resolution sequence that prevails in soap operas:

> everybody else. <$1> **No no no no no no** Andrew has to
> <$1> Anyone I know? <$3> Oh **no no no** Dermot was grand so <G5+> I had
> a socio-political thing. <$1> **No no no** I don't think so it's eh the world
> mbarrassment to you? <$1> **No** God **no no no** I'd love you to be there
> e on account of Yvonne. <$2> **No no no** it's fine no she's not working today.
> e a friend of yours? <$2> **No no no** just I no just I know her a bit
> everybody else. <$1> **No no no no no no** Andrew has to
> like everybody else. <$1> **No no no no no no** Andrew has to get
> home with your mother? <$2> **No no no no no** she is just minding my son
> home with your mother? <$2> **No no no no no** she is just minding my son for
> like everybody else. <$1> **No no no no no no** Andrew has to get
> disturb you. <$1> **No no no no** I understand look
> horne with your mother? <$2> **No no no no** she is just minding my son
> I'm sorry I shouldn't. <$1> **No no no** you are okay. <$2> I suppose

Figure 7.6 Concordance lines for *no* reduplication from *Fair City* soap opera scripts.

What are you is another item, in this context of use, which suggests conflict:

(7.20)

A: **What are you doing** with my things?
B: Jo eh we need to talk.
A: <$E> sighs <$E>.

(7.21)

A: **What are you** doing back?
B: I missed you. Is Billy with you?

(7.22)

A: Oh we all make mistakes it's no reason make a song and dance of it you did good work.

B: **What are you** doing?

C: I'm sick of this.

B: What's the problem?

A: Is there a problem?

(7.23)

A: God she is really putting the screws on you isn't she?

B: So **what are you** going to do?

(7.24)

A: **What are you** looking so smug about?

B: Me?

A: Yeah you.

(7.25)

A: You're talking about Mick?

B: Talking about me best friend going snooping behind me back. **What are you** doing asking Mick about gangs coming after Billy Tracey?

Problematisation in the context of the soap opera data is also reflected in high frequency items such as *I don't think*:

(7.26)

A: What's the problem?

B: Is there a problem?

C: Oh yeah there're plenty of problems but **I don't think** either of you are capable of solving any of them.

(7.27)

A: No like he said he's moved on so have I.

B: Are you sure?

A: Anyway **I don't think** he's really that interested in Jessica he's still mad at me yeah that's why he had a go.

(7.28)

A: No I think it's because he's black and I'm white.
B: Oh you mean you get strange looks.
A: Yeah **I don't think** that I deal with it very well.
B: You like him don't you?
A: Is that obvious?
B: Then go with your instincts.

7.5 CONCLUSION

In this chapter we have taken a look at a number of discourse domains so as to exemplify how different approaches can be taken to exploring the pragmatically-specialised ways in which language is used. It is crucial to start by looking at different domains of language use in terms of how their contextual conditions differ from the outset. Itemising the register characteristics (cf. Table 7.1) helps to tease out the reasons behind the differing use of language across contexts. It is when we explore details such as the mode of communication, the role relationships, the shared situational conditions, and so on, that we gain insight into what is behind the language.

We stressed here the need for comparison of data. By bringing different data side-by-side and looking at it from perspectives of turn sequences, word frequencies and keywords, we can bring into relief the differences that contextual conditions bring to bear on how we use language. It is also important to read the texts/recordings so as to gain depth of insight and trigger hypotheses which can be substantiated by follow up searches. Also, by looking at how key words and high frequency items cluster, pragmatics specialisations become more apparent. Frequently, pragmatic markers (discourse markers, markers of shared knowledge, response tokens) co-occur as do vagueness markers and hesitation devices.

We also stress that pragmatically-specialised patterns emerge even from very small corpora of data. If a collection of data is concentrated around a very specific domain of discourse, not much data is required to show pragmatically-specialised patterns of use. Findings can be corroborated by comparison with larger datasets. Finding out more about the pragmatics of specific domains of discourse also has a pedagogical implication because it tells us more about the lexical and grammatical contexts of use beyond the purely semantic and syntactical level. We devote our entire final chapter to the topic of pragmatics and English Language Teaching.

7.6 FURTHER READING

Barron, A. and **Schneider, K. P.** (eds) (2005) *The Pragmatics of Irish English*. Berlin: Mouton de Gruyter.
This volume focuses on the pragmatics of Irish English in private, official and public spheres. These different contexts prove useful as the basis for comparison with other varieties of

English. Such contexts include: discourse markers in literature, responding to thanks in Irish and American English, offering in Irish and British English, politeness in family discourse, relational strategies in institutional settings, indirectness in business negotiations, politeness in service encounters, pragmatics of question forms in a radio phone-in and relevance theory in the context of advertising. The data for the studies are collected using a variety of methodologies such as DCTs, questionnaires, ethnographical methods and corpora.

Cutting, J. (2008) *Pragmatics and Discourse*, 2nd edn. London: Routledge.
This book provides a comprehensive introduction to pragmatics and discourse, covering the core areas such as context, co-text, speech acts, conversation, Co-operative Principle and politeness. In terms of pragmatics in specific domains, it uses real examples from many different contexts of use, including from TV programmes such as *Who Wants to be a Millionaire* and *Dalziel and Pascoe*, mobile text messages and literature.

Finegan, E. and **Biber, D.** (1994) 'Register and social dialect variation: An integrated approach', in D. Biber and E. Finegan (eds), *Sociolinguistic Perspectives on Register*. Oxford: Oxford University Press.
This chapter is essential reading as it brings together in an integrated, and controversial, way how register and dialect variation can be examined. While it might appear to be of more relevance to sociolinguists, the chapter covers many important issues and concepts in relation to how we look at register variation and context of use.

Leech G., Grayson, P. and **Wilson, A.** (2001) *Word Frequencies in Written and Spoken English*. London: Longman.
This is essentially a reference text and one that anyone interested in using a corpus to compare data with should use. It contains frequency lists from the British National Corpus and so one can readily access results in either alphabetical or rank order for words from the spoken and written BNC, as well as sub-divisions of it. It also contains a very useful introduction, which includes information on the construction of the BNC and significance and dispersion statistics.

Sacks, H., Schegloff, E. A. and **Jefferson, G.** (1974) 'A simplest systematics for the organisation of turn-taking for conversation', *Language* 50: 696–735.
This ground-breaking article sets out the principles for simplest organisation of turn-taking in conversation. The authors based their findings on observations of real conversations. Conversational structure, they propose, hinges around the activities of turn construction and turn allocation. The authors propose that the system which they identify is universal across languages. It might therefore be a worthwhile project to investigate this further in different languages (as researchers have done) and to look at how these 'universals' may differ in specific discourse domains.

CHAPTER 8

Pragmatics and language teaching

8.1 INTRODUCTION

In this final chapter, we return again to the notion of defining pragmatics (see Chapter 1). We do so because understanding what pragmatics is is important if we are to explore how to teach it. Traditional areas of language teaching have clear-cut taxonomies: we can talk about word classes, grammatical structures and competencies and so on. How does all of this translate to the area of pragmatics? According to Yule (1996), within language analysis there is a traditional contrast drawn between pragmatics and semantics and syntax. Semantics is the study of how meaning is encoded in these linguistic forms. Syntax, on the other hand, is the study of how linguistic forms are arranged in a sequence that can be deemed grammatically 'acceptable' or not. In terms of the language classroom, semantics is primarily concerned with vocabulary teaching whereas syntax can be broadly equated with the grammatical rules taught. Both vocabulary and grammar can be taught in a relatively formal and structured way at word and sentence level, isolated from any reference to the speaker (or writer) or indeed listener (or reader). However, it is this reference to language users such as the speaker and listener that separates pragmatics from syntax or semantics. When any definition of pragmatics is examined, the interpersonal nature of pragmatics is readily apparent. Take for example Yule's assertion that 'pragmatics is the study of the *relationship between linguistic forms and the users of these forms*. In this three-part distinction [syntax–semantics–pragmatics], only pragmatics allows humans into the analysis' (1996: 4; emphasis added).

Similarly, Leech (1983) and Kasper and Rose (2001) describe pragmatics as the study of the way speakers and writers have to get things done while at the same time attending to the relationships they have with others. Therefore, *lexical* and *grammatical competence* equate to the learner's knowledge of semantics and syntax in the target language. *Pragmatic competence*, on the other hand, relates to 'a set of internalised rules of how to use language in socio-culturally appropriate ways, taking into account the participants in a communicative interaction and features of the context within which the interaction takes place' (Celce-Murcia and Olshtain, 2000: 19).

Numerous publications have underlined the fact that second language pragmatics is increasingly receiving attention (Barron, 2002; Rose, 2005; Belz, 2007; Cohen, 2008; Vásquez and Sharpless, 2009). Vásquez and Sharpless (2009: 8) have cited a 'burgeoning interest in pragmatics and language learning at the level of scholarly publications', a trend referred to by Cohen (2008: 215) as a 'veritable upsurge'. Therefore, the studies examined

Pragmatic competence involves both *pragmalinguistic* and *sociopragmatic* competences (Leech, 1983; Thomas, 1983). Pragmalinguistics refers to knowledge of the range of options available for performing various pragmatic actions and sociopragmatics refers to the knowledge of how to select an appropriate choice given a particular goal in a particular setting.

in this chapter are a small cross-section of what is available. It is hoped that these, in conjunction with the annotated bibliography at the end of the chapter, will provide adequate guidance for those who wish to pursue a more in-depth, detailed analysis. The chapter begins with a focus on pragmatics in the language classroom which puts forward the arguments for the inclusion of pragmatic instruction in this context. The chapter also provides some suggestions on how to practically address the teaching of different areas of pragmatic competence within the language classroom itself.

8.2 PRAGMATICS IN THE LANGUAGE CLASSROOM

Koike and Pearson (2005) examined the use of suggestions and the mitigation of these suggestions with Spanish learners of English. They observed that their control group made more use of statements and commands as strategies for suggestion (for example, *You go to the store and you ask for a cheaper one*), whereas the groups that received instruction appeared to have more options to express suggestions (for example, *Why don't you ...?* or *I suggest that...*) and also showed a raised awareness of the importance of mitigating their suggestions and their suggestion responses. Similar results were noted by Alcón Soler (2005) who examined direct and conventionally indirect request strategies (for example, *Can I? Could you?*) in Spanish speakers of English. She found that, again, learners' awareness of requests benefited from instruction (and feedback) in contrast to learners who received no input.

The teaching of pragmatics in the language classroom is important for two reasons: (1) it has been demonstrated that there is a need for it; and (2) quite simply, it has proven to be effective. Bardovi-Harlig (2001) asserts that, without instruction, differences in pragmatics show up in the English of learners regardless of their first language background or language proficiency. As the research into pragmatics across cultures has demonstrated, pragmatic transfer between languages can, on occasion, make non-native speakers (NNSs) appear rude or insincere. According to Bardovi-Harlig and Mahan-Taylor (2003a: 38), 'the consequences of pragmatic differences ... are often interpreted on a social or personal level', thereby increasing the sensitivity of the NS because of the difficulty in remaining objective about these mistakes. Therefore, instruction in pragmatics is desirable in order to help prevent the consequences of pragmatic failure. It also appears that pragmatic competence does not develop in conjunction with grammatical competence, or, as Bardovi-Harlig and Dörnyei (1998) put it, a good level of grammatical competence does not imply a good level of pragmatic competence. They point out that 'the disparity between learner's and NS's pragmatic competence may be attributed to two key factors related to input and the salience of relevant linguistic features in the input from the point of view of the learner' (ibid: 234). Furthermore, it has been claimed that exposure to an L2 alone is insufficient for the acquisition of pragmatic competence (see Rose, 2005). Schmidt (1993) and Kasper and Rose (2002) contend that pragmatic considerations are often not salient to the learner and so are not likely to be noticed despite prolonged exposure. For example, speaker turns that occur around expressions of gratitude may not be noticeable to learners (see Schauer and Adolphs, 2006). Similarly, Bardovi-Harlig and Mahan-Taylor (2003a) argue that the difference between speaker-orientated requests (*Can I?*) and hearer-orientated (*Can you?*) might not be immediately apparent to learners.

Pragmatic instruction is particularly necessary in a foreign language context. The two areas of pragmatic competence, pragmalinguistic and sociopragmatic, appear to be particularly difficult for English as a Foreign Language (EFL) learners and this has motivated much of the research in this area (see for example, Rose, 2001; Alcón Soler, 2005; Takimoto, 2009, among many others). Bardovi-Harlig and Dörnyei (1998) suggest that in the EFL classroom micro-level grammatical accuracy is being prioritised at the expense of macro-level pragmatic appropriateness. They tested the appropriateness of utterances in different contexts by examining both learners and their teachers in two countries – Hungary and the United States. They found that EFL learners and their teachers (those in Hungary) consistently ranked grammatical errors as more serious than pragmatic errors whereas English as a Second Language (ESL) learners and their teachers (those in the USA) ranked pragmatic errors as more serious. The preference for grammatical competence amongst the EFL cohort is, they claim, due to the prevalence of examinations as indicators of success in this context. One could also add that the pragmatic errors may not be seen as a priority also because of the EFL context (that is where all of the learners are living where their L1 is the first language). In this case, the classroom context may be the only place in which they use the target language and hence their opportunity for 'pragmatic conflict' is low in contrast to ESL learners who are based in the target language environment. This is confirmed by Bardovi-Harlig and Dörnyei (1998) when they say that, in terms of the ESL cohort, although examination is a consideration, successful communication with NSs is also an area that provides reward.

The treatment of pragmatics in both EFL and ESL textbooks has also highlighted the need for a more considered approach in the classroom. Bardovi-Harlig (2001: 25) maintains that 'in general, textbooks cannot be counted on as a reliable source of pragmatic input for classroom language learners'. This is because they often contain insufficient specific input or insufficient interpretation of language use. Corpus studies (for example, McCarthy and Carter, 1995; Römer, 2004a, 2004b; Gilmore, 2004; Jiang, 2006) have highlighted the inconsistencies between the English that is found in textbooks and the English that occurs in spoken and written corpora. The English found in textbooks has, in the past, been based on author intuition, whereas the English found in corpora is produced by a range of different speakers and/or writers (see also Schauer and Adolphs, 2006).

Vellenga (2004) maintains that despite a decade of complaint regarding the authenticity of the language contained in textbooks, little seems to have changed. Vellenga examined eight ELT textbooks in order to determine the amount and quality of pragmatic information included. She found a dearth of information for students in the areas of politeness, appropriacy, register, cultural information and speech act information, and maintains that 'in some cases, the focus on speech acts in textbooks may actually be pragmatically inappropriate for students' (Vellenga, 2004: 10). Crandall and Basturkmen (2004) also underline the inadequate approach for the teaching of speech acts taken by most English for Academic Purposes (EAP) textbooks. They claim that EAP textbooks appear to assume that learners know when it is appropriate to employ a particular speech act. Instead of being shown when and for what purposes to use a speech act, learners are instead provided with a list of 'useful expressions'. As discussed elsewhere in the book (Chapters 5 and 6, in particular), so much research into speech acts shows that non-native speakers find it very challenging to navigate the nuances of enacting a speech act in a foreign language (see for example, Boxer, 1993; Bardovi-Harlig, 2001; Félix-Brasdefer, 2003). While NNSs might easily know when an apology, invitation, or expression of gratitude is required, they may inadvertently end up over-apologising, being too forceful in an invitation, not expressing the right amount of gratitude, and so on, based on their L1 pragmatic norms. Vellenga (2004) concludes that a 'pragmatically friendly' textbook should include pragmatic awareness-raising activities that equip learners with the contextual information, variety of form and in-depth cultural information necessary to make the correct pragmalinguistic (the range of forms available) and sociopragmatic (the right form for the right situation) choices.

Perhaps the most convincing argument for the teaching of pragmatics is that it has proven to be effective. In terms of more recent studies, Takimoto (2009) looked at the effectiveness of instruction for teaching polite requests to Japanese learners of English. She found that the treatment groups, those who received instruction, outperformed the control group, who received no instruction in the speech act. One important pedagogic outcome of this study is the need for teachers to be aware that 'effective learning occurs when the tasks provide learners with opportunities for processing both pragmalinguistic and sociopragmatic features of the target structures' (p. 22). Takimoto maintains that this is due, in part, to the deeper processing that arises when learners focus on the pragmalinguistic-sociopragmatic connections of a target language feature.

Thomas (1983: 104) offers a caveat for the language teacher in relation to error correction and pragmatics:

... correcting pragmatic failure stemming from sociopragmatic miscalculation is a far more delicate matter for the language teacher than correcting pragmalinguistic failure. Sociopragmatic decisions are *social* before they are linguistic, and while foreign learners are fairly amenable to corrections that they regard as linguistic, they are justifiably sensitive about having their social (or even political, religious or moral) judgement called into question.

Studies that focus on pragmatic features other than speech acts show similar results. In a corpus-based study, Belz and Vyatkina (2005) report on the effectiveness of teacher intervention in NNSs' use of German modal particles. They found that intervention positively influenced the range, frequency and accuracy of the learners' usage of these particles. Yoshimi (2001) used an experimental group design similar to that of Alcón Soler (2005) and Koike and Pearson (2005) above to examine the effects of instruction on the use of discourse markers by English speakers of Japanese. She found that the instructed learners showed a dramatic increase in the frequency of these discourse markers, whereas in the control group, no similar increase was observed. Wishnoff (2000) examined the use of hedging devices in the academic writing of ESL learners. She found that although an increase in the use of hedges occurred in both the instructed group and the control group, the instructed group's hedging devices showed a statistically significant five-fold increase on the control group. Finally, although research suggests that explicit instruction is more effective than implicit (see Kasper, 2001), Rose (2005) and Jeon and Kaya (2006) note that the seemingly superior effects of explicit pragmatic instruction need to be more thoroughly examined (see for example, Takimoto, 2009).

Bardovi-Harlig and Mahan-Taylor (2003a) recommend three key pedagogical practices in the teaching of pragmatics to L2 learners: (1) the use of authentic language samples; (2) input first followed by interpretation and/or production; and (3) the introduction of the teaching of pragmatics at early levels. They maintain that the classroom provides a safe place for the acquisition of pragmatic competence. The language teacher can provide the learner with instant feedback and this can lead to greater insight into the 'secret' realm of pragmatics.

The language teacher also needs to consider the context of the classroom itself when designing pragmatic awareness exercises. The teacher–learner relationship is both an institutional and hierarchical one, in which the teacher is the power-role holder and this context normally produces a limited range of discourse patterns (see Lörscher, 1986; Ellis, 1990). Indeed, Cohen (2008) recommends that the teacher give the learner initial guidance in the form of direction to, for example, specific websites where learners can interact with different speech acts enacted in different situations and leave the actual learning of pragmatics to the learner according to their own interests. Cohen and his associates have built an excellent online resource for teaching Spanish pragmatics which is well worth exploring for ideas on how to approach teachings areas of pragmatic in a learner centred way (see website for the Centre for Advanced Research on Language Acquisition, CARLA: http://www.carla.umn.edu). For example, students can explore speech acts such as expressing gratitude, leave-taking, apologising, requesting, apologising, inviting, advising, suggesting, disagreeing, complimenting, complaining and reprimanding, as well as the social context of service encounters. For example, in the case of expressing gratitude, students are asked to assess when an expression of gratitude is needed in Spanish. Tick box options include borrowing an item, having someone else buy your lunch, getting a tour of the city, receiving a gift, the use of someone's time, borrowing money, receiving a favour, having someone serve you dinner. Students can then check their answers for feedback. The feedback window includes information such as:

> You should always be aware of situations that require more thanks than others. This will vary between language varieties. For example, in English, it is very common to thank someone profusely for their time, especially if they are very busy. In fact, it is a commonly used formulaic expression: *Thanks for your time!* However, in Spanish such a large expression of gratitude may not be necessary, or may even be rude. Other simple, formulaic thanking expressions are used much more often in English than they are in Spanish ... When learning to be pragmatically appropriate in Spanish, it is important to take note of the cases that require big thanks and those in which a simple *muchas gracias* is sufficient.
>
> (http://www.carla.umn.edu/speechacts/sp_pragmatics/
> gratitiude_leave_taking/enc_grat.html)

The site also includes video clips which the user is asked to notice certain pragmatic features, and so on.

8.3 WHAT CAN BE TAUGHT?

Olshtain and Blum-Kulka (1985) suggest that it can take ten years or more for learners to perform pragmatics in a way indistinguishable from natives. For many this assertion might well render the whole attempt to teach anything to do with pragmatics futile. On the other hand, Olshtain and Blum-Kulka's point forces us to consider the teaching of pragmatics in two ways. First, what can be attained in the short term? Second, what can we hope to achieve in the longer term? No less than for first language acquisition, the development of pragmatic competence is an incremental process. What L2 learners have to their advantage is that they already operate within the norms and exponents of the pragmatics of their first language and so they are open to awareness-raising and 'noticing' tasks (after Schmidt, 1990, 1993 and 1994). However, we note that, as with the language system itself, there can both positive and negative transfer between L1 and L2 pragmatics and as we have discussed elsewhere, while there may be parallels in areas such as speech acts, they may manifest differently and to differing degrees in the L2.

Short-term and long-term goals

Short-term goals for language teachers should be to systematically raise core issues of pragmatics. This is a matter of consciousness-raising and noticing. The longer-term goal is that, as a result of consistent awareness building, learners will be able to 'perform' L2 pragmatics, at least to some degree.

Some aspects of pragmatics are not easily transferable to the language classroom; however, many are, and in this section we will focus on those aspects of pragmatics that cut across everything we teach, whether it be vocabulary, grammar, skills development and so on. We will look at how short-term and long-term goals can be achieved in a practical

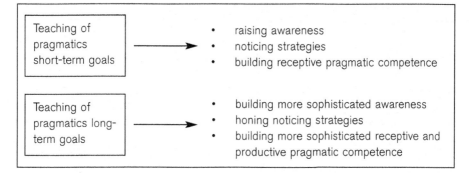

Figure 8.1 Short- and long-term goals in teaching pragmatic competence.

way within the parameters of those aspects of pragmatics which are most relevant and 'teachable'. As mentioned earlier, Kasper (2001) notes that explicit instruction is more effective than implicit. We provide suggestions for classroom tasks that allow for explicit teaching of pragmatics but we also note that there is a lot of scope for implicit work on pragmatics in the classroom because it permeates so many levels of language teaching. The tasks which we suggest here have been framed around positive and negative politeness (for a detailed treatment of theories of politeness, see Chapter 4). These are prototypical tasks and if they are to be used in class, they may need to be modified for the level of the students. We suggest adhering to the principle of 'grade the task not the language'.

We note that the area of speech acts could also have been covered here because it too spans so many levels of language teaching and so much research has been done in the area. However, we have opted to devote the remainder of the chapter to teaching politeness so as to give it a more detailed treatment. We strongly advise readers to look at what has been done by the University of Minnesota's Centre for Advanced Research on Language Acquisition (CARLA) as a model for teaching speech acts.

8.4 TEACHING POLITENESS

It is reasonable to question what and how much we can expect learners to assimilate in the short and long term in relation to politeness. It is obviously unreal to attempt to lecture language learners on positive and negative politeness. However, it is not an unattainable goal to communicate consistently across what we teach, from beginners' level upwards, that we show politeness in English in two ways:

(1) Showing people that we respect and value them (positive politeness);
(2) Making what you say or write less direct so as not to sound too forceful (negative politeness).

Teachers are generally aware of these concepts and intuitively address issues relating to positive and negative politeness in students' speaking and writing when it is produced. For example, if a student is over- or under-formal in their writing, a teacher will normally mark this. When teaching formal letter writing, students are made familiar with the conventions of address at openings and closings (*Dear Sir or Madam / To Whom it May Concern / Yours sincerely / Yours faithfully*). This is an example of positive politeness.

When students make overly direct requests, such as *I want some information about the times of the bus*, a teacher will usually alert them to a more indirect form of request, such as *Can you give me some information . . . please?* This is an example of negative politeness. It is important to acknowledge that this intuitive level of teaching of pragmatics already takes place in language classes. A more beneficial course of action however would be to address pragmatics in a more pre-emptive and systematic manner by developing noticing strategies for students.

The very first step in a systematic approach to pragmatics is to identify in practical terms what constitutes the language of politeness. How can it be broken down into actual categories and tangible forms (the pragmalinguistic knowledge)? A notable step in this direction is the inclusion of aspects of pragmatics in two major ELT grammar reference books, Biber *et al.* (1999) and Carter and McCarthy (2006). In both of these grammars, attention is given to aspects of politeness. Carter and McCarthy cover it extensively and break it down into tangible categorisations with corpus-based examples. Both Biber *et al.* (1999) and Carter and McCarthy (2006) draw clear distinctions between spoken and written grammar (see Carter and McCarthy, 1994 for more on spoken grammar). Carter and McCarthy (2006) dedicate a whole chapter of their grammar to politeness, entitled 'From discourse to social context', which includes aspects of positive politeness such as greetings and farewells, openings and closings, and the discourse functions of vocatives. They also address negative politeness under headings such as pragmatic markers (which includes discourse markers, interactional markers and response tokens), stance markers, vague language and hedges. Making such explicit reference to aspects of pragmatics within a grammar of English is a welcome step towards formalising an awareness of the central role of pragmatics in actual communication, both spoken and written.

Teaching positive politeness

Positive politeness is about showing people that we respect and value them and it is something that most teachers and course books address to some degree, as discussed. What we say when we greet or address someone is crucially important in both spoken and written interactions. Even when people are communicating in informal situations, it is still important to know the appropriate language for the interaction (i.e. sociopragmatic knowledge). Here we collate a summary of the typical formulaic language which we can introduce to our students at different stages and through different types of materials. Teaching contexts for these are often incorporated into language course books. Typically these include role-plays and simulations, structured and semi-structured dialogues, listening activities and task-based activities which promote student interaction and language production practice.

The important pragmatic lessons from the introduction of the formulaic language in Table 8.1 are the following:

• Language varies according to social relationship between speaker and listener, and writer and reader, and we need to be ever-sensitive to these contextual variables.

Table 8.1 Formulaic address in different spoken and written contexts

Spoken contexts	
Relational context	*Example exponents*
Addressing/greeting someone you know face to face	*Hi* *Hi* [first name], *how are you?* *Hi* [first name], *great to see you again.*
Addressing/greeting someone you do not know face to face	*Hello* *Hello* [*title + surname*]. *Pleased to meet you* *Hello. Nice to meet you.*
Addressing/greeting someone you know on the telephone	*Hi* *Hi* [first name], *how are you?*
Addressing/greeting someone you do not know on the telephone	If you receive the call: *Hello,* [first name + surname] *speaking* If you make the call: *Hello, my name is* [first name + surname]
Addressing a customer in a shop or restaurant	*May I help you?* *May I take your order sir/madam?* *Shall I take your coat madam?*
Addressing a customer at a hotel desk	*Here is your room key Mr Collins.* *Have a pleasant stay.*
Asking someone for directions or other requests (e.g. the time)	*Excuse me, could you tell me how to get to Markham St?* *Excuse me (sir) could I ask you the time?*
Other social politeness formulae: When someone is going on a trip When someone is ill When you want to thank someone for a gift	 *Have a safe trip / bon voyage* [in a get well card] *Get well soon* [in a thank you card] *Thank you for your wonderful gift.*
When you want to wish someone luck before an exam Just before you start a meal	*Best of luck in your exam* *Bon appetite / enjoy your meal* (formal) *Okay, tuck in / eat up / get stuck in* (informal)
Written contexts	
Addressing someone in a formal letter or email when you don't know the name of the addressee(s) Signing off	*To whom it may concern,* *Yours faithfully,*
Addressing someone in a formal letter or email when you do know their name and title Signing off	*Dear Prof. Rice,* *Yours sincerely,*
Addressing/greeting someone you know in informal writing (e.g. email)	*Hi* [first name] *Hi there* *Hiya*

Table 8.1 Continued

Written contexts	
Relational context	*Example exponents*
Addressing someone you know well but who is not a close friend in an informal letter or email, e.g. at work.	*Hi there* *[First name]* (on its own, e.g. *John*)
Signing off	*All the best* *Best wishes* *Best* (used as a short form of *Best wishes*) *Cheers*
Addressing someone you know and are very friendly with in an informal letter or email	*Hi* [first name] *Hiya* [first name] *Hey*
Signing off	*Cheers* *Lots of love* etc.

- Language varies according to context and mode of communication and we need to build up an awareness of how to show, in an appropriate way, that we respect and value our listener or reader through what we say or write.

We now look at some sample tasks which might be used to consolidate the language in Table 8.1.

Sample task A

Look up the *Business Letter Corpus* on the internet (http://www.someya-net.com/concordancer/index.html, at the time of writing). Select the personal letters corpus using the drop-down menu. Use this to help you find phrases to write an email to a friend for her first wedding anniversary. For example, use search words such as *anniversary, congratulations, wish you, together, happy.*

Sample task B

In which of the following contexts would you say or write the expressions in the table below?

(a) When you thank someone for a gift
(b) When someone is unwell
(c) Just before you start a meal
(d) When someone is going on holiday
(e) When you want to wish someone luck before an exam

	Say it or write it?	Context?
Have a great time.		
I wish you a speedy recovery.		
Thank you so much. It was so thoughtful of you.		
Best of luck!		
Bon appetite!		

Sample task C

Here is an email from a student to a professor asking her for more time to finish an assignment. Identify what is wrong about the way the student has addressed the professor and how she has ended the email. Write a corrected version:

```
— — — — — — Message — — — — — — —
From: Maria Vitale [mailto:Mariev@mm.uk]
Sent: 17 June 2009 10:38
To: Sharon Miles
Subject: class essay

Professor Sarah

I need more time for my essay. Can I give it to you on
Friday?

Your student

Maria
```

Teaching aspects of negative politeness

The second aspect of politeness which can be addressed consistently by language teachers is that of directness, or more precisely indirectness, that is the importance of making what you say or write less direct so as not to sound too forceful (negative politeness). This cuts across areas such as modal verbs, vocabulary and grammatical structures. Here we break down the notion of negative politeness into teachable areas and provide some sample classroom tasks. Table 8.2 illustrates in broad terms how negative politeness can be categorised in spoken language across hedging, vague language and approximation and pragmatic marking (which includes discourse markers, interactional markers and response tokens) based on the framework of Carter and McCarthy (2006). These features will be discussed in greater detail below.

Table 8.2 Ways in which we make what we say less direct (marked in bold)

Feature	Example
Hedging	It was too expensive **at least that's what I think**.
Vague language and approximation	There were lots of dirty dishes and saucepans **and that kind of thing.** We'll be there at **about** eight.
Pragmatic marking	Discourse markers **Anyway**, she's decided not to apply for the job. . . Interactional markers **You see** I've never been to college. Response tokens A: I've decided to take a year off work to travel. B: **Really!**

Hedging

Hedging is pervasive in both spoken and written English. However, it varies in terms of type and degree. Depending on the type of writing, there may be different degrees of hedging. There has been a proliferation of research into the use of hedging in academic writing (for example, Hyland, 1994, 1996a, 1996b, 1998, 1999a, 1999b; Hinkel, 2004). Hyland's (1998) study, which refers to hedging in scientific writing, asserts that writers hedge because they want to reduce their commitment to the truthfulness of their assertions. Hinkel (2004), writing in the context of teaching English as a Second Language (ESL), explains hedging in academic writing as the use of devices to show hesitation or uncertainty, to display politeness and indirectness and to defer to the reader's point of view (see also Hinkel, 1996, 1997). Hinkel sees the function of hedging in academic prose as having multifaceted social and rhetorical purposes; she stresses that it can take many forms, including adjectives, adverbs, modal and mental (or emotive) verbs, and conjunctions. Importantly, Hinkel makes the case that the overt teaching of hedges is crucial in English Language Teaching because hedging is not called for in many non-Anglo-American rhetorical traditions: 'the desirability of hedging statements, generalizations, and claims is not an obvious consideration for many NNSs. Therefore the need for hedging in academic prose has to be explicitly addressed' (2004: 315).

Here are some examples of hedging from PhD theses:

The second criterion **suggests that it is necessary** for members to gather together to actively pursue their goals, and that the members, as a collective, jointly negotiate these goals.

However, **we consider that** this sample **can allow us to identify** whether the strategies chosen in the soap opera dialogues correspond to the ones found in casual conversation . . .

If these statements were not hedged, they would look something like this:

The second criterion states that members gather together to actively pursue their goals, and that the members, as a collective, jointly negotiate these goals.

However, this sample will identify whether the strategies chosen in the soap opera dialogues correspond to the ones found in casual conversation . . .

The unhedged examples are still grammatically correct but they impose the ideas of the author more forcefully than is the norm for a PhD thesis or academic research paper. The hedges provide a polite deferential buffer between the writer and the reader. This is what is expected in English academic writing.

Sample task D

Below is an extract from a journal article by Beard (2008) on 'Advertising and audience offense: the role of intentional humor' taken from the *Journal of Marketing Communications.* Identify what hedging language the author has used and discuss the impact of these hedges on the reader. Two examples in the first sentence are identified for you:

Example:
In the first sentence of the extract, we see the use of the hedged reporting verb *suggest* and the modal verb *may*: 'Although prior research suggests advertising humor may be associated with offense when it is used in advertisements for certain products and services or combined with potentially offensive themes, this has not been confirmed empirically.'

Although prior research *suggests* advertising humor *may* be associated with offense when it is used in advertisements for certain products and services or combined with potentially offensive themes, this has not been confirmed empirically. For instance, researchers conclude that humor is used infrequently for products and services that are serious, intimate and high-involvement (Bauerly, 1990; Beard, 2006; Burnett *et al.,* 1987; Fugate *et al.,* 2000; Madden and Weinberger, 1984; McCullough and Taylor, 1993; Weinberger and Spotts, 1989). Conversely, humor is believed to be most appropriate for low-involvement and low-risk consumer goods and services (Alden and Hoyer, 1993; Alden *et al.,* 1993; Spotts *et al.,* 1997; Toncar, 2001; Weinberger *et al.,* 1995). Thematically, Weinberger and Gulas (1992) note that, 'Some forms of humor, such as satire, sexual humor, and other forms of aggressive humor, may generate strong positive feelings in some audience members while eliciting strong negative feelings in others' (p. 57).

Fugate (1998), however, suggests humor might enhance the persuasiveness of advertising for some unsought and controversial services by distracting consumers and reducing perceptual defenses. Other research similarly suggests humor might be effective when used to advertise uncomfortable products (McCullough and Taylor, 1993) or even reduce the likelihood of an offensive response, especially among men and younger audiences (Advertising Standards Authority, 2002).

Sample task E

Compare the two emails below:

(1) Which one is more polite?
(2) Which hedge words and phrases make it more polite?
(3) Which would you prefer to receive and why?

EMAIL A

From: xxxxx
Sent: 27 April 2009 15:29
To: Melissa Ryan
Subject: Chapters to print

Dear Melissa

Whenever you have a chance, could you print two copies of the attached documents and send one set of copies to McHales Ltd? Would you mind stapling them separately and sending me a copy as well if possible by Friday.

Thanks a million.
Lynn

EMAIL B

From: xxxxx
Sent: 27 April 2009 15:29
To: Melissa Ryan
Subject: Chapters to print

Dear Melissa

Please print two copies of the attached documents and send one set of copies to McHales Ltd. Staple them separately and send a copy to me as well by Friday.

Regards,
Lynn

Sample task F

[Note: while this task focuses on hedges, it could be used to explore aspects of politeness, e.g. positive politeness: *please* and *thank you* at service encounters; discourse markers: *okay, so* etc.]

In pairs, compare text A and B. One is adapted from a corpus and one is invented. Which one seems most natural to you and why?

Text A

Server:	Hello
Customer:	Can I have a bag of potatoes, please?
Server:	The four ninety-nine bag, is it?
Customer:	Yes, please.
Server:	Seven eighty-three, so please. (sound of till)
Customer:	Now thanks very much.
Server:	Now thanks a lot.
Customer:	Last of all is there anyone around that would lift it for me.
Server:	Oh right. I'll get someone for you. Now see the man there he'll lift it for you. Okay?
Customer:	Okay. Thank you very much.

Text B

Server:	Hello
Customer:	A bag of potatoes.
Server:	The four ninety-nine bag?
Customer:	Yes.
Server:	Seven eighty-three. (sound of till)
Customer:	I need someone to lift it for me.
Server:	Oh right. I'll get someone for you. See the man there he'll lift it.
Customer:	Okay.

A summary of the forms commonly used to hedge is listed in Table 8.3.

Vague language

Vague language and approximation are features of both spoken and written genres. However, as is the case with hedging, they may manifest differently. For example, if we look up the word *estimated* in the British National Corpus, we find that in written news reports, it occurs more than four times as often and it is almost exclusively used as an approximator of numbers whereas in the BNC spoken corpus, this pattern with numbers is in the minority:

Most frequent patterns for *estimated + number(s)* in the BNC news (written) (frequency = 472.5 times per 10 million words):

Pattern	Example
an estimated X amount	But **an estimated** *£30 million of loans and grants is still missing.*
to be + estimated at	*... his personal wealth* **is estimated at** *around £100m*
to be + estimated that	*It* **is estimated that** *more than £12 billion a year is spent*
to be + estimated to be	*About 150* **are estimated to be** *still in jail.*

Table 8.3 A summary of hedging forms

Form	Example
Modal verbs: can, could, may, might, should, would, etc.	Part completion **may** be considered. Other options **could** be explored. Future research **should** take these factors into consideration.
Verbs with modal meaning: appear, assume, believe, consider, estimate, suppose, seem, suggest, suspect, think, tend, indicate, propose, speculate	This practice is **believed** to have originated in Ancient Rome. Tools **tended** to be very rudimentary. McCann (2008) **proposes** that … This research **suggests** four options …
Nouns: assumption, claim, possibility, estimate, suggestion	Based on the **assumption** that the rate of flow will remain constant … Our **claim** is that this will result in greater efficiency and productivity …
Adverbs: actually, apparently, arguably, broadly, evidently, frequently, generally, just, only, really, likely, maybe, necessarily, normally, partially, probably, quite, relatively, roughly, seemingly, surely, typically, usually	This is **arguably** the most important finding in relation to this process … It is **likely** that more software of this kind exists … This is just one **possible** cause of the MRSA superbug's rampant spread.
Prepositional phrases (Carter and McCarthy 2006): in a way in some/many respects generally/broadly/roughly speaking	**Broadly speaking**, this new policy document has been welcomed. It has **more or less** been established that …

in most cases
in the majority of cases
more or less
in principle
in a sense
in some senses

Grammatical choices: e.g. choosing 'softer' question forms.
The prototypical question forms (*wh-* questions, *yes-no* questions and *declarative questions*) are more direct than:

double questions

Tag questions

Questions which are prefaced

Questions which are mitigated with hedges and other politeness devices such as using someone's name.

- Compare: *wh-* question with double question
  Why have you applied for this job?
  Why have you applied for this job? Is it because you feel you have a lot to offer?
- Compare: yes-no question with tag question
  Have you paid the electricity bill?
  You've paid the electricity bill, haven't you?
- Compare: declarative question with prefaced (indirect) question
  This is the way out?
  Do you mind me asking if this is the way out?
- Compare: unmitigated *wh-* question with mitigated *wh-* question
  Where have you left the keys?
  ***John**, where **might** you have left the keys?*

Most frequent patterns for *estimated + number(s)* in the BNC spoken (frequency = 111.7 times per 10 million words):

Pattern	Example
to be + estimated that	*It's **estimated that** over 10 million people now earn less . . .*
to be + estimated at	*And then another lunch **was estimated at** £280.45 . . .*

Sample task G

Look up the words *miles, kilometers, pounds, dollars* in a corpus. You could use The Bank of English corpus online, the BNC or Webcorp. Make a list of the different words and patterns that are used to make the amounts of *miles, kilometers, pounds, dollars* more approximate. Is there a difference between spoken and written words and patterns?

As you will have found when looking up the words in task G, when we use numbers in speaking and in writing, we usually use a vague expression to hedge the directness of a bare factual numeric statement. Here are further examples from written sources in the British National Corpus:

This 'five-star' community service costs **in the region of** £1,000 per annum for a two-bedroom flat.

The easiest way to make the journey, of **just over** 20 miles from Munich, is by the suburban railway (S-Bahn), one of whose lines ends at Erding.

A corpus is an excellent source of vocabulary for approximation. You simply use a number or unit of time (*minute, hour, year, time,* etc.) as your search word. The approximation generally comes before the number but it may come after (see below: *Four hours, I think*). Note that in many corpora, numbers may be written alphabetically rather than alphanumerically (unless they are beyond three digits). Figures 8.2 and 8.3 show some examples from corpora:

Out in a boat for about **three hours** you know? hour and a half maybe
it took us about **three hours** to get there from where we night.
kept going You'd about **two hours** sleep last night I'd none myself.
ean stay home for a couple of **hours**? They stopped feeding her through a
I'd say the latest one. **Four hours, I think** they're they're gonna
ly about **two and a half three hours** really. By car? Yeah. And how long
in the space of a few **hours** like and I went to the doctors and
You've had nearly an **hour's** sleep now Well I watched
sleep experts. **Ten or twelve hours** sleep is really bad for you. Ten or
ad for the last **three** or **four hours** which has allowed all the other
approximately **twenty-four hours** they're unloaded they're they're

---

Figure 8.2 Concordance lines from LCIE using the search word *hours*.

> mine said that it took her **about a year**
> **more than** six hundred pounds **a year**.
> Dried mushrooms keep for **at least a year** and
> Even if he remembers, it's **a year and more**
> philosophical time, producing work once **a year or less.**
> of allergy, although this varies and can take **a year or longer**.
> He seeks more time and he has asked for **a year or more**.
> o go erm in prison for about more than **a year or so**.

Figure 8.3 Concordance lines from BNC using the search word *year*.

Sample task H

Using a corpus, look up three numbers (you may need to spell them) and three time expressions (e.g. *minute, hour, week, month, year*) and make a list of the vague expressions that occur with them. Note whether the expression comes before or after the search word.

Certain suffixes, words and phrases exist to make what we say vaguer and less direct. Below is a sample task which illustrates some of these and how they might be introduced in class.

Sample task I

Make these spoken statements vague by using one of the items below:

| *or whatever* | *and so on* | *sort of* | *like* | *kind of* |
| *-ish* | *a bit* | *about* | *around* | *or something* |

(a) It's cold in here.
(b) This exercise is difficult.
(c) It was a blue car.
(d) I'll see you at five.
(e) Would you like tea?

Pragmatic markers

We use the term 'pragmatic marker' (see Fraser, 1996) as an umbrella term for a number of items that occur outside the clause. They operate more at a discourse level than at a grammatical level. While they may have low syntactic or semantic value, they have high pragmatic value. Carter and McCarthy (2006) include three distinct areas under this term:

discourse markers, interactional markers and response tokens. Items which variously fall into these categories, such as *well, however, anyway, right, you know, I see, really, okay,* share the fact that they are small but very frequently used words. Much debate has abounded over the years as to the definition and categorisation of these items; see, for instance, Blakemore (1987, 1992), Brinton (1996), Fraser (1988, 1990, 1996), Redeker (1990, 1991) and Schiffrin (1987). Fraser (1990) proposes that the non-propositional part of sentence meaning can be called a pragmatic marker. He points out that these markers, taken as separate and distinct from the propositional content of the sentence (or utterance), are the linguistically encoded clues which signal the speaker's potential communicative intentions. Hence, we can also look at these items as having acquired pragmatic specialisations as markers at discourse level rather than sentence or clause level (that is outside of the propositional content). For example, in extract 8.1 below from a conversation between two teachers (from the BNC), we can see the pragmatic markers in bold. The extract would be grammatically and semantically complete without the pragmatic markers. On paper, some would argue that it would be neater and tidier without them. However, in real-time they are pragmatically essential to the interaction:

(8.1)

A: You're looking at three weeks before you've got all them round. And you've only got six weeks left to kind of do anything for any of the kids.

B: **Yeah. Yeah. Well I mean** this is the last time I'm gonna do any group work with them.

A: **So** what happened anyway in [name of class]? You haven't told me about what happened in that lesson.

B: **Right. Erm** they came in and I said 'You four you're sitting separately remember'. And they instantly went to sit together.

A: **Mm**.

B: I said 'No. You're sitting separately'. **So** they moved. **And then** I said 'But not very far away'. I said 'Well it doesn't matter cos I'm moving you all into groups in a minute'.

A: **Mhm**.

B: **Right. So I erm** explained what we were gonna do and they all was like 'Yeah yeah. That's that's fine'. I thought 'Oh it is gonna be a good lesson'.

A: **Mm**.

B: And **erm then** I put them all in groups. And Michael decided that that was it. He wasn't gonna look at me. He wasn't gonna talk to me. He wasn't gonna do anything because he was with two girls that he didn't wanna be with and that was it. And then the others were either disrupting their group or doing the same. Just not talking to anyone in the group. And not participating . . .

(BNC)

Pragmatic markers: discourse markers

In the language classroom, discourse markers are given reasonable coverage in terms of formal written contexts. Typically, items such as evaluative, viewpoint and linking adverbs feature in textbook material for English for Academic Purposes (EAP), with a particular focus on linking adverbs:

> evaluative adverbs: *strangely, oddly*
> viewpoint adverbs: *personally, professionally*
> linking adverbs: *however, consequently.*

The main function of discourse markers is to organise stretches of text or conversation. They have many micro-functions which learners can be made aware of. Though the main textbook focus is on their function in a written text, they are pervasive in speaking and add greatly to the discourse repertoire of a learner in terms of oral fluency. Table 8.4 illustrates some of the core functions of discourse markers in speaking (discourse markers are marked in bold).

Table 8.4 Examples of discourse markers (in bold) and their core functions in speaking

Function	Example from a corpus
Marking openings	🗣 [Context: at the beginning of a politics lecture] **A: Okay so.** Anybody paying any attention to the US election? **B:** Yeah. **A:** Yeah? Any news so far? <div align="right">(LIBEL)</div>
Marking closings	🗣 [Context: the end of a radio phone-in call. A is the caller and B is the presenter] **A:** ... here's another one of these tourists coming again you know give them a wide berth and perhaps we'd be nice nicer to them you know. **B: Right okay. Okay** all sorts of spin off benefits **okay listen** Brian thank you very much indeed for talking to us. **A: Right** you are Marian. **B:** All the best cheers bye bye. [Commercial Break] <div align="right">(LCIE)</div>
Marking the introduction of a new topic	🗣 [Context: referring to the refrigerator] **A:** No fresh meat goes on the bottom. **B: So** are you working on the tapes now at the moment? **C:** Yeah. This is my second one. <div align="right">(LCIE)</div>
Marking a move to a new part of a story or argument	🗣 **A:** ... she has a sister do you know what happened her sister? **B:** No **A:** The sister was doing all the same subjects that Kathryn is doing except the sister was made do biology instead of accounting as Mrs Finn has a thing that everyone has to do a science subject right. **B:** Right.

Table 8.4 Continued

Function	Example from a corpus
	A: So anyway her sister hated biology blah blah blah anyway her sister is now working as an accountant but she hasn't got her degree in accounting so she going to school at night time you know to become an accountant . . . (LCIE)
Focusing on or emphasising a topic	🗣 [Context: a student asking a question in an accountancy class] **A:** Oh is that it I thought you said to direct. **So** you're changing the direct debit from our account to the company account? (LIBEL)
To mark a return to an earlier topic after an interruption or digression	🗣 [Context: a family talking. A is the daughter, B is the father and C is the mother] **A:** That's the tart Dad. Will you have some of that now? I'll give you some of that with your tea so. **B:** Oh no. I won't have any of it. No. **C:** Did you ever have blueberries Jim? **B:** Never. **C:** You did. Anyway I got them in Roches. **B:** Why did you ask me so? **C:** Cos I thought you would have long ago. Would they not grow on the bushes? **B:** Oh them kind of berries? Blackberries you mean? **B:** I don't know like. I haven't a clue like. **C:** I'm only asking you. **B:** I don't remember them. **C: Anyway** they're nice. I got them there for a recipe in a book. (LCIE)
Marking the sequence of items in a list	🗣 [Context: a caller to a radio phone-in programme near the end of his call] **A:** And **finally** I think that we have to recognise that the main bottle necks in Irish society today are bottle necks in Irish government. The government is responsible for the road services . . . (LCIE)

Pragmatic markers: interactional markers

Interactional markers, most typically items such as *you know (what I mean)*, *I mean*, *you see*, *the thing is*, are a central feature of conversation. As noted by Carter and McCarthy (2006), their main function is as monitors, on the part of the speaker, of the ongoing delivery of speech. Hence, they are very much listener-oriented devices. The speaker uses them in an attempt to make the message clearer and to mark what is shared as well as what is new information. In terms of broaching these items in the classroom, they have quite explicit functions so they can be the focus of awareness building tasks. Table 8.5 lists some of the typical functions and the markers which are most associated with each.

Table 8.5 Examples of interactional markers (in bold) and their functions

Function	Corpus example with typical marker(s)
Making something clearer	**A:** Have you ever come across a book by General Tom McEoin? **B:** I might have yeah **A:** Ah **I mean** he is well he's more or less a poet. <div align="right">(LCIE)</div>
Expanding on a point	[Context: from a radio phone-in] **A:** ... Why are they so untouchable these people? **B:** Well **I mean** the judges are judges you know. They sit up on benches. **C:** They're like Gods. <div align="right">(LCIE)</div>
Correcting what has been said	**A:** She's gone to Geneva. **I mean** Zurich. I always confuse Geneva and Zurich. <div align="right">(LCIE)</div>
Marking what the speaker assumes to be shared (or old) information for the listener	**A:** ... the keynote speaker on the Sunday is always someone very prestigious. They had Robert Fisk one year. **You know** the famous middle-east correspondent and so on. And they had amm I forget who they had this year ... <div align="right">(LIBEL)</div>
Marking what the speaker hopes the listener will agree with	[Context: Bolton Wanderers is the name of a British football team] **A:** Bolton Wanderers are a team down at the very bottom they lose four games in one month that's their season over. Therefore they have **you know what I mean** their attendance will drop sharply. So therefore you've got to kind of even this one example **you know what I mean** that even that one example it would point out both grounds both grounds are in the same industry. They're both doing the exact same thing but one factor will affect one small factor will affect one rather than the other. <div align="right">(LIBEL)</div>
Marking what the speaker assumes is new information for the listener	**A:** ... and you're almost half way to winning the ah the presidency by taking these three states. But **the thing is** that in each state it's it's the votes within the state that count. <div align="right">(LIBEL)</div>

Sample task J

The following concordance lines contain examples of *I mean* from the LIBEL corpus. Examine each line and decide which of the following functions it is being used for in each case.

(1) Making something clearer
(2) Correcting what has been said
(3) Expanding a point

Example	Making something clearer	Correcting what has been said	Expanding a point
1. . . . if you don't use commas it's more difficult to understand. **I mean** a comma is like a small stop. So if you're speaking . . .			
2. . . . and that isn't just words from my mouth which wouldn't be good enough. **I mean** the British Medical Journal, the Lancet, backs the legalisation of it.			
3. But always if your sentence is quite long then you must have a comma. Now **I mean** you can always use a comma in all of your writing whether it's long or not . . .			
4. Am what tense is gone? **I mean** it exists but it's not right here. What would it be?			
5. . . . why should that be so? **I mean** a self-employed person doesn't have courses of that kind offered to him by anybody . . .			
6. There are Irish movies that are made in Ireland with Irish money but there are very few of them. **I mean** most of them still have to get money from the B B C or Channel four.			
7. When we divide it up into sentences **I mean** sorry paragraphs . . .			

Pragmatic markers: response tokens

Response tokens refer to the short utterances, such as *mm, mmhmm, yeah, oh really, that's a pity* etc. and non-verbal surrogates such as head nods and shoulder shrugs that listeners utter or make by way of response to what a speaker is saying. They have been given extensive coverage in research literature over the years (Fries, 1952; Kendon, 1967; Yngve, 1970; Maynard, 1989, 1990, 1997; Tottie, 1991; Drummond and Hopper, 1993a, 1993b; McCarthy, 2002; Gardner, 2002; O'Keeffe and Adolphs, 2008). According to Kendon (1967), these signals are produced by the listener as an accompaniment to a speaker. Kendon suggests that the speaker relies to some degree upon these signals for guidance as to how the message is being received by the listerner(s). In extract 8.2 below, from a radio phone-in, we see how the use of the word *yeah* by the presenter functions to signal to the caller that she should continue telling her story.

(8.2) [Context: an elderly caller to a radio phone-in explains how, when she was young, a local woman used to do home ear-piercing, using a thick darning needle, olive oil, some string and a cork]

Caller:	The way this was done was a Scottish lady who lived across the road from us.
Presenter:	**Yeah**.
Caller:	And she would soak some grey wool. A length of grey wool in a saucer with olive oil.
Presenter:	**Yeah**.
Caller:	And then she'd thread it through an extremely large darning needle.
Presenter:	**Yeah**.
Caller:	Then there was a cork held together ... and she just threaded the needle with the wool straight through your ear and into the cork ...

(LCIE)

As we can see from this example, the presenter wants to signal that she is listening and that she wants the caller to continue telling her story, but she does not want to take over the speaking turn (or the 'floor'). Tottie aptly refers to these tokens as functioning to 'grease the wheels of the conversation' while not constituting a 'claim to take over the turn' (1991: 255).

McCarthy (2002) and O'Keeffe *et al.* (2007), among others, argue for the importance of introducing learners to these items. They see them as key vocabulary items for fluency in oral communication. It is important to remember that these items exist in all languages so language learners will not find them unusual. They are best treated as vocabulary items, as these sample tasks illustrate:

Sample task K

Use some of the following words and phrases in response to what is said below:

great news!	how about that!	how scary!	quite	perfect	of course
right	absolutely	great	cool	definitely	certainly
sounds great!	me too	sure	true	wonderful	lucky for you!
oh no!	too bad!	exactly	wow	excellent	fine
gosh	lovely	really	good		

(a) This weather is just great!
(b) My sister is getting married next week.
(c) I love this soup.
(d) There was a terrible accident here last year.
(e) He's been offered a new job.

Sample task L

Look at the following extracts from real conversations from LCIE. What is the function of the following responses in each extract: *That's a lot, That's amazing, Oh that's awful, That's bad*

[Context: a mother and daughter talking about a local lottery draw]
Daughter: How much did you say the Lotto was worth this week, Mom?
Mother: Nearly a hundred.
Daughter: **That's a lot.**
Mother: Tis I suppose. That's the last one in a while.

[Context: two friends chatting. Cherry Orchard is a football club]
A: ... and ah Cherry Orchard are able to go out and have trials at the start of the year they could have forty or fifty coming to trials and pick the best twenty so+
B: **That's amazing.**
A: +for us to take a team like that is unreal really.

[Context: two friends talking about a car accident]
A: And did he die?
B: No the child the baby girl died.
C: Oh she was lovely.
B: She was in the car with him?
A: Yeah she was. No she was in the other car.
B: Oh and the mother of that child that died is pregnant again is it?
A: Yeah sure it's little consolation now.
B: **Oh that's awful.**

[Context: two friends gossiping about another friend's boyfriend]
A: ... he's such a miserable fella. He'd get her to pay if they stayed in a hotel and she paid her half of the hotel and he paid his half
B: **That's bad**.
A: He wouldn't pay the hotel.

8.5 CONCLUSION

In this chapter we have just looked at the area of pragmatics and language teaching. There is scope to write much more on areas such as figurative language and creativity and speech act development. In the interest of concision, we have limited our focus to politeness by way of illustration as to what can be done, especially in how real language can be used in tasks. Another important point we have not raised here is how we can appraise pragmatic competence and also the issue of whether it should become part of assessment programmes and international examinations. Cohen (2004a) discusses the assessment of speech acts and surveys many attempts to address it in language teaching. He notes that the question still arises – despite an ever-growing body of work on speech acts – as to whether we really know enough about speech acts to be able to adequately assess them in terms of performance in a language classroom. Many of the points Cohen raises ring true for other aspects of pragmatics too, which have been illustrated here as 'teachable items'. He notes that the problem is that 'sociocultural and sociolinguistic behaviour are by their very nature variable . . . there will be few "right" and "wrong" responses, but rather tendencies in one direction or another' (ibid: 322).

Most fundamental of all is the need for pragmatics to be a core part of language teacher education programmes. If pragmatics is to become more central to language teaching, it is going to have to be given more focus (see Vásquez and Sharpless, 2009). Just as teachers of a foreign language are equipped with know-how in relation to the vocabulary and grammar of the language which they are going to teach, so too they need to be made aware of the core concepts of pragmatics and in particular they need to have an awareness of how pragmatic norms differ between languages.

As we come to the end of the book, we hope to have covered the canon of concepts in the area of pragmatics in a way that puts them in context. We have tried to illuminate theory with actual use. This can prove a messy enterprise because real language is not neat and tidy. Real spoken language happens in real time and between real people who are constantly attending to how their message will be received by their listener(s).

8.6 FURTHER READING

Bardovi-Harlig, K. and **Mahan-Taylor, R.** (eds) (2003b) *Teaching Pragmatics.* Washington, DC: United States Department of State.
A wide-ranging volume containing 30 papers on a range of aspects relating to the teaching of pragmatics. The papers divide under five themes: awareness, conversational management, conversation openings and closings, requests, and assorted speech acts. The book is very suited to teacher education programmes as it is very practical and is not theory-heavy. It goes into detail on many basic aspects of interaction in a range of contexts, such as polite ways of correcting and contradicting, making contrasts, keeping a conversation going, complaining successfully in service encounters, among others.

Carter, R. and **McCarthy, M**. (2006) *Cambridge Grammar of English: A Comprehensive Guide to Spoken and Written English Grammar and Usage.* Cambridge: Cambridge University Press.
The opening chapters of this book are entitled 'Spoken language' and 'Grammar and discourse' respectively, and address many areas core to pragmatics. It is a milestone to see them not only in a major grammar of English but also placed at the start of the book before moving on to the more traditional grammatical areas such as *word and phrase classes*. The chapters cover pragmatic markers particularly well but also turn to structure and organisation, hedging, vague language, deixis, the pragmatics of address in English, among other areas. Speech acts are also addressed in the book under the generic heading of 'Notions and functions'.

Cohen, A. (2004) 'Assessing speech acts in a second language', in D. Boxer and A. D. Cohen (eds), *Studying Speaking to Inform Second Language Learning.* Clevedon, England: Multilingual Matters.

Roever, C. (2004) 'Difficulty and practicality in tests of interlanguage pragmatics', in D. Boxer and A. D. Cohen (eds), *Studying Speaking to Inform Second Language Learning*. Clevedon, England: Multilingual Matters.

Two important chapters from the same volume. They deal with the under-addressed topic of assessment of speech acts in language learning. Roever's chapter also provides a very useful survey of existing attempts to assess speech acts as well as an appraisal of the difficulties faced in this area. Much of what is said here has relevance for all aspects of teaching pragmatics. Cohen's paper goes into greater depth on the challenges of assessing speech acts and offers many practical suggestions.

References

Adolphs, S. (2006) *Introducing Electronic Text Analysis: A Practical Guide for Language and Literary Studies*. London and New York: Routledge.

— (2008) *Corpus and Context: Investigating Pragmatic Functions in Spoken Discourse*. Amsterdam: John Benjamins.

Adolphs, S., Atkins, S. and Harvey, K. (2007) 'Caught between professional requirements and interpersonal needs: vague language in health care contexts', in J. Cutting (ed.), *Vague Language Explored*. Basingstoke: Palgrave.

Adolphs, S., Crawford, P., Brown, B., Sahota, O. and Carter, R. (2004) 'Applying corpus linguistics in a health care context', *International Journal of Applied Linguistics* 1(1): 44–9.

Aijmer, K. (1996) *Conversational Routines in English*. London: Longman.

— (2002) *English Discourse Particles*. Amsterdam: John Benjamins.

Aijmer, K. and Simon-Vandenbergen, A. M. (eds) (2006) *Pragmatic Markers in Contrast*. Oxford: Elsevier.

Alcón Soler, A. (2005) 'Does instruction work for learning pragmatics in the EFL context?', *System* 33: 417–35.

Amador Moreno, C., O'Riordan, S. and Chambers, A. (2006) 'Integrating a corpus of classroom discourse in language teacher education: the case of discourse markers', *ReCALL* 18: 83–104.

Anderson, W. and Corbett, J. (2009) *Exploring English with Online Corpora: An Introduction*. Basingstoke, Hampshire: Palgrave Macmillan.

Argaman, E. (2007) 'With or without "it": the role of empathetic deixis in mediating educational change', *Journal of Pragmatics* 39: 1591–1607.

Atkins, S., Clear, J. and Ostler, N. (1992) 'Corpus design criteria', *Literary and Linguistic Computing* 7(1): 1–16.

Atkinson, J. M. (1979) 'Sequencing and shared attentiveness to court proceedings', in G. Psathas (ed.), *Everyday Language: Studies in Ethnomethodology*. New York: Irvington.

Atkinson, J. M. and Drew, P. (1979) *Order in Court: The Organization of Verbal Interaction in Judicial Settings*. London: Macmillan.

Austin, J. L. (1962) *How to Do Things with Words*. Oxford: Clarendon Press.

Baker, P. (2006) *Using Corpora in Discourse Analysis*. London: Continuum.

Bakhtin, M. M. (1986) *Speech Genres and Other Late Essays*. Trans. Vern W. McGee. Austin, TX: University of Texas Press.

Bardovi-Harlig, K. (2001) 'Evaluating the empirical evidence: grounds for instruction in pragmatics?', in K. Rose and G. Kasper (eds), *Pragmatics in Language Teaching*. London: Routledge.

Bardovi-Harlig, K. and Dörnyei, Z. (1998) 'Do language learners recognise pragmatic violations? Pragmatic versus grammatical awareness in instructed L2 learning', *TESOL Quarterly*, 32(2): 233–59.

Bardovi-Harlig, K. and Griffin, R. (2005) 'L2 pragmatic awareness: evidence from the ESL classroom', *System* 33: 401–15.

Bardovi-Harlig, K. and Hartford, B. (1993) 'Learning the rules of academic talk: a longitudinal study of pragmatic development', *Studies in Second Language Acquisition* 15: 279–304.

Bardovi-Harlig, K. and Mahan-Taylor, R. (2003a) *Introduction to Teaching Pragmatics*. Available online: <http://exchanges. state.gov/englishteaching/forum/archives/docs/03–41–3-h. pdf> (accessed 18 June 2009).

— (eds) (2003b) *Teaching Pragmatics*. Washington, DC: United States Department of State.

Bardovi-Harlig, K. and Salsbury, T. (2004) 'The organization of turns in the disagreements of L2 learners: a longitudinal perspective', in D. Boxer and A. Cohen (eds), *Studying Speaking to Inform Second Language Learning*. Clevedon: Multilingual Matters.

Bargiela-Chappini, F. (2003) 'Face and politeness: new (insights) for old (concepts)', *Journal of Pragmatics* 35: 1453–69.

Barron, A. (2003) *Acquisition in Interlanguage Pragmatics. Learning How to do Things with Words in a Study Abroad Context.* Amsterdam: John Benjamins.

— (2005) 'Offering in Ireland and England', in A. Barron and K. P. Schneider (eds), *The Pragmatics of Irish English*. Berlin/New York: Mouton de Gruyter.

Barron, A. and K. Schneider (eds) (2005) *The Pragmatics of Irish English*. Berlin: Mouton de Gruyter.

Beard, F. K. (2008) 'Advertising and audience offense: the role of intentional humor', *Journal of Marketing Communications* 14(1): 1–17.

Beebe, L. M. and Cummings, M. C. (1996) 'Natural speech act data versus written questionnaire data: how data collection method affects speech act performance', in S. M. Gass, and N. Joyce (eds), *Speech Acts across Cultures: Challenges to Communication in a Second Language*. Berlin: Mouton de Gruyter.

Beebe, L. and Zhang Waring, H. (2004) 'The linguistic encoding of pragmatic tone: adverbials as words that work', in D. Boxer and A. Cohen (eds), *Studying Speaking to Inform Language Learning*. Clevedon: Multilingual Matters.

Beebe, L., Takahashi, T. and Uliss-Weltz, R. (1990) 'Pragmatic transfer in ESL refusals', in R. Scarcella, E. Andersen and S. Krashen (eds), *Developing Communicative Competence in a Second Language*. New York: Newbury House.

Belz, J. (2007) 'The role of computer mediation in the instruction and development of L2 pragmatic competence', *Annual Review of Applied Linguistics* 27: 45–75.

Belz, J. and Vyatkina, N. (2005) 'Learner corpus analysis and the development of L2 pragmatic competence in networked inter-cultural language study: the case of German modal particles', *Canadian Modern Language Review* 62(1): 17–48.

Bergman, M. and Kasper, G. (1993) 'Perception and performance in native and non-native apology', in G. Kasper and S. Blum-Kulka (eds), *Interlanguage Pragmatics*. Oxford: Oxford University Press.

Berry, M. (1981) 'Systemic linguistics and discourse analysis: a multi-layered approach to exchange structure', in M. Coulthard and M. Montgomery (eds), *Studies in Discourse Analysis*. London: Routledge.

Biber, D. (1988) *Variation across Speech and Writing*. Cambridge: Cambridge University Press.

— (1993) 'Representativeness in corpus design', *Literary and Linguistic Computing* 8(4): 243–57.

— (1995) *Dimensions of Register Variation: A Cross-Linguistic Comparison*. Cambridge: Cambridge University Press

Biber, D. and Conrad, S. (1999) 'Lexical bundles in conversation and academic pros', in H. Hasselgard and S. Oksefjell (eds), *Out of Corpora: Studies in Honor of Stig Johansson*. Amsterdam: Rodopi.

— (2009) *Register, Genre, and Style*. Cambridge: Cambridge University Press.

Biber, D. and Finegan, E. (eds) (1994) *Sociolinguistic Perspectives on Register*. New York: Oxford University Press.

Biber, D., Conrad, S. and Reppen, R. (1998) *Corpus Linguistics: Investigating Language Structure and Use*. Cambridge: Cambridge University Press.

Biber, D., Johansson, S., Leech, G., Conrad, S. and Finegan, E. (1999) *The Longman Grammar of Spoken and Written English*. London: Longman.

Billmyer, K. and Varghese, M. (2000) 'Investigating instrument-based pragmatic variability: effects of enhancing discourse completion tests', *Applied Linguistics* 21(4): 517–52.

Binchy, J. (2000) *Relational Language and Politeness in Southern-Irish Service Encounters*. Unpublished MA dissertation, University of Limerick.

Bird, C. (2005) 'How I stopped dreading and learned to love transcription', *Qualitative Inquiry* 11: 226–48.

Blakemore, D. (1987) *Semantic Constraints on Relevance*. Oxford: Blackwell.

— (1992) *Understanding Utterances*. Oxford: Blackwell.

Blum-Kulka, S. (1982) 'Learning to say what you mean in a second language: a study of speech act performance of learners of Hebrew as a second language', *Applied Linguistics* 3: 29–59.

— (1989) 'Playing it safe: the role of conventionality and indirectness', in S. Blum-Kulka, J. House and G. Kasper (eds), *Cross-Cultural Pragmatics: Requests and Apologies*. Norwood, NJ: Ablex.

— (1997) *Dinner Talk: Cultural Patterns of Sociability and Socialisation in Family Discourse*. London: Lawrence Erlbaum.

Blum-Kulka, S. and Olshtain, E. (1984) 'Requests and apologies: a cross-cultural study of speech act realization patterns CCSARP', *Applied Linguistics* 5: 196–213.

Blum-Kulka, S., House, J. and Kasper, G. (eds) (1989) *Cross-Cultural Pragmatics: Requests and Apologies*. Norwood: Ablex.

Bollobás, E. (2007) 'Performing texts/performing readings: a pragmatic understanding of the revisionist interpretation of American literature', *Journal of Pragmatics* 39(12): 2332–44.

Botley, S. and McEnery, T. (2001) 'Demonstratives in English: a corpus-based study', *Journal of English Linguistics* 29(1): 7–33.

Bousfield, D. (2008) *Impoliteness in Interaction*. Amsterdam: John Benjamins.

Boxer, D. (1993) 'Complaints as positive strategies: what the learner needs to know', *TESOL Quarterly* 27(2): 277–99.

— (2002) 'Discourse issues in cross-cultural pragmatics', *Annual Review of Applied Linguistics* 22: 150–67.

Boxer, D. and Cohen, A. (eds) (2004) *Studying Speaking to Inform Second Language Learning*. Clevedon, England: Multilingual Matters.

Brinton, L. J. (1996) *Pragmatic Markers in English: Grammaticalization and Discourse Functions*. Berlin: Mouton de Gruyter.

Brown, G. and Yule, G. (1983) *Discourse Analysis*. Cambridge: Cambridge University Press.

Brown, P. and Levinson S. (1978) 'Universals in language usage: politeness phenomena', in E. Goody (ed.), *Questions and Politeness: Strategies in Social Interaction*. Cambridge: Cambridge University Press.

— (1987) *Politeness: Some Universals in Language Usage*. Cambridge: Cambridge University Press.

Bühler, K. (1934) *Sprachtheorie*. Jena: Fisher (reprinted Stuttgart: Fisher, 1965).

Burton, D. (1981) 'Analysing spoken discourse', in M. Coulthard and M. Montgomery (eds), *Studies in Discourse Analysis*. London: Routledge

Caballero, R. (2007) 'Manner-of-motion verbs in wine description', *Journal of Pragmatics* 39(12): 2095–2114.

Cameron, D. and Hills, D. (1990) '"Listening in": negotiating relationships between listeners and presenters on radio phone-in programmes', in G. McGregor and R. White (eds), *Reception and Response: Hearer Creativity and the Analysis of Spoken and Written Texts*. London: Routledge & Kegan Paul.

Cameron, L. and Deignan, A. (2003) 'Combining large and small corpora to investigate tuning devices around metaphor in spoken language', *Metaphor and Symbol* 18(3): 149–60.

Carter, R. and McCarthy, M. (1997) *Exploring Spoken English*. Cambridge: Cambridge University Press.

— (1999) 'The English *get*-passive in spoken discourse: description and implication for an interpersonal grammar', *English Language and Literature* 3(1): 41–58.

— (2006) *Cambridge Grammar of English: A Comprehensive Guide to Spoken and Written Grammar and Usage*. Cambridge: Cambridge University Press.

Celce-Murcia, M. and Olshtain, E. (2000) *Discourse and Context in Language Teaching: A Guide for Language Teachers*. Cambridge: Cambridge University Press.

Chang, P. (2002) 'Who's behind the personal pronouns in talk radio? Cartalk: a case study', in A. Sánchez Macarro (ed.), *Windows on the World: Media Discourse in English*. Valencia: University of Valencia Press.

Charteris-Black, J. (2004a) *Corpus Approaches to Critical Metaphor Analysis*. Basingstoke: Palgrave-MacMillan.

— (2004b) 'Why "an angel rides in the whirlwind and directs the storm": a corpus-based comparative study of metaphor in British and American political discourse', in K. Aijmer and B. Altenberg (eds), *Advances in Corpus Linguistics: Papers from the 23rd International Conference on English Language Research on Computerized Corpora (ICAME 23)*. Amsterdam: Rodopi.

— (2006) 'Britain as a container: immigration metaphors in the 2005 Election Campaign', *Discourse and Society* 17(6): 563–82.

Charteris-Black, J., Seale, C. and Ziebland, S. (2006) 'Gender, cancer experience and internet use: a comparative keyword analysis of interviews and online cancer support groups', *Social Science and Medicine* 62: 2577–90.

Chen, H. J. (1996) 'Cross-cultural comparison of English and Chinese metapragmatics in refusal', ERIC document reproduction service (No. ED 408 860).

Cheng, W. (2003) *Intercultural Conversation*. Amsterdam: John Benjamins.

Cheng, W. and Warren, M. (2007) 'Checking understanding: comparing textbooks and a corpus of spoken English in Hong Kong', *Language Awareness* 16(3), 190–207.

Cheng, W., Greaves, C. and Warren, M. (2008) *A Corpus-driven Study of Discourse Intonation: The Hong Kong Corpus of Spoken English (Prosodic)*. Amsterdam: John Benjamins.

Christie, C. (2000) *Gender and Language: Towards a Feminist Pragmatics*. Edinburgh: Edinburgh University Press.

Clancy, B. (2005) '*You're fat. You'll eat them all*. Politeness strategies in family discourse', in K. P. Schneider and A. Barron (eds), *The Pragmatics of Irish English*. Berlin: Mouton de Gruyter.

— (2010) '*Hurry up baby son all the boys is finished their breakfast*: a socio-pragmatic analysis of Irish settled and Traveller family discourse', unpublished thesis, Mary Immaculate College/University of Limerick.

Clemen, G. (1997) 'The concept of hedging: origins, approaches and definitions', in R. Markkanen and H. Schröder (eds), *Hedging and Discourse: Approaches to the Analysis of a Pragmatic Phenomenon in Academic Texts*. Berlin: Mouton de Gruyter.

Clift, R. (1999) 'Irony in conversation', *Language in Society* 28: 523–53.

Cohen, A. (1996) 'Speech acts', in S. L. McKay and N. H. Hornberger (eds), *Sociolinguistics and Language Teaching*. Cambridge: Cambridge University Press.

— (2004a) 'Assessing speech acts in a second language', in D. Boxer and A. Cohen (eds), *Studying Speaking to Inform Second Language Learning*. Clevedon, England: Multilingual Matters.

— (2004b) 'The interface between interlanguage pragmatics and assessment', paper presented at The Interface between Interlanguage, Pragmatics and Assessment: Proceedings of the 3rd Annual JALT Pan-SIG Conference, Tokyo, 22–23 May 2004. Available online: http://jalt.org/pansig/2004/HTML/Cohen.htm (accessed 26 July 2010).

— (2008) 'Teaching and assessing L2 pragmatics: what can we expect from learners?' *Language Teaching* 41(2), 213–35.

Cook, G. (1994) *Discourse and Literature*. Oxford: Oxford University Press.

— (2007) '"This we have done": the vagueness of poetry and public relations', in J. Cutting (ed.), *Vague Language Explored*. Basingstoke: Palgrave.

Cotterill, J. (2003) *Language and Power in Court: A Linguistic Analysis of the O. J. Simpson Trial*. Basingstoke: Palgrave.

— (2007) '"I think he was kind of shouting or something": uses and abuses of vagueness in the British courtroom', in J. Cutting (ed.), *Vague Language Explored*. Basingstoke: Palgrave.

Coulmas, F. (1979) 'On the sociolinguistic relevance of routine formulae', *Journal of Pragmatics* 3: 239–66.

Cowie, A. P. (1988) 'Stable and creative aspects of vocabulary use', in R. Carter and M. McCarthy (eds), *Vocabulary and Language Teaching*. London: Longman.

Crandall, E. and Basturkmen, H. (2004) 'Evaluating pragmatics-focused materials', *ELT Journal* 58(1): 38–49.

Crystal, D. (1985) *A Dictionary of Linguistics and Phonetics*. Oxford: Blackwell.

Culpeper, J. (1996) 'Towards an anatomy of impoliteness', *Journal of Pragmatics* 25: 349–67.

— (2005) 'Impoliteness and *The Weakest Link*', *Journal of Politeness Research* 1(1): 35–72.

Culpeper, J., Bousfield, D. and Wichmann, A. (2003) 'Impoliteness revisited: with special reference to dynamic and prosodic aspects', *Journal of Pragmatics* 35: 1545–79.

Cutting, J. (ed.) (2007) *Vague Language Explored*. Basingstoke: Palgrave.

— (2008) *Pragmatics and Discourse*. London: Routledge.

Dahlmann, I. and Adolphs, S. (2009) 'Spoken corpus analysis: multi-modal approaches to language description', in P. Baker (ed.), *Contemporary Approaches to Corpus Linguistics*. London: Continuum Press.

Danielsson, P. (2003) 'Automatic extraction of meaningful units from corpora: a corpus-driven approach using the word *stroke*', *International Journal of Corpus Linguistics* 8(1): 109–27.

Davies, B. (2007) 'Grice's cooperative principle: meaning and rationality', *Journal of Pragmatics* 39(12): 2308–31.

Demeter, G. (2007) 'Role-plays as a data collection method for research on apology speech acts', *Simulation and Gaming* 38(1): 83–90.

Diessel, H. (1999) *Demonstratives: Form, Function and Grammaticalization*. Amsterdam: John Benjamins.

Downing, A. (2006) 'The English pragmatic marker *surely* and its functional counterparts in Spanish', in K. Aijmer and A. M. Simon-Vandenbergen (eds), *Pragmatic Markers in Contrast*. Oxford: Elsevier.

Drew, P. and Chilton, K. (2000) 'Calling just to keep in touch: regular and habitual telephone calls as an environment for small talk', in J. Coupland (ed.), *Small Talk*. London: Longman.

Drummond, K. and Hopper, R. (1993a) 'Some uses of *yeah*', *Research on Language and Social Interaction* 26: 203–312.

— (1993b) 'Backchannels revisited: acknowledgement tokens and speakership incipiency', *Research on Language and Social Interaction* 26: 157–77.

Dufon, M., Kasper, G., Takahashi, S. and Yoshinaga, N. (1994) 'Bibliography on linguistic politeness', *Journal of Pragmatics* 21: 527–78.

Dunning, T. (1993) 'Accurate methods for the statistics of surprise and coincidence', *Computational Linguistics* 19(1): 61–74.

Durkheim, E. (1915) *The Elementary Forms of the Religious Life*. London: G. Allen and Unwin.

Eelen, G. (2001) *A Critique of Politeness Theories*. Manchester: St. Jerome.

Eisenstein, M. and Bodman, J. W. (1986) '"I very appreciate": expressions of gratitude by native and non-native speakers of American English', *Applied Linguistics* 7(2): 167–85.

— (1993) 'Expressing gratitude in American English', in G. Kasper and S. Blum-Kulka (eds), *Interlanguage Pragmatics*. Oxford: Oxford University Press

Ellis, R. (1990) *Instructed Second Language Acquisition*. Oxford: Blackwell.

— (1994) *The Study of Second Language Acquisition*. Oxford: Oxford University Press.

Erickson, F. and Schultz, J. (1982) *The Counsellor as Gatekeeper*. New York: Academic Press.

Evison, J. (2010) 'What are the basics of analysing a corpus?', in A. O'Keeffe and M. McCarthy (eds), *The Routledge Handbook of Corpus Linguistics*. London: Routledge.

Evison, J., McCarthy M. and O'Keeffe A. (2007) '"Looking out for love and all the rest of it": vague category markers as shared social space', in J. Cutting (ed.), *Vague Language Explored*. Basingstoke: Palgrave.

Farr, F. (2005) 'Relational strategies in the discourse of professional performance review in an Irish academic environment: the case of language teacher education', in K. P. Schneider and A. Barron (eds), *The Pragmatics of Irish English*. Berlin: Mouton de Gruyter.

— (2007) 'Engaged listenership in spoken academic discourse: the case of student–tutor meetings', in W. Teubert and R. Krishnamurthy (eds), *Corpus Linguistics: Critical Concepts in Linguistics*. London: Routledge.

Farr, F. and O'Keeffe, A. (2002) '*Would* as a hedging device in an Irish context: an intra-varietal comparison of institutionalised spoken interaction', in R. Reppen, S. Fitzmaurice and D. Biber (eds), *Using Corpora to Explore Linguistic Variation*. Amsterdam: John Benjamins.

Farr, F., Murphy B. and O'Keeffe, A. (2004) 'The Limerick Corpus of Irish English: design, description and application', *Teanga* 21: 5–30.

Fasold, R. (1990) *The Sociolinguistics of Language*. Oxford: Blackwell.

Félix-Brasdefer, J. C. (2003) 'Declining an invitation: a cross-cultural study of pragmatic strategies in American English and Latin American Spanish', *Multilingua* 22: 225–55.

Fernando, C. (1996) *Idioms and Idiomaticity*. Oxford: Oxford University Press.

Fillmore, C. (1997) *Lectures on Deixis*. Stanford, CA: CSLI Publications.

Finegan, E. and Biber, D. (1994) 'Register and social dialect variation: an integrated approach', in D. Biber and E. Finegan (eds), *Sociolinguistic Perspectives on Register*. Oxford: Oxford University Press.

Fraser, B. (1975) 'Hedged performatives', in P. Cole and J. Morgan (eds), *Syntax and Semantics, vol. 3, Speech Acts*. New York: Academic Press.

— (1988) 'Types of English discourse markers', *Acta Linguistica Hungarica* 38(1–4): 19–33.

— (1990) 'An approach to discourse markers', *Journal of Pragmatics* 14: 383–95.

— (1996) 'Pragmatic markers', *Pragmatics* 6(2): 167–90.

Fries, C. C. (1952) *The Structure of English*. New York: Harcourt, Brace.

Fung, L. and Carter R. (2007) 'Discourse markers and spoken English: native and learner use in pedagogic settings', *Applied Linguistics* 28(3): 410–39.

Gao, G. (1996) 'Self and other: a Chinese perspective on interpersonal relationships', *Journal of Pragmatics* 25: 1–32.

Gardner, R. (2002) *When Listeners Talk: Response Tokens and Listener Stance*. Amsterdam: John Benjamins.

Garside R. and Smith, N. (1997) 'A hybrid grammatical tagger: CLAWS4', in R. Garside, G. Leech and A. McEnery (eds), *Corpus Annotation*. London: Longman.

Gilmore, A. (2004) 'A comparison of textbook and authentic interactions', *ELT Journal* 58(4): 363–74.

Godard, D. (1977) 'Same setting, diffferent norms: phone call beginnings in France and the United States', *Language in Society* 6: 209–19.

Goffman, E. (1956) 'The nature of deference and demeanour', *American Anthropologist* 58: 473–502.

— (1959) *The Presentation of Self in Everyday Life*. New York: Doubleday.

— (1967) *Interaction Ritual: Essays in Face-to-Face Behaviour*. New York: Random House.

— (1981) *Forms of Talk*. Oxford: Basil Blackwell.

Golato, A. (2003) 'Studying compliment responses: a comparison of DCTs and recordings of naturally occurring talk', *Applied Linguistics* 21(1): 90–121.

Grant, L. and Starks, D. (2001) 'Screening appropriate teaching materials: closings from textbooks and television soap operas', *International Review of Applied Linguistics* 39: 39–50.

Greaves, C. and Warren, M. (2010) 'What can a corpus tell us about multi-word units?', in A. O'Keeffe and M. McCarthy (eds), *The Routledge Handbook of Corpus Linguistics*. London: Routledge.

Green, K. (1995) 'Deixis: a re-evaluation of concepts and categories', in K. Green (ed.), *New Essays in Deixis*. Amsterdam: Rodopi.

Grice, H. P. (1975) 'Logic and conversation', in P. Cole and J. Morgan (eds), *Syntax and Semantics, vol. 3, Speech Acts*. New York: Academic Press.

— (1989) *Studies in the Way of Words*. Harvard, MA: Harvard University Press.

Grundy, P. (2008) *Doing Pragmatics*, 3rd edn. London: Hodder Education.

Halliday, M. A. K. (1978). *Language as Social Semiotic: The Social Interpretation of Language and Meaning*. Maryland: University Park Press.

Halliday, M. and Hasan, R. (1976) *Cohesion in English*. London: Longman.

Halmari, H. (1993) 'Intercultural business telephone conversations: a case of Finns vs. Anglo-Americans', *Applied Linguistics* 14(4): 408–30.

Hammond, J. and Deriwianka, B. (2001) 'Genre', in R. Carter and D. Nunan (eds), *The Cambridge Guide to Teaching English to Speakers of Other Languages*. Cambridge: Cambridge University Press

Hanks, W. (1992) 'The indexical ground of deictic reference', in A. Duranti and C. Goodwin (eds), *Rethinking Context: Language as an Interactive Phenomenon*. Cambridge: Cambridge University Press.

Hartford, B. S. and Bardovi-Harlig, K. (1992) 'Experimental and observational data in the study of interlanguage pragmatics', in L. F. Bouton and Y. Kachru (eds), *Pragmatics and Language Learning*, vol. 3. University of Illinois, Urbana-Champaign: Division of English as an International Language.

Hasan, R. (1985) 'The structure of a text', in M. A. K. Halliday and R. Hasan (eds), *Language, Context, and Text: Aspects of Language in a Social-Semiotic Perspective*. Cambridge: Cambridge University Press.

— (1999) 'Speaking with reference to context', in M. Ghadessy (ed.), *Text and Context in Functional Linguistics*. Amsterdam: John Benjamins.

Hinkel, E. (1996) 'When in Rome: evaluations of L2 pragmalinguistic behaviors', *Journal of Pragmatics* 26(1): 51–70.

— (1997) 'Appropriateness of advice: DCT and multiple choice data', *Applied Linguistics* 18: 1–26.

— (1997) 'Indirectness in L1 and L2 academic writing', *Journal of Pragmatics* 27(3): 360–86.

— (2002) *Second Language Writers' Text*. New Jersey: Lawrence Erlbaum.

— (2004) *Teaching Academic ESL Writing: Practical Techniques in Vocabulary and Grammar*. New Jersey: Lawrence Erlbaum Associates.

— (2005) 'Hedging, inflating, and persuading in L2 academic writing', *Applied Language Learning* 14(2): 29–54.

Holmes, J. (1995) *Women, Men and Politeness*. London: Longman.

— (1998) 'Generic pronouns in the Wellington Corpus of spoken New Zealand English', *Kōtare* 1(1). Available online: <http://www. nzetc.org/tm/scholarly/tei-Whi011Kota-t1-g1-t5. html> (accessed 14 April 2010).

Hopper, R. (1989) 'Sequential ambiguity in telephone openings: "What are you doin"', *Communication Monographs* 56(3): 240–52.

— (1992) *Telephone Conversation*. Bloomington: Indiana University.

Hopper, R. and Drummond, K. (1992) 'Accomplishing interpersonal relationship: the telephone openings of strangers and intimates', *Western Journal of Communication* 56: 185–99.

Hopper, R., Doany, N., Johnson, M. and Drummond, K. (1991) 'Universals and particulars in telephone openings', *Research on Language and Social Interaction* 24: 369–87.

House, J. (1988) '"Oh excuse me please . . .": apologising in a foreign language', in B. Kettermann, P. Bierbaumer, A. Fill and A. Karpf (eds), *Englisch als Zweitsprache*. Tübingen: Narr.

House, J. and Kasper, G. (1981) 'Politeness markers in English and German', in F. Coulmas (ed.), *Conversational Routine: Explorations in Standardized Communication Situations and Prepatterned Speech*. The Hague: Mouton.

House-Edmondson, J. (1986) 'Cross-cultural pragmatics and foreign language learning', in K. Bausch, F. Königs and R. Kogelheide (eds), *Probleme und Perspektiven der Sprachlehrforsuchung*. Frankfurt am Main: Scriptor.

Huang, Y. (2007) *Pragmatics*. Oxford: Oxford University Press.

Hunston, S. and Francis, G. (2000) *Pattern Grammar: A Corpus-Driven Approach to the Lexical Grammar of English*. Amsterdam: John Benjamins.

Hutchby, I. (1991) 'The organisation of talk on talk radio', in P. Scannell (ed.), *Broadcast Talk*. London: Sage.

— (1996a) *Confrontation Talk: Arguments, Asymmetries, and Power on Talk Radio*. Mahwah, NJ: Lawrence Erlbaum Associates.

— (1996b) 'Power in discourse: the case of arguments on a British talk radio show', *Discourse and Society* 7(4): 481–97.

— (1999) 'Frame attunement and footing in the organisation of talk radio openings', *Journal of Sociolinguistics* 3(1): 41–63.

Hyland, K. (1994) 'Hedging in academic writing and EAP coursebooks', *English for Specific Purposes* 13(3): 239–56.

— (1996a) 'Writing without conviction? Hedging in science research articles', *Applied Linguistics* 17(4): 433–54.

— (1996b) 'Nurturing *hedges* in the ESP curriculum', *System* 24(4): 477–90.

— (1998) *Hedging in Scientific Research Articles*. Amsterdam: John Benjamins.

— (1999a) 'Academic attribution: citation and the construction of disciplinary knowledge', *Applied Linguistics* 20(3): 341–67.

— (1999b) 'Disciplinary discourses: writer stance in research articles', in C. N. Candlin and K. Hyland (eds), *Writing: Texts, Processes and Practices*. Harlow: Longman.

Hyland, K. and Milton, J. (1997) 'Hedging in L1 and L2 student writing', *Journal of Second Language Writing* 6: 183–206.

Hymes, D. (1972) 'Models of the interaction of language and social life', in J. Gumperz and D. Hymes (eds), *Directions in Sociolinguistics: The Ethnography of Communication*. Oxford: Blackwell.

— (1974) *Foundations of Sociolinguistics*. Philadelphia: University of Pennsylvania Press.

Ide, S. (1989) 'Formal forms and discernment: two neglected aspects of universals of linguistic politeness', *Multilingua* 8(2/3): 223–48.

Jautz, S. (2008) 'Gratitude in British and New Zealand radio programmes: nothing but gushing?', in K. Schneider and A. Barron (eds), *Variational Pragmatics: A Focus on Regional Varieties in Pluricentric Languages*. Amsterdam: John Benjamins.

Jeon, E. and Kaya, T. (2006) 'Effects of L2 instruction on interlanguage pragmatic development: a meta-analysis', in J. Norris and L. Ortega (eds), *Synthesising Research on Language Learning and Teaching*. Amsterdam: John Benjamins.

Jesperson, O. (1965) *The Philosophy of Grammar*. New York: Norton.

Jiang, X. (2006) 'Suggestions: what should ESL students know?', *System* 34: 36–54.

Johansson, S. (2006) 'How well can *well* be translated? On the English discourse particle *well* and its correspondences in Norwegian and German', in K. Aijmer and A. M. Simon-Vandenbergen (eds), *Pragmatic Markers in Contrast*. Oxford: Elsevier.

Jones, P. (1995) 'Philosophical and theoretical issues in the study of deixis: a critique of the standard account', in K. Green (ed.), *New Essays in Deixis*. Amsterdam, Rodopi.

Jucker, A. H. and Taavitsainen, I. (eds) (2008) *Speech Acts in the History of English*. Amsterdam: John Benjamins.

Jucker, A. H., Schreier, D. and Hundt, M. (eds) (2009) *Corpora: Pragmatics and Discourse*. Amsterdam/New York: Rodopi.

Jung, E. (2004) 'Interlanguage pragmatics, apology speech acts', in C. L. Moder and A. Martinovic-Zic (eds), *Discourse across Languages and Cultures*. Philadelphia: John Benjamins.

Kasper, G. (1990) 'Linguistic politeness', *Journal of Pragmatics* 14: 193–218.

— (2000) 'Data collection in pragmatics research', in H. Spencer-Oatey (ed.), *Culturally Speaking*. London: Continuum.

— (2001) 'Four perspectives on L2 pragmatic development', *Applied Linguistics* 22(4): 502–30.

Kasper, G. and Dahl, M. (1991) *Research Methods in Interlanguage Pragmatics*. Honolulu, HI: University of Hawaii Press.

Kasper, G. and Roever, C. (2005) 'Pragmatics in second language learning', in E. Hinkel (ed.), *Handbook of Research into Second Language Teaching and Learning*. London: Routledge.

Kasper, G. and Rose, K. (1999) 'Pragmatics and SLA', *Annual Review of Applied Linguistics* 19: 81–104.

— (2001) 'Pragmatics in language teaching', in K. Rose and G. Kasper (eds), *Pragmatics in Language Teaching*. London: Routledge.

— (2002) 'The role of instruction in learning second language pragmatics', *Language Learning* 52(1): 237–73.

Kendon, A. (1967) 'Some functions of gaze-direction in social interaction', *Acta Psychologia* 20: 22–63.

Kenning, M. M. (2010) 'What are parallel and comparable corpora and how can we use them?', in A. O'Keeffe and M. McCarthy (eds), *The Routledge Handbook of Corpus Linguistics*. London: Routledge.

Knight, D. and Adolphs, S., (2008) 'Multi-modal corpus pragmatics: the case of active listenership', in J. Romeo-Trillo (ed.), *Corpus and Pragmatics*. Berlin: Mouton de Gruyter.

Knight, D., Evans, D., Carter, R. and Adolphs, S. (2009). 'Redrafting corpus development methodologies: blueprints for 3rd generation "multimodal, multimedia" corpora', *Corpora* 4(1): 1–32.

Kochman, T. (1981) *Black and White Styles in Conflict.* Chicago: University of Chicago Press.

Koester A. (2007) '"About twelve thousand or so": vagueness in North American and UK offices', in J. Cutting (ed.), *Vague Language Explored.* Basingstoke: Palgrave.

Koike, D. and Pearson, L. (2005) 'The effect of instruction and feedback in the development of pragmatic competence', *System* 33: 481–501.

Konishi, K. and Tarone, E. (2004) 'English constructions used in compensatory strategies: baseline data for communicative EFL instruction', in D. Boxer and A. Cohen (eds), *Studying Speaking to Inform Language Learning.* Clevedon: Multilingual Matters.

Kotani, M. (2002) 'Expressing gratitude and indebtedness: Japanese speakers' use of "I'm sorry" in English conversation', *Research on Language and Social Interaction* 35(1): 39–72.

Kramsch, C. (1993) *Context and Culture in Language Teaching.* Oxford: Oxford University Press.

Kübler, N. and Aston, G. (2010) 'Using corpora in translation', in A. O'Keeffe and M. McCarthy (eds), *The Routledge Handbook of Corpus Linguistics.* London: Routledge.

Labov, W. (1972) *Language in the Inner City.* Philadelphia: University of Pennsylvania Press.

Lakoff, G. (1972) 'Hedges: a study in meaning criteria and the logic of fuzzy concepts', *Journal of Philosophical Logic* 2: 458–508.

Lakoff, R. (1973) 'The logic of politeness; or, minding your p's and q's', in *Papers from the Ninth Regional Meeting of the Chicago Linguistics Society.* Chicago: Chicago Linguistics Society.

—— (1974) 'Remarks on this and that', in M. Lagaly, R. Fox and A. Brook (eds), *Papers from the Tenth Regional Meeting of the Chicago Linguistic Society.* Chicago: Chicago Linguistic Society.

LeBaron, C. D. and Jones, S. E. (2002) 'Closing up closings: showing the relevance of the social and material surround to the completion of interaction', *Journal of Communication* 52(3): 542–65.

Lee, D. Y. W (2008) 'Bookmarks for corpus linguistics.' Available online: <http://personal. cityu.edu.hk/~davidlee/devotedtocorpora/CBLLinks.htm> (accessed 14 April 2010).

—— (2010) 'What corpora are available?', in A. O'Keeffe, and M. McCarthy (eds), *The Routledge Handbook of Corpus Linguistics.* London: Routledge.

Leech, G. (1983) *Principles of Pragmatics.* London: Longman.

—— (1999) 'The distribution and function of vocatives in American and British English conversation', in H. Hasselgård and S. Oksefjell (eds), *Out of Corpora: Studies in Honour of Stig Johansson.* Amsterdam: Rodopi.

Leech, G., Grayson, P. and Wilson, A. (2001a) *Word Frequencies in Written and Spoken English: Based on the British National Corpus.* London: Longman.

—— (2001b) *Word Frequencies in Written and Spoken English: Based on the British National Corpus.* Companion website. Available online: <http://ucrel.lancs.ac.uk/bncfreq/lists/2_3_writtenspoken. txt> (accessed 24 September 2009).

Levinson, S. (1983) *Pragmatics.* Cambridge: Cambridge University Press.

—— (2004) 'Deixis', in L. Horn and G. Ward (eds), *The Handbook of Pragmatics.* Oxford: Blackwell.

Lewis, D. M. (2005) 'Arguing in English and French asynchronous online discussion', *Journal of Pragmatics* 37(11): 1801–18.

— (2006) 'Contrastive analysis of adversative relational markers, using comparable corpora', in K. Aijmer and A. M. Simon-Vandenbergen (eds), *Pragmatic Markers in Contrast*. Oxford: Elsevier.

Liang, G. and Han, J. (2005) 'A contrastive study on disagreement strategies for politeness between American English and Mandarin Chinese', *Asian EFL Journal* 7(1): 1–12.

Lin, G. Y. H. (2007) 'Expressions of gratitude: a cross-cultural comparison between Chinese speakers in Taiwan and English speakers in the U.S.', paper presented at the Annual Meeting of the American Council on the Teaching of Foreign Languages, San Antonio, Texas, 12 November 2007.

Lindblom, K. (2001) 'Cooperating with Grice: a cross-disciplinary metaperspective on uses of Grice's cooperative principle', *Journal of Pragmatics* 33: 1601–23.

Lörscher, W. (1986) 'Conversational structures in the foreign language classroom', in G. Kasper (ed.), *Learning, Teaching and Communication in the Foreign Language Classroom*. Aarhus: Aarhus University Press.

Louw, B. (1993) 'Irony in the text or insincerity in the writer: the diagnostic potential of semantic prosodies', in M. Baker, G. Francis and H. Tognini-Bonelli (eds), *Texts and Technology: In Honour of John Sinclair*. Amsterdam: John Benjamins.

Lyons, J. (1977) *Semantics, vols 1 and 2*. Cambridge: Cambridge University Press.

Maeshiba, N., Yoshinaga, N., Kasper, G. and Ross, S. (1996) 'Transfer and proficiency in interlanguage apologising', in M. Gass and J. Neu (eds), *Speech Acts across Cultures: Challenges to Communication in a Second Language*. Berlin: Mouton de Gruyter.

Mao, L. R. (1994) 'Beyond politeness theory: "face" revisited and renewed', *Journal of Pragmatics* 21: 451–86.

Markkanen, R. and Schröder, H. (1997) 'Hedging: a challenge for pragmatics and discourse analysis', in R. Markkanen and H. Schröder (eds), *Hedging and Discourse: Approaches to the Analysis of a Pragmatic Phenomenon in Academic Texts*. Berlin: Mouton de Gruyter.

Markus, H. and Kitayama, S. (1991) 'Culture and the self: implications for cognition, emotion, and motivation', *Psychological Review* 98: 224–53.

— (eds) (1994) *Emotion and Culture: Empirical Studies of Mutual Influence*. Washington, DC: American Psychological Association.

Marmaridou, S. (2000) *Pragmatic Meaning and Cognition*. Amsterdam: John Benjamins.

Márquez Reiter, R. and Placencia, M. E. (2005) *Spanish Pragmatics*. Basingstoke: Palgrave.

Morris, C. (1938) 'Pierce, Mead and Pragmatism', *Philosophical Review* 47(2): 109–27.

Mason, I. and Şerban, A. (2003) 'Deixis as an interactive feature in translations from Romainian into English', *Target* 15(2): 269–94.

Matsumoto, Y. (1988) 'Re-examination of the universality of face: politeness phenomena in Japanese', *Journal of Pragmatics* 12: 403–26.

Maynard, D. W. (2003) *Bad News, Good News: Conversational Order in Everyday Talk and Clinical Settings*. Chicago: University of Chicago Press.

Maynard, D. W. and Heritage, J. (2005) 'Conversation analysis, doctor–patient interaction and medical communication', *Medical Education* 39: 428–35.

Maynard, S. K. (1989) *Japanese Conversation: Self-contextualization through Structure and Interactional Management*. Norwood, NJ: Ablex.

— (1990) 'Conversation management in contrast: listener response in Japanese and American English', *Journal of Pragmatics* 14: 397–412.

— (1997) 'Analysing interactional management in native/non-native English conversation: a case of listener response', *IRAL* 35: 37–60.

McCarthy, M. (1998) *Spoken Language and Applied Linguistics.* Cambridge: Cambridge University Press.

— (2002) 'Good listenership made plain: British and American non-minimal response tokens in everyday conversation', in R. Reppen, S. Fitzmaurice and D. Biber (eds), *Using Corpora to Explore Linguistics Variation.* Amsterdam: John Benjamins.

McCarthy, M. and Carter, R. (1995) 'Spoken grammar: what is it and how can we teach it?', *ELT Journal* 49(3): 207–18.

McCarthy, M. and Handford, M. (2004) '"Invisible to us": a preliminary corpus-based study of spoken business English', in U. Connor and T. A. Upton (eds), *Discourse in the Professions.* Amsterdam: John Benjamins.

McCarthy, M., O'Keeffe, A. and Walsh, S. (2009) *The Vocabulary Matrix: Understanding, Learning, Teaching.* London: Cengage Learning.

McEnery, T., Xiao, R. and Tono, Y. (2006) *Corpus-based Language Studies: An Advanced Resource Book.* London: Routledge.

McKellin, W. H., Shahin, K., Hodgson, M., Jamieson, J. and K. Pichora-Fuller (2007) 'Pragmatics of conversation and communication in noisy settings', *Journal of Pragmatics* 39(12): 2159–84.

Meier, A. J. (1995) 'Defining politeness: universality in appropriateness', *Language Sciences* 17(4): 345–56.

Mey, J. (1991) 'Pragmatic gardens and their magic', *Poetics* 20: 233–45.

Mills, S. (2003) *Gender and Politeness.* Cambridge: Cambridge University Press.

Mitchell, T. F. (1957) 'The language of buying and selling in Cyrenaica', *Hesperis* 44: 31–71.

Moon, R. (1994) 'The analysis of fixed expressions in text', in M. Coulthard (ed.), *Advances in Written Text Analysis.* London: Routledge.

— (1997) 'Vocabulary connections: multiword items in English', in N. Schmitt and M. McCarthy (eds), *Vocabulary Description, Acquisition and Pedagogy.* Cambridge: Cambridge University Press.

— (1998) *Fixed Expressions and Idioms in English: A Corpus-based Approach.* Oxford: Clarendon.

Morgan, J. L. (1978) 'Two types of convention in indirect speech acts', in P. Cole (ed.), *Syntax and Semantics, vol. 9, Pragmatics.* New York: Academic Press.

Morris, C. (1938) 'Foundations of the theory of signs', in O. Neurath, R. Carnap and C. Morris (eds), *International Encyclopaedia of Unified Science.* Chicago: University of Chicago Press.

Mühlhäusler, P. and Harré, R. (1990) *Pronouns and People: The Linguistic Construction of Social and Personal Identity.* Oxford: Blackwell.

Müller, S. (2005) *Discourse Markers in Native and Non-native English Discourse.* Amsterdam: John Benjamins.

Nattinger, J. R. and DeCarrico, J. (1992) *Lexical Phrases and Language Teaching.* Oxford: Oxford University Press.

O'Keeffe, A. (2002) 'Exploring indices of national identity in a corpus of radio phone-in data from Irish radio', in A. Sánchez Macarro (ed.), *Windows on the World: Media Discourse in English.* Valencia: Universidad de Valencia.

— (2005) 'You've a daughter yourself? A corpus-based look at question forms in an Irish radio phone-in', in A. Barron and K. Schneider (eds), *The Pragmatics of Irish English*. Berlin: Mouton de Gruyter.

— (2006) *Investigating Media Discourse*. London: Routledge.

O'Keeffe, A. and Adolphs, S. (2008) 'Using a corpus to look at variational pragmatics: response tokens in British and Irish discourse', in K. Schneider and A. Barron (eds), *Variational Pragmatics: A Focus on Regional Varieties in Pluricentric Languages*. Amsterdam: John Benjamins.

O'Keeffe A. and McCarthy, M. (eds) (2010) *The Routledge Handbook of Corpus Linguistics*. London: Routledge.

O'Keeffe, A., McCarthy, M. and Carter, R. (2007) *From Corpus to Classroom: Language Use and Language Teaching*. Cambridge: Cambridge University Press.

Olshtain, E. and Blum-Kulka, S. (1985) 'Degree of approximation: non-native reactions to native speech act behavior', in S. Gass and C. Madden (eds), *Input in Second Language Acquisition*. Rowley, MA: Newbury House.

Olshtain, E. and Weinbach, L. (1993) 'Interlanguage features of the speech act of complaining', in G. Kasper and S. Blum-Kulka (eds), *Interlanguage Pragmatics*. Oxford: Oxford University Press.

Orpin, D. (2005) 'Corpus linguistics and critical discourse analysis: examining the ideology of sleaze', *International Journal of Corpus Linguistics* 10(1): 37–61.

Palma Fahey, M. (2005) *A cross-cultural discourse and pragmatic analysis of two soap operas Fair City and Amores de Mercado compared*. Unpublished PhD thesis, Mary Immaculate College, University of Limerick.

Partington, A. (1998) *Patterns and Meanings: Using Corpora for English Language Research and Teaching*. Amsterdam: John Benjamins.

Pawley, A. and Syder, F. (1983) 'Two puzzles for linguistic theory: nativelike selection and nativelike fluency', in J. Richards and R. Schmidt (eds), *Language and Communication*. New York: Longman.

Placencia, M. E. and García, C. (eds) (2007) *Research on Politeness in the Spanish-Speaking World*. Mahwah, NJ: Lawrence Erlbaum.

Plas, P. (2007) 'Voicing folk for the academy: interdiscursivity and collective identity in a north Dalmatian ethnography, 1899–1900', *Journal of Pragmatics* 39(12): 2244–72.

Prodromou, L. (2008) *English as a Lingua Franca: A Corpus-based Analysis*. London: Continuum.

Redeker, G. (1990) 'Ideational and pragmatic markers of discourse structure', *Journal of Pragmatics* 14(3): 367–81.

— (1991) 'Review article: linguistic markers of discourse structure', *Linguistics* 29(6): 1139–72.

Reppen, R. (2010) 'Building a corpus: what are the key considerations?', in A. O'Keeffe and M. J. McCarthy (eds), *The Routledge Handbook of Corpus Linguistics*. London: Routledge.

Rintell, E. and Mitchell, C. (1989) 'Studying requests and apologies: an inquiry into method', in S. Blum-Kulka, J. House and G. Kasper (eds), *Cross-cultural Pragmatics: Requests and Apologies*. Norwood, NJ: Ablex.

Roberts, C. (1997) 'Transcribing talk: issues of representation', *TESOL Quarterly* 31(1): 167–72.

Roever, C. (2004) 'Difficulty and practicality in tests of interlanguage pragmatics', in D. Boxer and A. Cohen (eds), *Studying Speaking to Inform Second Language Learning*. Clevedon: Multilingual Matters.

—— (2006) 'Validation of a web-based test of ESL pragmalinguistics', *Language Testing* 23(2): 229–56.

Römer, U. (2004a) 'Comparing real and ideal language learner input: the use of an EFL textbook corpus in corpus linguistics and language teaching', in G. Aston, G. Bernardini and D. Stewart (eds), *Corpora and Language Learners*. Amsterdam: John Benjamins.

—— (2004b) 'Textbooks: a corpus-driven approach', in J. Sinclair (ed.), *How to Use Corpora in Language Teaching*. Amsterdam: John Benjamins.

Romero-Trillo, J. (ed.) (2008) *Pragmatics and Corpus Linguistics: A Mutualistic Entente*. Berlin: Mouton de Gruyter.

Rose, K. (1994) 'On the validity of discourse completion tests in non-western contexts', *Applied Linguistics* 15(1): 1–14.

—— (2001) 'Compliments and compliment responses in film: implications for pragmatics research and language teaching', *International Review of Applied Linguistics* 39: 309–26.

—— (2005) 'On the effects on instruction in second language pragmatics', *System* 33: 385–99.

Rosendale, D. (1989) 'Role-play as a data generation method', *Simulation and Gaming* 20(4): 487–92.

Rühlemann, C. (2007) *Conversation in Context: A Corpus-Driven Approach*. London: Continuum.

—— (2010) 'What can a corpus tell us about pragmatics?' in A. O'Keeffe and M. McCarthy (eds), *The Routledge Handbook of Corpus Linguistics*. London: Routledge.

Sacks, H. (1992) *Harvey Sacks: Lectures on Conversation,* vols 1–2, (ed.) G. Jefferson. Oxford: Blackwell.

Sacks H., Schegloff, E. A., Jefferson, G. (1974) 'A simplest systematics for the organisation of turn-taking for conversation', *Language* 50 (4): 696–735.

Sadock, J. M. (1974) *Toward a Linguistic Theory of Speech Acts*. New York: Academic Press.

Sasaki, M. (1998) 'Investigating EFL students' production of speech acts: a comparison of production questionnaires and role plays', *Journal of Pragmatics* 30: 457–84.

Schauer, G. and Adolphs, S. (2006) 'Expressions of gratitude in corpus and DCT data: vocabulary, formulaic sequences and pedagogy', *System* 34: 119–34.

Schegloff, E. A. (1968) 'Sequencing in conversational openings', *American Anthropologist* 70(6): 1075–95.

—— (1986) 'The routine as achievement', *Human Studies,* 9: 111–52.

Schegloff, E. A., Jefferson, G. and Sacks, H. (1977) 'The preference for self-correction in the organization of repair in conversation', *Language* 53: 361–82.

Schiffrin, D. (1987) *Discourse Markers*. Cambridge: Cambridge University Press.

Schmidt, R. (1990) 'The role of consciousness in second language learning', *Applied Linguistics* 11: 129–58.

—— (1993) 'Consciousness, learning and interlanguage pragmatics', in G. Kasper and S. Blum-Kulka (eds), *Interlanguage Pragmatics*. Oxford: Oxford University Press.

—— (1994) 'Implicit learning and the cognitive unconscious: of artificial grammars and SLA', in N. Ellis (ed.), *Implicit and Explicit Learning of Languages*. London: Academic Press.

—— (ed.) (2004) *Formulaic Sequences*. Amsterdam: John Benjamins.

Schneider, K. P. and Barron, A. (2008) 'Where pragmatics and dialectology meet: introducing variational pragmatics', in K. Schneider and A. Barron (eds), *Variational Pragmatics: A Focus on Regional Varieties in Pluricentric Languages*. Amsterdam: John Benjamins.

Scollon, R. and Scollon, S. (1995) *Intercultural Communication: A Discourse Approach*. Oxford: Blackwell.

Scott, M. (1997) 'PC analysis of key words – and key key words', *System* 25(2): 233–45.

— (2009) *WordSmith Tools Version 5.0*. Liverpool: Lexical Analysis Software Ltd.

— (2010) 'What can corpus software do?', in A. O'Keeffe and M. McCarthy (eds), *The Routledge Handbook of Corpus Linguistics*. London: Routledge.

Searle, J. R. (1969) *Speech Acts*. Cambridge: Cambridge University Press.

— (1975) 'Indirect speech acts', in P. Cole and J. L. Morgan (eds), *Syntax and Semantics*, vol. 3. New York: Academic Press.

— (1976) 'The classification of illocutionary acts', *Language in Society* 5: 1–24.

Sifianou, M. (1989) 'On the telephone again. Differences in telephone behaviour: England versus Greece', *Language and Society* 18(4): 527–44.

Simpson, R. C., Briggs, S. L., Ovens, J. and Swales, J. M. (2002) *The Michigan Corpus of Academic Spoken English*. Ann Arbor, MI: The Regents of the University of Michigan.

Sinclair, J. M. (1987) 'Collocation: a progress report', in R. Steele and T. Threadgold (eds), *Language Topics: Essays in Honour of Michael Halliday*. Amsterdam: John Benjamins.

— (1991) *Corpus, Concordance, Collocation*. Oxford: Oxford University Press.

— (1996) 'The search for the units of meaning', *Textus* 9(1): 75–106.

— (2003) *Reading Concordances*. London: Longman.

Sinclair, J. M. and Coulthard, M. (1975) *Towards an Analysis of Discourse*. London: Oxford University Press.

Sohn, H. (1983) 'Intercultural communication in cognitive values: Americans and Koreans', *Language and Linguistics* (Seoul) 9: 93–136.

Spencer-Oatey, H. (2002) 'Managing rapport in talk: using rapport sensitive incidents to explore the motivational concerns underlying the management of relations', *Journal of Pragmatics* 34: 529–45.

Sperber, D. and Wilson, D. (1995) *Relevance: Communication and Cognition*. Oxford: Blackwell.

— (2006) 'Relevance theory', in L. Horn and G. Ward (eds), *The Handbook of Pragmatics*. Oxford: Blackwell.

Stenström, A. B. (2006) 'The Spanish discourse markers *o sea* and *pues* and their English correspondences', in K. Aijmer and A. M. Simon-Vandenbergen (eds), *Pragmatic Markers in Contrast*. Oxford: Elsevier.

Strauss, S. (2002) '*This, that* and *it* in spoken American English: a demonstrative system of gradient focus', *Language Sciences* 24: 131–52.

Stubbs, M. (1995) 'Collocations and semantic profiles: on the cause of the trouble with quantitative methods', *Functions of Language* 2(1): 1–33.

Takimoto, M. (2009) 'The effects of input-based tasks on the development of learners' pragmatic proficiency', *Applied Linguistics* 30(1): 1–25.

Tanck, S. (2002) 'Speech acts sets of refusal and complaints: a comparison of native and non-native English speakers' production'. Available online: <http://www.american.edu/tesol/wptanck.pdf#search> (accessed 10 April 2006).

Tannen, D. (2007) 'Power manoeuvres and connection manoeuvres in family interaction', in D. Tannen, S. Kendall and C. Gordon (eds), *Family Talk: Discourse and Identity in Four American Families*. Oxford: Oxford University Press.

Tao, H. (1998) 'An interactional account of generic *you* expressions in spoken English', paper presented at the International Pragmatics Association Conference, Reims, France, July 1998.

Thomas, J. (1983) 'Cross-cultural pragmatic failure', *Applied Linguistics* 4(2): 91–112.

Tognini-Bonelli, E. (2001) *Corpus Linguistics at Work*. Amsterdam: John Benjamins.

Tottie, G. (1991) 'Conversational style in British and American English: the case of backchannels', in K. Aijmer and B. Altenberg (eds), *English Corpus Linguistics*. London: Longman.

Tracy, K. (1997) 'Interactional trouble in emergency service requests: a problem of frames', *Research on Language and Social Interaction* 30(4): 315–43.

Tracy, K. and Anderson, D. L. (1999) 'Relational positioning strategies in calls to the police: a dilemma', *Discourse Studies* 1: 201–26.

Tribble, C. (2010) 'What are concordances and how are they used?', in A. O'Keeffe and M. McCarthy (eds), *The Routledge Handbook of Corpus Linguistics*. London: Routledge.

Trosborg, A. (1987) 'Apology strategies in native and non-native speakers of English', *Journal of Pragmatics* 11(1): 147–67.

—— (1995) *Interlanguage Pragmatics: Requests, Complaints, Apologies*. Berlin: Mouton de Gruyter.

Tsui, A. (1994) *English Conversation*. Oxford: Oxford University Press.

Varghese, M. and Billmyer, K. (1996) 'Investigating the structure of discourse completion tests', *Working Papers in Educational Linguistics* 12(1): 39–58.

Vásquez, C. and Sharpless, D. (2009) 'The role of pragmatics in the master's TESOL curriculum: findings from a nationwide survey', *TESOL Quarterly* 43(1): 5–28.

Vaughan, E. (2007) '*I think we should just accept . . . our horrible lowly status*: analysing teacher–teacher talk within the context of community of practice', *Language Awareness* 16(3): 173–89.

—— (2008) '"Got a date or something?": an analysis of the role of humour and laughter in the workplace meetings of English language teachers', in A. Ädel and R. Reppen (eds), *Corpora and Discourse: The Challenge of Different Settings*. Amsterdam: John Benjamins.

—— (2010) 'How can teachers use a corpus for their own research?', in A. O'Keeffe and M. McCarthy (eds), *The Routledge Handbook of Corpus Linguistics*. London: Routledge.

Vellenga, H. (2004) 'Learning pragmatics from ESL and EFL textbooks: How likely?', *TESL-EJ* 8(2). Available online: <http://www-writing.berkeley.edu/TESL-EJ/ej30/a3.html> (accessed 17 June 2009).

Ventola, E. (1987) *The Structure of Social Interaction: A Systemic Approach to the Semiotics of Service Encounters*. London: Frances Pinter.

Verschueren, J. (1999) *Understanding Pragmatics*. London: Arnold.

Wales, K. (1996) *Personal Pronouns in Present-Day English*. Cambridge: Cambridge University Press.

Walsh, S. (2006) *Investigating Classroom Discourse*. London: Routledge.

Walsh, S., O'Keeffe, A. and McCarthy, M. (2008) '. . . *post-colonialism, multi-culturalism, structuralism, feminism, post-modernism and so on and so forth*: a comparative analysis of vague category markers in academic discourse', in A. Ädel and R. Reppen (eds), *Corpora and Discourse: The Challenges of Different Settings*. Amsterdam: John Benjamins.

Washburn, G. (2001) 'Using situation comedies for pragmatic language teaching and learning', *TESOL Journal* 10(4): 21–6.

Watts, R. (1989) 'Relevance and relational work: linguistic politeness as politic behaviour', *Multilingua* 8(2/3): 131–66.

— (2003) *Politeness*. Cambridge: Cambridge University Press.

Watts R., Ide S. and Ehlich, K. (eds) (2005) *Politeness in Language*, 2nd edn. Berlin: Mouton de Gruyter.

Whalen, M. R. and Zimmerman, D. H. (1987) 'Sequential and institutional context in calls for help', *Social Psychology Quarterly* 50(2): 172–85.

White, W. and Chan, E. (1983) 'A comparison of self-concept scores of Chinese and White graduate students and professionals', *Journal of Non-White Concerns* 19: 138–41.

Wierzbicka, A. (1985) 'Different cultures, different languages, different speech acts', *Journal of Pragmatics* 9: 145–78.

— (2003) *Cross-Cultural Pragmatics: The Semantics of Human Interaction*. Berlin: Mouton de Gruyter.

Wilson, D. (1994) 'Relevance and understanding', in G. Brown, M. Malmkjaer, A. Pollitt and J. Williams (eds), *Language and Understanding*. Oxford: Oxford University Press.

Wishnoff, J. (2000) 'Hedging your bets: L2 learners' acquisition of pragmatic devices in academic writing and computer mediated discourse', *Second Language Studies* 19(1): 119–48.

Wolfram, W. and Schilling-Estes, N. (2006) *American English*. Oxford: Blackwell.

Wray, A. (2002) *Formulaic Language and the Lexicon*. Cambridge: Cambridge University Press.

Yngve, V. (1970) 'On getting a word in edgewise', *Papers from the 6th Regional Meeting, Chicago Linguistic Society*. Chicago: Chicago Linguistic Society.

Yoon, Y. B. and Kellogg D. (2002) '"Ducks" and "parrots": elaboration, duplication and duplicity in a cartoon discourse completion test', *Evaluation and Research in Education* 16(4): 218–39.

Yoshimi, D. (2001) 'Explicit instruction and JFL learners' use of interactional discourse markers', in K. Rose and G. Kasper (eds), *Pragmatics in Language Teaching*. London: Routledge.

Yuan, Y. (2001) 'An inquiry into empirical pragmatics data-gathering methods: written DCTs, oral DCTs, field notes, and natural conversations', *Journal of Pragmatics* 33(2): 271–92.

Yule, G. (1996) *Pragmatics*. Oxford: Oxford University Press.

Yus Ramos, F. (1998) 'A decade of relevance theory', *Journal of Pragmatics* 30: 305–45.

Index

academic language 148–9
actional pragmatic variation 111
address terms 55–6, 67–8
Adolphs, S. 3, 9, 15, 23, 111–12
adverbs 152, 157; of space 39; of time 39, 50–3
advertising 149
advisives 97
agreement maxim 105
Aijmer, K. 94, 102
Alcón Soler, A. 138
Amador Moreno, C. 31
American English 23, 110–11
American National Corpus (ANC) 8
anaphora 45–6, 54
apologies 25–6, 107, 109
approbation maxim 105
approximation 148, 151–5
argumentation 131–2
Asian cultures 105–6
assessment 162–3
attested data 21
Austin, J.L. 84–6; revised Speech Act Theory 85–6

background knowledge 1, 45
bald FTA 65
banter 72–3
Bardovi-Harlig, K. 26–7, 100, 107, 108, 138–9, 141
Barron, A. 110–11, 112–13
Basturkmen, H. 140
Beebe, L. 22, 108
Belz, J. 141
Bergman, M. 109
Biber, D. 115–16, 144
Billmyer, K. 23–4
Blum-Kulka, S. 56
Bollobás, E. 19
Bousfield, D. 71, 72

Boxer, D. 23, 25, 101, 102–3, 108–9
British National Corpus (BNC) 4, 7, 9, 10, 28, 121, 151–4, 155
broad transcription 29, 30
Brown and Levinson's theory of politeness 59, 60–71, 104, 105

Caballero, R. 19–20
call openings 117–20
caller inhalations 128–30
CANCODE 15
canonical turn sequence 116–20
Carter, R. 144, 155–6
cataphora 45–6
Centre for Advanced Research on Language Acquisition (CARLA) 141–2, 143
Chen, H.J. 23
Cheng, W. 106
Chilton, K. 118
Chinese speakers 23
choice 108, 153
Christie, C. 1, 2
classification of speech acts 86–7; in discourse analysis 96–8
clusters 10–11, 130–5
coding time (CT) 50
cognitive effects 75
Cohen, A. 23, 25, 141, 162–3
collegiality 66–7
colligation 14
Collins and Birmingham University International Language Database (COBUILD) 7
collocation 14
commissives 86, 92–3
communicative competence 2
comparability 115; of corpora across language varieties 16; at the level of turns 116–20; using a corpus 120–6
complex adverbs of time 50, 52–3

concordance lines 12–16, 122–4, 125–6, 127, 133

conflict 133–4

confrontation 131–2

consent forms 28

constatives 84–5

Constituent-Likelihood Automatic Word Tagging System (CLAWS) 11

content 2, 108

context 1–2, 3; deixis and 45–8, 48–9; politeness and 74, 76; speech act context 93–5

contextual implication 75

conventionalised indirect speech acts 69, 87, 88, 90

conversation analysis (CA) 116–20

conversational implicature 62, 88

co-operation drift 18

Co-operative Principle *see* Grice's Co-operative Principle

Corpus of Contemporary American English (COCA) 4, 8, 14–15

corpus linguistics/corpora 3–4, 6–16, 80–1; comparability using a corpus 120–6; concordance lines 12–16, 122–4, 125–6, 127, 133; corpora as language data 7–8; corpus data 28–34, 97–8; and deixis 36–7; extralinguistic information 127–30; keyword lists 11–12, 122, 123, 124–5; multi-word units 10–11, 130–5; using a corpus to study pragmatics 8–16; word frequency lists 9–11, 57–8, 121; *see also under individual corpora*

Corpus of Meetings of English Language Teachers (C-MELT) 4, 12, 124–6

co-text 13

co-textual context 1, 45

Coulthard, M. 96

Crandall, E. 140

cross-cultural communication 103–4

cross-cultural pragmatics 6, 100–14; defining 102–4; pragmatic variation within the same language 109–12; research 107–9, 138–9; universality of pragmatic norms 104–6

Cross-Cultural Speech Act Realisation Project (CCSARP) 107

Crystal, D. 18

Culpeper, J. 71, 72, 73

cultural knowledge 1, 45

cultural ranking 71

Cutting, J. 1, 45, 59

data collection approaches 20–34; attested data 21; corpus data 28–34; elicited data 21–4; interviews 26–7; questionnaires 27; role-plays 25–6

Davies, B. 18, 19–20

days of the week 51–2

declarations 87

definitions of pragmatics 1–2, 18, 137

deictic centre (origo) 42–4, 48–9

deixis 5, 32, 36–58; basic categories of 44–57; deictic vs non-deictic expression 37–9; gestural vs symbolic 39–42

Demeter, G. 25–6

Democrat 14–15

demographic information 15

demonstratives 37–8, 56–7; *see also that, this*

dinner, politeness at 77

direct speech acts 87

directives 86, 92–3, 96–7

discourse analysis, speech act classification in 96–8

Discourse Completion Tasks/Tests (DCTs) 3, 21–4, 26, 91–2, 107

discourse deixis 54–5

discourse domains, specific *see* specific discourse domains

discourse markers 31, 120, 127, 141; teaching politeness 148, 156, 157–8

distal–proximal distinction 48–9, 50

diversity of studies in pragmatics 19–20

Dörnyei, Z. 139

downtoning 68

Drew, P. 118

early corpora 7

Eastern cultures 105–6

egocentric origo 42–3

elicitation speech acts 96

elicited data 21–4

ellipsis 129

emergency phone calls 117–18

emotional deixis 57

empathetic deixis 56–7

English for Academic Purposes (EAP) 140

English as a Foreign Language (EFL) 100, 139

English language teaching (ELT) 6, 137–64

English as a Second Language (ESL) 139

error correction 140

essential conditions 85–6

estimated + numbers 151–4

evaluative adverbs 157

exclusive we 47–8

explicit performatives 84

expressives 86

extralinguistic information 127–30

face 63–6, 104, 105–6; in Western vs Asian cultures 106

face threatening acts (FTAs) 64–71

face-work 63

Fair City scripts 131–5
family discourse: deixis 47–8, 53–4, 55; phone calls between intimates 118–19; politeness 73–4, 76–8, 79
Fasold, R. 1, 36
felicity conditions 85–6
Félix-Brasdefer, J.C. 108
folk identities 19–20
form 2, 108–9
formal pragmatic variation 111–12
formulaic language 144–7
fragmented multi-word units 10–11, 130–1
frames 94–5
Fraser, B. 156
frequency lists 9–11, 57–8, 121; multi-word units 10–11, 130–5

García, C. 110
general corpora 7–8
generic you 37
generosity maxim 105
genre theory 94–5
genuine impoliteness 72, 73–4
gestural deixis 39–42
Goffman, E. 63
grammatical competence 2, 137, 139
gratitude 101–2, 141–2
Grice's Co-operative Principle 18, 19–20, 60–3, 75, 104, 105; indirect speech acts and 88–90
Griffin, R. 107
Grundy, P. 103–4

Halliday, M.A.K. 115
Han, J. 23, 24
Hartford, B. 108
he 45–7, 57–8
head nods 33
hedges/hedging 9, 10, 31, 126, 141; common forms 152–3; negative politeness 69–71; teaching politeness 148–51
here 48–9
hesitation devices 128–30
Hinkel, E. 148
historical corpora 7
Hong Kong Corpus of Spoken English 29–30
hours 154
humour 89–90, 149
Hyland, K. 148
Hymes, D. 2, 93–4, 95

I 42–3, 44–5, 47, 57–8
I don't know 132
I don't think 134–5
I think 70
idiom 90

illocutionary acts 85, 87
illocutionary force 54–5, 87
impoliteness 60, 71–4
inclusive we 47–8, 67
indirect complaints 108–9
indirect speech acts 87–91; and the Co-operative Principle 88–90
informative speech acts 96
inhalations, caller 128–30
inherent impoliteness 72, 73–4
intentional impoliteness 71–2
interactional markers 148, 156, 158–60
interactional pragmatic variation 111
intercultural communication 103–4
interlanguage pragmatics (IP) 3, 6, 102–14; defining 102–4; research 107–9; universality of pragmatic norms 104–6
International Corpus of English (ICE) 8
interpersonal knowledge 1, 45
interviews 26–7
intracultural communication 104, 109–12
intuitive data 21
Irish Travellers 56
it 57–8
it's 124

Jones, P. 43
Journal of Pragmatics 19–20
just 122–4

Kasper, G. 27, 109, 137
Kellogg, D. 22
Kendon, A. 160
Key Word in Context (KWIC) 13
keyword lists 11–12, 122, 123, 124–5
kinship networks 56
kinship terms 43, 55–6
Koike, D. 138
Konishi, K. 25
Kotani, M. 109

language learning 112–13
language teaching 6, 137–64; hedging 148–51; politeness 143–62; pragmatic markers 155–62; pragmatics in the language classroom 138–42; short-term and long-term goals 142–3; vague language 151–5
learner corpora 7, 8
Leech, G. 18, 101, 137; politeness maxims 104, 105
lemmatised frequency lists 9
levels of pragmatic variation 111–12
Levinson, S. 36, 44; Brown and Levinson's theory of politeness 59, 60–71, 104, 105
Lewis, D.M. 31
lexical competence 137

Liang, G. 23, 24
Limerick and Belfast Corpus of Academic
  Spoken English (LIBEL CASE) 4, 29, 130
Limerick Corpus of Irish English (LCIE) 4, 9, 10,
  12, 15, 57–8, 154; frequency of please
  79–80; personal pronouns in frequency list
  44, 45, 57–8; shop counter recordings 127
linking adverbs 157
Liveline radio phone-ins 32, 33
locational deixis 42, 48–9
locutionary acts 85
long-term goals 142–3
Lyons, J. 56

Mahan-Taylor, R. 138, 139, 141
mandatives 97
manner 61–2, 88, 105
manner-of-motion verbs 19–20
Márquez Reiter, R. 109–10
McCarthy, M. 110–11, 144, 155–6
McKellin, W.H. 19
meaning 1–2, 3
media scripts 131–5
metadata 15
mitigation of an FTA 68
mock impoliteness 72–3
modesty maxim 105
monitor corpora 7
Morgan, J.L. 90
Morris, C. 1
Müller, S. 31
multi-modal corpora 16, 33, 98
multiple choice questionnaires 27
multi-word units 10–11, 130–5

narrow transcription 29–30
native speakers 31, 108–9
negative face 63–4, 68, 69
negative impoliteness strategies 72
negative keyword lists 11, 12
negative politeness 67, 68–71, 143–4;
  teaching 147–62
NHS Direct corpus 4, 89–90, 119–20, 121–4,
  128–30
nicknames 55–6, 67–8
no 133
node word 13
noisy settings 19
non-conventionalised indirect speech acts 87
non-egocentric origo 43
non-native speakers 31, 108–9, 140
non-verbal communication 33, 39–42, 97–8
norms, universality of 104–6
Nottingham Multi-Modal Corpus (NMMC) 4
nouns 152
now 13, 39, 41, 127

O'Keeffe, A. 9, 15, 111–12
online pragmatics exercises 141–2
organisational pragmatic variation 111
origo (deictic centre) 42–4, 48–9

parallel corpora 7
parent-child interactions 43
part-of-speech (POS) tagging 11, 13
Pearson, L. 138
performatives 84–5
perlocutionary acts 85
person deixis 42, 44–8
personal pronouns 9, 32, 33, 37, 42–3, 44–8
PhD supervision 95
PhD theses 148–9
phone calls *see* telephone calls
place deixis 42, 48–9
Placencia, M.E. 109–10
Plas, P. 19–20
please 79–80
polite behaviour 78–80
politeness 5, 59–82, 101; Brown and
  Levinson's theory 59, 60–71, 104, 105;
  linguistic study of 59–60; politeness1 vs
  politeness2 76–8; teaching 143–62; Watt's
  theory 59–60, 74–80; *see also* impoliteness
politic behaviour 78–80
positive cognitive effect 75
positive face 63–4, 66
positive impoliteness strategies 72
positive keyword lists 11, 12
positive politeness 66–8, 143–4; teaching
  144–7
post-observation teacher training interaction
  115–16
power difference 71
pragmalinguistics 138, 139, 140
pragmatic competence 112–13, 137, 138,
  139
pragmatic failure 101
pragmatic markers 31–2, 148; teaching
  155–62
pragmatic tagging 33
preparatory conditions 85–6
prepositional phrases 152–3
primary illocutionary acts 87
problematisation 134–5
processing effort 75
pronouns, personal 9, 32, 33, 37, 42–3, 44–8
proposals 97
propositional conditions 85–6
proximal–distal distinction 48–9, 50

quality 61–2, 88, 89, 105
quantity 61–2, 88, 89, 105
questionnaire data 27

radio phone-ins 32, 33, 68, 115–16, 160–1
receiving time (RT) 50
redress 65, 66
reference corpus 12, 120
referent 37, 41
register 115–16
relevance (relation maxim) 61–2, 88, 89–90, 105
relevance theory (RT) 75–6
religious references 111–12
representativeness of a corpus 30–1
representatives 86
Republican 14–15
requestives 96–7
research 5, 18–35; data collection methods 20–34; diversity of studies 19–20; pragmatics across languages and cultures 107–9, 138–9
response tokens 9, 15, 111–12, 120, 121, 122, 148, 156; teaching politeness 160–2
revisionist interpretation 19
Roever, C. 27
role-plays 3, 25–6, 91–2
Romero-Trillo, J. 2, 3, 33
Rose, K. 23, 137
routinised language 90–1
Rühlemann, C. 33, 44–5, 46, 56, 57

Salsbury, T. 26–7
Schauer, G. 3, 23
Schegloff, E.A. 117
Schilling-Estes, N. 110
Schneider, K.P. 110–11
Searle, J.R. 85–6, 86–7, 93
secondary illocutionary acts 87
self 106
semantic preference 14
semantic prosodies 14–15, 16
semantics 1, 90–1, 137
sequences 10–11, 130–5
seven-step process for concordance analysis 14
she 45–7
shop counter service 94–5, 127
short-circuited implicature 90
short-term goals 142–3
sincerity conditions 85–6
Sinclair, J.M. 13, 14, 96
situational context 1, 45
soap opera scripts 131–5
social deixis 55–6
social distance 71
social variables 71
sociopragmatics 138, 139, 140
sort 122–4
space, adverbs of 39

Spanish 109–10, 141–2
spatial deixis 42, 48–9
specialised corpora 7, 8
specific discourse domains 6, 115–36; comparability at the level of turns 116–20; comparability using a corpus 120–6; extralinguistic information 127–30; multi-word units 130–5
Speech Act Theory 84–91
speech acts 5–6, 16, 23, 33, 83–99; classification 86–7; classification in discourse analysis 96–8; context 93–5; cross-cultural pragmatics research 107–9; direct 87; identifying and analysing 91–3; indirect 87–91; online pragmatic exercises 141–2
speech events 93, 94–5
speech situations 93–4
Sperber, D. 75–6
spoken genre range 115–16
strategic impoliteness 71–2
suggestions 92–3, 97
swear words 111–12
symbolic deixis 39–42
sympathy maxim 105
syntax 1, 137

tact maxim 105
Takimoto, M. 140
Tanck, S. 22, 24
Tarone, E. 25
teachers 66–7, 124–6
telephone calls: caller inhalations 128–30; openings 117–20; radio phone-ins see radio phone-ins
tense 53–4
textbooks 139–40
thanking 101–2, 141–2
that 38, 40, 49, 55, 56–7, 57–8
then 50–1
there 39, 40–1, 48–9, 57–8
they 45–7, 57–8
think 12, 70
this 37–8, 39–40, 49, 54–5
this year 52–3
Thomas, J. 100, 101, 140
time 154–5; adverbs of 39
time deixis 42, 50–4
today 51–2
tomorrow 51–2
topic pragmatic variation 111
Tottie, G. 110–11
transcription 16, 29–30, 97–8
transcultural communication 104
Travelling community 56
Tsui, A. 96–7
turns 116–20

unanchored utterances 50
universality of pragmatic norms 104–6

vagueness markers 32, 122–4, 129–30,
   148; teaching 151–5
Varghese, M. 23–4
variation: situational 115, 116; within the
   same language 109–12; *see also* specific
   discourse domains
variational pragmatics 110–12
Vellenga, H. 139–40
verbs: modal 152; with modal meaning
   152
Verschueren, J. 20
viewpoint adverbs 157
Vyatkina, N. 141

Wales, K. 43
Watts, R. 59–60, 74–80
we 12, 47–8, 124–6; inclusive 47–8, 67
websites 141–2

Western cultures 69, 105–6
Whalen, M.R. 117
what are you 133–4
what do you 131
Wierzbicka, A. 104–5
Wilson, D. 75–6
Wishnoff, J. 141
Wolfram, W. 110
word frequency lists 9–11, 57–8, 121;
   see also multi-word units

years 155
yesterday 51–2
Yoon, Y.B. 22
Yoshimi, D. 141
you 37, 41, 42–3, 44–5, 47, 57–8
Yuan, Y. 27
Yule, G. 137

Zhang Waring, H. 22
Zimmerman, D.H. 117

CPSIA information can be obtained
at www.ICGtesting.com
Printed in the USA
LVOW03s2134071217
558796LV00003B/85/P